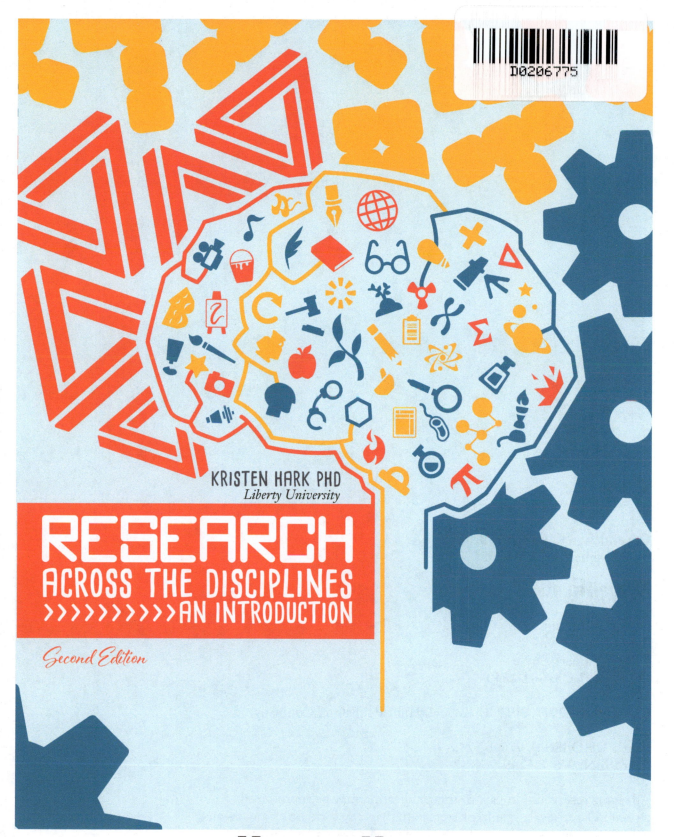

KRISTEN HARK PHD
Liberty University

RESEARCH
ACROSS THE DISCIPLINES
>>>>>>>>>>AN INTRODUCTION

Second Edition

Kendall Hunt
publishing company

Cover design © Joshua Wilson
www.JoshuaWilsonArt.com

Kendall Hunt
publishing company

www.kendallhunt.com
Send all inquiries to:
4050 Westmark Drive
Dubuque, IA 52004-1840

Text + KHQ ISBN: 978-1-5249-9647-5
Text ISBN: 978-1-5249-9648-2

Published in the United States of America

Table of Contents

Preface

Welcome to *Research Across the Disciplines an Introduction*! Through this textbook we hope you will learn to share our excitement about research. Your authors are researchers who—amazingly enough—love doing research. We may be crazy, and we may be academic nerds, but that's not why we love research. We think research is FUN! We feel investigating, following leads, and solving puzzles is exciting.

It is our hope that this book gives you enough information about the foundations of research methods, the choices as scholars make, and the methodological decisions driving to balance your desire to know and inquire into interesting communication questions while instilling an enthusiasm about the process.

Doing research is like being a detective. Both researchers and detectives are trying to find out something. Both are asking and answering questions. Both are trying to put together a puzzle to come up with a solution. In both, answering questions leads to more questions. And, in both, seeing patterns is crucial to solving the puzzle.

There is much about the social world that most of us think we know already; yet, there is also much left to learn his book, we will ask you to question what you know, why you know what you know, and where that belief came from. Some Research Methods may not be an "easy A" class, but it's worth the effort. You'll learn a lot in this class—and hopefully it will be information you'll use the rest of your career. We encourage you to talk with each other about this material. We often overlook the powerful learning tool of informally discussing what we learn in the classroom. As you learn to talk about these conceptual ideas, you will begin to crystallize your understanding of research methods and theory.

We hope that through this course you'll discover your own joy in conducting research. Some students are intimidated when they first encounter research methods. We'd like to lessen the intimidation factor for you. To do this, we want to introduce to you a model of the stages of learning (Dubin, 1962; Howell & Fleishman, 1982; Kirkpatrick, 1971).

You're in Step 1 right now—Unconscious Incompetence. That means you know so little, you don't even know what you don't know. This is a pretty blissful place to be ("ignorance is bliss"), but we're about to move you out of your comfort zone. We're about to move you to Step 2—Conscious Incompetence. We're about to tell you what you don't know. We're going to teach you how to do things, which will move you to Step 3—Conscious Competence, and you will spend much of this course moving between Steps 2 and 3. We'll teach you something, and you'll be very conscious of the fact that you're learning something new. By the end of the term, you will have mastered many skills and competencies, and you will be in Step 4—Unconscious Competence for much of the course content. These stages are always uncomfortable because new learning feels awkward. Remember

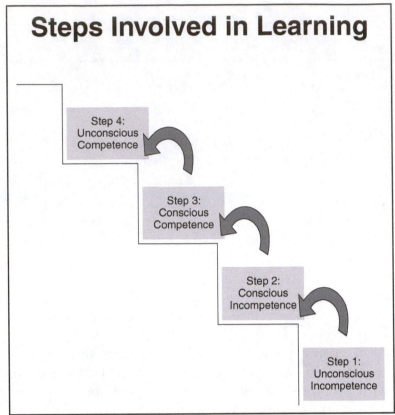

Steps Involved in Learning

Step 4:
Unconscious
Competence

Step 3:
Conscious
Competence

Step 2:
Conscious
Incompetence

Step 1:
Unconscious
Incompetence

Courtesy Christine Davis and Kenneth Lachlan. Copyright © Kendall Hunt Publishing Company

when you were first learning how to drive a car? There was a time when you had to remind yourself to push in the brake, and check your rear view mirror, and for a while that felt very uncomfortable. Luckily for you (and your parents), that stage didn't last long, and soon you were in the stage of Unconscious Competence in your driving—you could get in the car and drive without even thinking about it. We expect that by the end of the term, you will be in this final stage for research. You will be able to do things that, right now, you don't even know exist.

Much of this course is based on adult learning theory. Adult learning scholars suggest that learning for adults must be experiential—taking into account the learners' experiences, and integrating the materials into their own lives, combining active experimentation with theory and practical life skills as participants learn both formally and informally through application of course materials to experiences (Dinmore, 1997; Knowles, 1984). Research has also shown that adult learners best remember concepts given to them as spaced repetition—repeated in intervals over time (Spieler & Balota, 1996). Therefore, we give you information in small chunks that build upon each other, repeating then expanding knowledge. We'll give you multiple passes over concepts—introducing you to concepts in early chapters; then telling you more about those concepts in subsequent chapters. That's why it's going to be important for you to keep up with the material throughout the term—you don't want to miss any of the early passes over the information.

Why do I have to take this course? We require that you take classes in Research Methods so you will learn how we know things, describe things, and decide if something is true or not. Have you ever wondered where all these things, facts, and theories came from? Did someone just make them up so you could have something to be tested on? We know sometimes it feels that way, but this term you'll learn how to do various types of research. You'll see firsthand how theories (and other research questions) begin as a curiosity—an "I wonder if . . ."—and how these musings and wonderings turn into full-blown research, then into facts, knowledge, and theories.

You'll also learn how people in our community prove a point. You'll learn that not everything you read or hear is true, and, as we said, you'll learn how to question what you hear and believe, and how to determine if you want to continue believing it. You'll learn how to make credible claims and how to back them up with evidence so other people will believe what you have to say.

Confused—or curious? For now, don't worry about what you don't yet know. Just sit back, relax, and enjoy the ride!

Student-Oriented Pedagogy

Because we recognize the importance of assessing student learning, we have included features in each chapter that facilitate student learning and help instructors measure learning outcomes.

- Chapter Outlines serve as a map to guide you through the content of the text and focus on key points.
- Key Terms list shows important terms to focus on as you read the chapter.
- Chapter Objectives help you focus on the overall concepts, theories, and skills discussed in the chapter.
- Running Glossary provides the definition of a key term in the margin for quick clarification when reading the material.
- So What? chapter summary reviews the key points explored in the text.
- Chapter Glossary serves as a helpful reference tool at the end of each chapter.
- References list documents the research cited within the chapter.

About the Contributors

Dr. Lucinda S. Spaulding earned her Ph.D. in Special Education and Educational Psychology, M.Ed. in Special Education, and B.S. in Elementary Education. She has taught general and special education in the United States and English as a Second Language in Japan. She is an Associate Professor in the School of Education at Liberty University where she serves as the Administrative Chair of Research. Dr. Spaulding was born and raised in Ottawa, Canada and currently resides in Forest, Virginia with her husband and three children.

Dr. Matthew Towles earned his Ph.D. in English at The University of Kentucky, M.A. in English from Longwood College and B.A. in English from Liberty University. His research interests include: Nineteenth- and Twentieth-Century American Literature, Regional Fiction and Faith and Literature. Dr. Towles has been teaching in higher education for over a decade and before returning to teach at Liberty in 2007, Dr. Towles taught at every level, from elementary school through high school to college.

Dr. Greg Raner has a Ph.D. in Biological Chemistry and taught Chemistry and Biochemistry for 19 years at the University of North Carolina at Greensboro and now serves as a Professor at Liberty University in the Department of Biology and Chemistry. Research has been an integral component of his teaching throughout his career, having trained over 100 undergraduate student researchers, with funding from Federal and private agency such as NSF, NIH, The American Chemical Society and Research Corporation. Dr. Raner has been married for over 30 years and has 3 children, and he enjoys spending time with his family hiking, biking, traveling, or just watching movies. He has been a worship leader in several churches and has a heart for ministering to people struggling with substance abuse through organizations such as Teen Challenge and Celebrate Recovery.

Kevin L. Rawls, Ph.D., M.B.A., M.A.R.
Dr. Kevin Rawls has been studying the concept of worldview for over 20 years. He holds a Ph.D. in Business Administration, a M.B.A., and a M.A. in Religion. A strong believer in the ubiquitous nature of the Gospel, Dr. Rawls sees the impact that a well-developed Biblical worldview can have on the lives of believers and the world. Dr. Rawls brings a breadth of study from various disciplines together in a way that allows for a broad understanding of Biblical worldview. Additionally, as an advocate and researcher in social entrepreneurship Dr. Rawls is continuing to advance the idea of business as a means to advance the Gospel. Dr. Rawls currently serves as an Associate Dean at Liberty University where he has been a part of the development of the online program for a number of departments and schools.

Elisa Rollins, M.L.I.S.

Born and raised just outside of Lynchburg in the Bedford County area, Elisa Rollins has long called southwest Virginia, home. Six years of absence only confirmed her love for the Blue Ridge Mountains and she returned after graduating from Johns Hopkins University with a Masters in Public Policy to take a job in a local public library and pursue a Masters in Library and Information Science degree from the University of South Carolina. The Lord led Elisa to Liberty University in 2013 and, now, as Assistant Vice Provost for Quality Enhancement of Undergraduate Education and Director of the Center for Research & Scholarship, Elisa supports faculty members' development and strengthening of their own research knowledge and skills in order to enhance students' abilities to develop and demonstrate research knowledge, values, and skills. Her weekend excursions usually involve trail runs, sailing, and fly fishing with her husband.

Darren Wu, Ed.D.

Dr. Wu earned his Ed.D. from Liberty University, his M.A.R. from Liberty Baptist Theological Seminary and his B.S.M.E. from the United States Naval Academy. Prior to returning to Liberty University in 2001, Dr. Wu served as a commissioned officer in the United States Navy with tours of duties in: Charleston, SC; the Republic of Panama; Norfolk, VA; and Washington DC. Dr. Wu currently serves as the Associate Director of the Center for Research & Scholarship. The Center for Research & Scholarship (CRS) coordinates and supports new and ongoing research initiatives for both faculty and students at Liberty University. CRS oversees the university's Quality Enhancement Plan (QEP), entitled "Illuminate: Cultivating a Community of Research and Scholarship," which focuses on improving research and scholarship among undergraduate residential students.

Dr. Wu, happily married to his wife Tracy for 13 years, met her at Liberty University while both were serving as Resident Directors. They have three children: Caleb, Karis, and Titus and together enjoy scuba diving and downhill skiing.

JoHannah Lowder serves as an academic and scholarship librarian at Liberty University, specializing in Scholarly Communications topics. She received her Master's degree in Library Science from the University of Illinois Urbana-Champaign after receiving her B.A. in History from Liberty University. JoHannah's professional interests range from Open Educational Resources to scholarly publishing. She enjoys exploring new ideas, especially through reading and traveling.

CHAPTER 1

Approaches to Research: Why Point of View Matters

CHAPTER OUTLINE

This chapter describes how our attitudes and perceptions of the natural world or society can have a significant impact on how we approach a research problem, and how they can shape our expected outcomes; particularly the types of questions we ask.

Upon successful completion of this chapter, you will be able to:

- Recognize different worldviews, paradigms, and attitudes.
- Understand the relationship between identified paradigms and associated research methods.

1

▼ Introduction

Have you ever wondered how you make decisions? Or what factors were the most important in making those decisions? Sometimes the main factor in decision-making is simply the benefit to you . . . or perhaps it is the voice of a family member reminding you to "do the right thing." And what is the "right" thing, anyway? That is the key question this chapter should prompt you to think about: how do your attitudes and perceptions of the world impact how you think?

Finding this answer isn't as easy as it may seem at first glance. You need to learn how to ask **good** questions. These should be questions that make you think about why you believe things to be a certain way. For instance, some people think _____, while others ____. Hence, it's ALL about perspective. Think about perspective as a pair of eyeglasses; the lens that you look through filters what you see. Geofilters can make your face into a puppy, or situate you at a café in Paris. In other words, there are myriad ways that you can alter your vision, your decisions, and your thinking. This chapter will help you "see" that (see what I did there?).

This framework, or paradigm, has a specific place in research. Essentially, a paradigm is a set of assumptions governing how we interact with and interpret the world. Every person has a personal paradigm, influenced by outside forces acting on them and their own experiences in support of the paradigm. Status and cultural situations are major contributing factors in determining the kind of paradigm you will have. Someone spending their formative years in southern suburban Atlanta will operate under a different paradigm than a person who grew up as a member of the Maasai in Africa. Paradigms need constant reinforcement to function. And, if events occur that cannot be explained by your current paradigm, a new paradigm might be generated.

A **scientific** paradigm, in the most basic sense of the word, is a framework containing all of the commonly accepted views about a subject. It then uses those views/assumptions to create a structure to determine what direction research should take and how it should be performed. Thomas Kuhn suggested that a paradigm defines "the practices that define a scientific discipline at a certain point in time."

The Selection of a Research Approach

▼ Three Components Involved in an Approach

The approach one takes to research involves philosophical assumptions as well as distinct methods or procedures. The broad research approach is the *plan or proposal to conduct research*, and involves the intersection of philosophy, research designs, and specific methods. A framework used to explain the interaction of these three components is seen in Figure 1.1. In planning a study, researchers need to think through the philosophical worldview assumptions that they bring to the study, the research design that is related to this worldview, and the specific methods or procedures of research that translate the approach into practice.

Philosophical Worldviews

Although philosophical ideas remain largely hidden in research (Slife & Williams, 1995), they still influence the practice of research and need to be identified. It's important for individuals preparing a research proposal or plan to make explicit the larger philosophical ideas they espouse. This information will help explain why they chose qualitative, quantitative, or mixed methods approaches for their research. In writing about worldviews, a proposal might include a section that addresses the following:

- The philosophical worldview proposed in the study
- A definition of basic ideas of that worldview
- How the worldview shaped their approach to research

I have chosen to use the term *worldview* as meaning "a basic set of beliefs that guide action" (Guba, 1990, p. 17). Others have called them *paradigms* (Lincoln, Lynham, & Guba, 2011; Mertens, 2010); *epistemologies* and *ontologies* (Crotty, 1998), or *broadly conceived research methodologies* (Neuman, 2009). I see worldviews as a general philosophical orientation about the world and the nature of research that a researcher brings to a study. Worldviews arise based on discipline orientations, students' advisors/

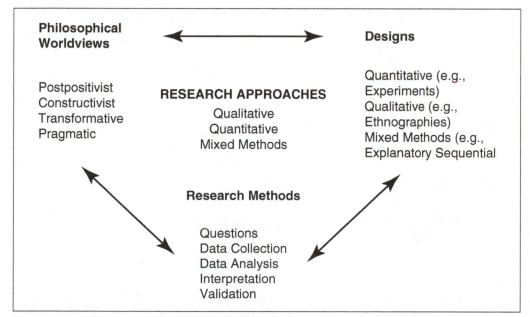

Figure 1.1. A Framework for Research—The Interconnection of Worldviews, Design, and Research Methods

mentors inclinations, and past research experiences. The types of beliefs held by individual researchers based on these factors will often lead to embracing a qualitative, quantitative, or mixed methods approach in their research. Although there is ongoing debate about what worldviews or beliefs researchers bring to inquiry, I will highlight four that are widely discussed in the literature: postpositivism, constructivism, transformative, and pragmatism. The major elements of each position are presented in Table 1.1.

The Postpositivist Worldview

The postpositivist assumptions have represented the traditional form of research, and these assumptions hold true more for quantitative research than qualitative research. This worldview is sometimes called the *scientific method*, or doing *science research*. It is also called *positivist/postpositivist research*, *empirical science*, and *postpositivism*. This last term is called postpositivism because it represents the thinking after positivism, challenging the traditional notion of the absolute truth of knowledge (Phillips & Burbules, 2000) and recognizing that we cannot be positive about our claims of knowledge when studying the behavior and actions of humans. The postpositivist tradition comes from 19th-century writers, such as Comte, Mill, Durkheim, Newton, and Locke (Smith, 1983) and more recently from writers such as Phillips and Burbules (2000).

Postpositivists hold a deterministic philosophy in which causes (probably) determine effects or outcomes. Thus, the problems studied by postpositivists reflect the need to identify and assess the causes that influence outcomes, such as those found in experiments. It is also reductionistic in that the intent is to reduce the ideas into a small, discrete set to test, such as the variables that comprise hypotheses and research questions. The knowledge that develops through a postpositivist lens is based on careful observation and measurement of the objective reality that exists "out there" in the world. Thus, developing numeric measures

Table 1.1. Four Worldviews

Postpositivism	Constructivism
• Determination	• Understanding
• Reductionism	• Multiple participant meanings
• Empirical observation and measurement	• Social and historical construction
• Theory verification	• Theory generation
Transformative	Pragmatism
• Political	• Consequences of actions
• Power and justice oriented	• Problem-centered
• Collaborative	• Pluralistic
• Change oriented	• Real-world practice oriented

of observations and studying the behavior of individuals becomes paramount for a postpositivist. Finally, there are laws or theories that govern the world, and these need to be tested or verified and refined so that we can understand the world. Thus, in the scientific method—the accepted approach to research by postpositivists—a researcher begins with a theory, collects data that either supports or refutes the theory, and then makes necessary revisions and conducts additional tests.

In reading Phillips and Burbules (2000), you can gain a sense of the key assumptions of this position, such as the following:

1. Knowledge is conjectural (and antifoundational)—absolute truth can never be found. Thus, evidence established in research is always imperfect and fallible. It is for this reason that researchers state that they do not prove a hypothesis; instead, they indicate a failure to reject the hypothesis.
2. Research is the process of making claims and then refining or abandoning some of them for other claims which are more strongly warranted. Most quantitative research, for example, starts with the test of a theory.
3. Data, evidence, and rational considerations shape knowledge. In practice, the researcher collects information on instruments based on measures completed by the participants or by observations recorded by the researcher.
4. Research seeks to develop relevant, true statements, ones that can serve to explain the situation of concern or that describe the causal relationships of interest. In quantitative studies, researchers advance the relationship among variables and pose this in terms of questions or hypotheses.
5. Being objective is an essential aspect of competent inquiry; researchers must examine methods and conclusions for bias. For example, standard of validity and reliability are important in quantitative research.

The Constructivist Worldview

Others hold a different worldview. Constructivism or social constructivism (often combined with interpretivism) is such a perspective, and it is typically seen as an approach to qualitative research. The ideas came from Mannheim and from works such as Berger and Luekmann's (1967) *The Social Construction of Reality* and Lincoln and Guba's (1985) *Naturalistic Inquiry*. More recent writers who have summarized this position are Lincoln and colleagues (2011), Mertens (2010), and Crotty (1998), among others. **Social constructivists** believe that individuals seek understanding of the world in which they live and work. Individuals develop subjective meanings of their experiences— meanings directed toward certain objects or things. These meanings are varied and multiple, leading the researcher to look for the complexity of views rather than narrowing meanings into a few categories or ideas. The goal of the research is to rely as much as possible on the participants' views of the situation being studied. The questions become broad and general so that the participants can construct the meaning of a situation, typically forged in discussions or interactions with other persons. The more open-ended the questioning, the better, as the researcher listens carefully to what people say or do in their life settings. Often these subjective meanings are negotiated socially and historically. They are not simply imprinted on individuals but are formed through interaction with others (hence social constructivism) and through historical and cultural norms that operate in individuals' lives. Thus, constructivist researchers often address the processes of interaction among individuals. They also focus on the specific contexts in which people live and work in order to understand the historical and cultural settings of the participants. Researchers recognize that their own backgrounds shape their interpretation, and they position themselves in the research to acknowledge how their interpretation flows from their personal, cultural, and historical experiences. The researcher's intent is to make sense of (or interpret) the meanings others have about the world. Rather than starting with a theory (as in postpositivism), inquirers generate or inductively develop a theory or pattern of meaning.

For example, in discussing constructivism, Crotty (1998) identified several assumptions:

1. Human beings construct meanings as they engage with the world they are interpreting. Qualitative researchers tend to use open-ended questions so that the participants can share their views.
2. Humans engage with their world and make sense of it based on their historical and social perspectives—we are all born into a world of meaning bestowed upon us by our culture. Thus, qualitative researchers seek to understand the context or setting of the participants through visiting this context and gathering information personally. They also interpret what they find, an interpretation shaped by the researcher's own experiences and background.
3. The basic generation of meaning is always social, arising in and out of interaction with a human community. The process of qualitative research is largely inductive; the inquirer generates meaning from the data collected in the field.

The Transformative Worldview

Another group of researchers holds to the philosophical assumptions of the transformative approach. This position arose during the 1980s and 1990s from individuals who felt that the postpositivist assumptions imposed structural laws and theories that did not fit marginalized individuals in our society or issues of power and social justice, discrimination, and oppression that needed to be addressed. There is no uniform body of literature characterizing this worldview, but it includes groups of researchers that are critical theorists; participatory action researchers; Marxists; feminists; racial and ethnic minorities; persons with disabilities; indigenous and postcolonial peoples; and members of the lesbian, gay, bisexual, transsexual, and queer communities. Historically, the transformative writers have drawn on the works of Marx, Adorno, Marcuse, Habermas, and Freire (Neuman, 2009). Fay (1987), Heron and Reason (1997), Kemmis and Wilkinson (1998), Kemmis and McTaggart (2000), and Mertens (2009, 2010).

In the main, these inquirers felt that the constructivist stance did not go far enough in advocating for an action agenda to help marginalized peoples. A **transformative worldview** holds that research inquiry needs to be intertwined with politics and a political change agenda to confront social oppression at whatever levels it occurs (Mertens, 2010). Thus, the research contains an action agenda for reform that may change lives of the participants, the institutions in which individuals work or live, and the researcher's life. Moreover, specific issues need to be addressed that speak to important social issues of the day, issues such as empowerment, inequality, oppression, domination, suppression, and alienation. The researcher often begins with one of these issues as the focal point of the study. This research also assumes that the inquirer will proceed collaboratively so as to not further marginalize the participants as a result of the inquiry. In this sense, the participants may help design questions, collect data, analyze information, or reap the rewards of the research. Transformative research provides a voice for these participants, raising their consciousness or advancing an agenda for change to improve their lives. It becomes a united voice for reform and change.

This philosophical worldview focuses on the needs of groups and individuals in our society that may be marginalized or disenfranchised. Therefore, theoretical perspectives may be integrated with the philosophical assumptions that construct a picture of the issues being examined, the people to be studied, and the changes that are needed, such as feminist perspectives, racialized discourses, critical theory, queer theory, and disability theory.

Although these are diverse groups and my explanations here are generalizations, it is helpful to view the summary by Mertens (2010) of key features of the transformative worldview or paradigm:

- It places central importance on the study of lives and experiences of diverse groups that have traditionally been marginalized. Of special interest for these diverse groups is how their lives have been constrained by oppressors and the strategies that they use to resist, challenge, and subvert these constraints.
- In studying these diverse groups, the research focuses on inequities based on gender, race, ethnicity, disability, sexual orientation, and socioeconomic class that result in asymmetric power relationships.
- The research in the transformative worldview links political and social action to these inequities.
- Transformative research uses a program theory of beliefs about how a program works and why the problems of oppression, domination, and power relationships exist.

The Pragmatic Worldview

Another position about worldviews comes from the pragmatists. Pragmatism derives from the work of Peirce, James, Mead, and Dewey (Cherryholmes, 1992). Other writers include Murphy (1990), Patton (1990), and Rorty (1990). There are many forms of this philosophy, but for many, pragmatism as a worldview arises out of actions, situations, and consequences rather than antecedent conditions (as in postpositivism). There is a concern with applications—what works—and solutions to problems (Patton, 1990). Instead of focusing on methods, researchers emphasize the research problem and use all approaches available to understand the problem (see Rossman & Wilson, 1985). As a philosophical underpinning for mixed methods studies, Morgan (2007), Patton (1990), and Tashakkori and Teddlie (2010) convey its importance for focusing attention on the research problem in social science research and then using pluralistic approaches to derive knowledge about the problem. Using Cherryholmes (1992), Morgan (2007), and my own views, pragmatism provides a philosophical basis for research:

- Pragmatism is not committed to any one system of philosophy and reality. This applies to mixed methods research in that inquirers draw liberally from both quantitative and qualitative assumptions when they engage in their research.
- Individual researchers have a freedom of choice. In this way, researchers are free to choose the methods, techniques, and procedures of research that best meet their needs and purposes.
- Pragmatists do not see the world as an absolute unity. In a similar way, mixed methods researchers look to many approaches for collecting and analyzing data rather than subscribing to only one way (e.g., quantitative or qualitative).
- Truth is what works at the time. It is not based in a duality between reality independent of the mind or within the mind. Thus, in mixed methods research, investigators use both quantitative and qualitative data because they work to provide the best understanding of a research problem.
- The pragmatist researchers look to the *what* and *how* to research based on the intended consequences—where they want to go with it. Mixed methods researchers need to establish a purpose for their mixing, a rationale for the reasons why quantitative and qualitative data need to be mixed in the first place.
- Pragmatists agree that research always occurs in social, historical, political, and other contexts. In this way, mixed methods studies may include a postmodern turn, a theoretical lens that is reflective of social justice and political aims.
- Pragmatists have believed in an external world independent of the mind as well as that lodged in the mind. But they believe that we need to stop asking questions about reality and the laws of nature (Cherryholmes, 1992). "They would simply like to change the subject" (Rorty, 1983, p. xiv).

- Thus, for the mixed methods researcher, pragmatism opens the door to multiple methods, different worldviews, and different assumptions, as well as different forms of data collection and analysis.

Quick Reference

Worldviews might seem ambiguous and unimportant (mostly because worldview isn't your focus of attention right now), but those beliefs that you hold DIRECTLY affect research. How? Because the approach you take toward research, the questions you choose to ask and the methods you use to seek out the answers, are all based off of your worldview. For example, you'll see that later in the book, quantitative and qualitative researchers begin with different foundational beliefs about the world around them. So, they are then looking through different lenses and that changes their research.

—*Kristen Hark*

---

*How Do We Know What We Know?

Where Does Knowledge Come From?

Of course, in order to answer these and other questions, we are forced to confront difficult issues concerning knowledge itself. These aren't likely to be questions that you ask yourself every day. Most of us go through our everyday lives with a fairly comfortable understanding of what is and what is not. Our view of the world may come from a variety of sources, and we generally don't stop to think about what those sources may be. We certainly don't often stop to ask ourselves the question: Where does knowledge come from?

The study of knowledge itself is known as **epistemology** (Babbie, 1995). Before examining communication research, the questions it asks, and methods of exploring those questions, it may be helpful to think about different ways of understanding what it is that we know to be true. This serves to illustrate both how we make sense of our world, and how scholarly inquiry may deviate from these means of gathering knowledge. The philosopher Charles Peirce identified four methods of knowing: tenacity, authority, a priori, and science (Buchler, 1955). We'll discuss these plus a few others—personal experience; traditions, customs and faith; magic, superstition, and/or mysticism; and intuition or hunches.

epistemology
The study of knowledge.

Much research is dedicated to things that we see in our everyday lives, the functionality of everyday interactions, and ways in which we make sense of the world around us. In fact, if we think about it for a minute, there are countless examples of everyday behaviors that can be informed by research.

Perhaps you are walking across campus one day, and someone approaches you and asks if you would like to buy some raffle tickets for a local charity. While you don't mind helping a good cause, you realize that before you knew it your wallet was out and you were handing over cash. How was this person so convincing? Why were you so willing to comply?

You get into an argument with your significant other. You don't feel that he is spending enough time with you, while he thinks he is doing the right thing by not trying to smother you or monopolize your time. How did this disconnect take place? How can two people in a relationship see that relationship so differently?

experience
A common way of understanding the social world.

Experience. One of our best teachers is often personal experience. Many of us learn much of understanding of the social world by experiencing. The easiest example of this type of knowledge conforms to the adage that sometimes we have to learn the hard way. Touching a hot stove with your hand is a pretty good teacher. Not many experiences with a hot stove are necessary before you have complete knowledge of what will happen if you touch another hot item. Our experience with people is no different. We may have had previous experiences with specific people, similar people, or situations that we can then use as a guide to anticipate and interpret a new experience and/or situation. This is known as generalizing and it is an important aim for some scientific research. The value of this type of knowing is that it can be a fruitful beginning upon which we build to gain knowledge.

tenacity
The assumption that something is true because it has always been said to be true.

Tenacity. Think of some things about the world that everybody knows. For example, "everybody knows" that if you toss a coin off the Empire State Building, it will kill whomever it lands upon. Likewise, "everybody knows" that a dog's mouth is actually cleaner than a human's; bad guys in the Old West always wore black hats; and when you cross the equator, toilets begin flushing in the opposite direction.

There is just one problem with all of these statements: None of them are true. A coin tossed off a skyscraper does not have enough mass, relative to resistance from the air below it, to accelerate to a speed that could kill someone. Think about how you bathe and how your dog bathes. Lawmen and outlaws in the Old West wore hats that came in a variety of colors. Toilets will flush in the direction that water enters them (usually counterclockwise), whether they are in New York or Melbourne. So how, then, do statements such as those above become accepted as "facts"?

Part of the reason may be our tendency to rely on tenacity as a method of knowing. Tenacity is simply the assumption that something is true because it always has been said to be true. Knowledge is passed from person to person and generation to generation through cultural norms and assumptions. You may believe that the sun rises in the morning because the sun god Ra wills it so; if you do, chances are it's because that's what your parents, grandparents, and great-grandparents believed. Furthermore, consensus plays a critical role in tenacity as a source of knowledge: the frequent repetition of these so-called facts makes them seem more likely to be true (Kerlinger, 1992).

Even in the face of conflicting information, people will hold onto their beliefs and rationalize away evidence that flies in the face of what they already hold to be true.

Of course, tenacity is not inherently bad as a means of knowing. It comes in handy in a variety of different scenarios, mostly because, as humans, we don't have the time or energy to consider all possible explanations for every observation we ever make. And very often, it provides us with knowledge that is useful and accurate. We don't really need to formally test the notion that stepping out in front of traffic is a bad idea, or that it is more likely to rain if it is cloudy outside, or that your lawn will grow if you water it. These are things that most of us have always accepted as being true, have heard repeated over and over, and for the most part are correct.

Authority. Another important instructor in everyday knowledge is authority. Authority is when we turn to experts to help us make sense out of a particular situation. Authority has less to do with the repetition of information and more to do with the perceived credibility of the source of that information. Very often, people realize they are not experts on a given subject, to the extent that they may not even be able to comprehend or make sense of their observations. In these instances, they often rely on someone in a position of power to tell them what is factual. This power may be derived from a variety of places, such as expertise, political power, religious authority, or interpersonal trust.

Consider this common example. Many people have someone they go to for information about anything having to do with computers, software, or technology. This person may have been assembling and disassembling computers since he was a child, or he may be more of a programmer type who enjoys cracking the source code on various software applications. In any case, this person can probably tell you how to turn on the computer, as this will be child's play given their level of expertise. This person could tell you practically anything, and you would assume it to be true (at least until you try it out, and even then you might assume that you are not following his or her instructions correctly, since he or she, after all, is the expert).

Advertisements using celebrity spokespersons are good examples of how authority guides our knowledge building. If Michael Jordan tells us to purchase Hanes underwear, then we think we should since we have trust in him. After all, Michael wouldn't lie to us, would he? Authority only works as a source of knowledge if I have faith in the authority figure or she has some control over me. For example, one of your authors once served on a jury. One of the experts brought in to testify in the case was a drug specialist for the state of North Carolina. Her job was to explain to us the laboratory tests conducted on the white substance found in the defendant's car and convince us that it was, in fact, crack cocaine. Due to her experience, her education, and the way in which she presented herself, the jury never debated over whether the substance was actually crack cocaine. Her authority created knowledge for us.

authority
The reliance upon someone in a position of power to determine what is factual. This power may be derived from a variety of places, such as expertise, political power, religious authority, or interpersonal trust.

Consider another example: Most of us have experienced our parents' authority, and you can probably remember how smart your parents were when you were a small child and how stupid they became when you reached adolescence! If they haven't already, they'll become much smarter in your eyes as you move through college and into adulthood. You probably believed your parents' authority when they told you that vegetables were good for your health, and you might someday use your mom's advice for making stock market picks.

Authority has value, if we believe the authority to be reliable, because it saves us time from having to find out everything for ourselves. What's the downside of relying on information from an authority without checking it out for ourselves? Authorities are sometimes wrong, or they may have biased information or opinions.

Traditions, Customs, and Faith. Traditions, customs, and faith are also great teachers. A perfect example is the adage "an apple a day keeps the doctor away." An adage is a type of tradition, and while we all know eating one apple a day really will not ensure our not getting sick, we also know that eating a healthy diet, including fruits, does increase the likelihood of living a healthy life.

Think about the things you've come to know by the traditions your family followed and the knowledge passed down from one generation to the next. Take the tradition of the Easter basket. In a recent conversation with another mother, who is a friend of one of your authors, we were discussing Easter baskets for our daughters. She detailed her search for just the right basket this year, as she couldn't reuse last year's basket, or her daughter might catch on. I responded that at our house the Easter bunny uses the basket that we already have, which I place out in the house for decoration during the Easter season. What our daughters know about the Easter bunny is based upon the traditions each family follows. Her daughter is convinced the Easter bunny is wealthy, while my daughter knows that the Easter bunny is concerned with the environment! Another great example comes from the same friend. She grew up in the South during the 1960s and 1970s and loved Pepsi. It was a treat not often allowed in her youth. Because her family expected each child to drink a glass of milk with each meal, Dianne would guzzle down her glass of milk, hoping for a chance to have her cherished beverage. However, Dianne's mother explained to her that drinking Pepsi after milk would upset her stomach and cause her to be sick. It was not until she was away at college that Dianne realized she had been duped. This demonstrates how we know or believe things to be true because we've been told or taught by others to believe them early in life. While the latter examples may not ring true, many customs, such as eating an apple a day, are based upon solid evidence.

Intuition or Hunches. Most of us also have some form of knowledge we believe is based upon intuition. Intuition is that feeling we get that we often call our *gut feeling*. It is some internal-based instinct we have about a situation, issue, or experience. It is not unusual for us to accept certain things as true, just because they make sense. Some people see intuition as a "leap of insight." Again, intuition can produce useful ideas, but since we are unable to explain why, it can be difficult to investigate.

A Priori Reasoning. The a priori way of knowing has its roots in early philosophers contemplating epistemology, such as Immanuel Kant. A priori knowledge refers to ways of knowing that are independent of empirical observation, that are known through personal reasoning or judgment.

For lack of a better way of putting it, a priori reasoning is based on logic, or the fact that there are some things you just simply know to be true. Based on universal truths, you might know something is true even if you haven't tested it.

For example, let's say you are trying to move an enormous couch into your apartment. It weighs about 300 pounds, and you and your roommate have been trying to get it up a stairwell for half an hour. It isn't working. You look over and see a large freight elevator. A priori knowledge tells you that using the elevator to move the couch will greatly increase your likelihood of success. You don't have to test the hypothesis or conduct an engineering test of the elevator—it's a universal truth that elevators reduce effort.

Of course, it's possible that the elevator is broken. This illustrates the major shortcoming of a priori reasoning: exceptions to logic. While accumulated experience in related matters may lead to an assumption about a specific experience, there is always the possibility that this particular scenario deviates from past experiences.

> **a priori**
> This form of reasoning is based on personal reasoning or logic, or the fact that there are some things you just simply know to be true.

· ▼

What's Wrong with Everyday Ways of Knowing?

While the everyday ways of knowing we have detailed above do provide a starting point for building knowledge, there are numerous problems inherent in these ways of knowing. People tend to place more trust in their beliefs from personal experience than from evidence that may be contrary to their own experience. We must consider some of these problems with everyday ways of knowing.

Accuracy

First, all in all, the majority of us are not very accurate at making observations. We tend to be pretty casual observers. Think back for a minute to the last person you saw. Who was that person? What was he or she wearing? What kind of shoes? Do you remember the details? Most of us do not.

Overgeneralization

Another problem with our everyday ways of knowing is overgeneralization. As individuals, we prefer our world to be orderly and, as such, we tend to generalize our knowledge to a broader reach. This can be problematic when we base this knowledge on just a few experiences or observations. For example, we might generalize that people with college degrees are less likely to get divorced. However, what if our experience is atypical? We need to be cautious when it comes to generalizing based on limited data in any form.

Cognitive Conservatism

cognitive conservatism
The idea that how someone views the world is often based upon his or her prior beliefs.

Yet another difficulty with everyday knowing is that, once we believe something, we tend to pay special attention to experiences and situations that are consistent with our beliefs, and disregard those that are inconsistent with our beliefs. This is called **cognitive conservatism**, the idea that how we view the world is often based upon our prior beliefs. Allport and Postman (1945) conducted a series of studies that demonstrate how cognitive conservatism works. In this research, they played a game called "Rumor," where a message is given to the first person who then must whisper in his or her neighbor's ear, each in turn, until the message is shared aloud by the last participant. For their study on racial prejudice, they showed white subjects a picture of a fight between a white man and a black man on a train. The white man was holding a razor to the black man in the picture. What do you suppose participants experienced? Yes, that's right; the razor typically changed hands. Allport and Postman noted information that does not fit the predisposition of a perceiver is likely to be forgotten or changed in memory.

Contradictory Knowledge

Everyday ways of knowing can lead to contradictions in what we know. For example, if you've ever been in a long-distance relationship, you've likely heard the expression "absence makes the heart grow fonder," and that makes logical sense. However, you might have also experienced the effects of "if you can't be with the one you love, love the one you're with." So you know that both could be true. Your parents or other authorities (including your friends) might have given you advice on one side or the other about that reality, and they could probably cite everyday evidence to support each claim.

scientific reasoning
A way of knowing where one has a hunch about how things ought to be, then tests that hunch by making observations.

hypotheses
Educated guesses about a social phenomenon based on prior observations.

Scientific Reasoning

This leads us to the final way of knowing, identified by Charles Pierce and cited by Buchler (1955): science. The scientific method attempts to address the problems with these everyday ways of knowing. **Scientific reasoning** begins with a priori assumptions, but goes a step further—it includes *self-correction* (Kerlinger, 1992). Under the method of science, one has an idea about how things ought to be, then tests this by making observations. These ideas are often called **hypotheses,** or educated guesses, about a social phenomenon based on prior observations. Scientists propose hypotheses and then make observations in order to test them.

One major misconception of science as a way of knowing is that science *proves* things. Scientific reasoning by its very nature is skeptical, and scientists don't make claims about the truth in black-and-white terms. Rather, scientists are more likely to talk about *probability* and confidence in their conclusions. They discuss their conclusions in terms of the likelihood of their explanations and observations being true. In fact, the process of scientific reasoning is largely concerned with the *disproving* of a priori statements, as opposed to looking for ways of finding out that they are correct. Scientists start from a position of skepticism, assuming their hunches to be wrong, and evaluate their observations in terms of how they may refute or fail to refute their hypotheses. They then repeat their procedures in order to build more confidence in these conclusions. In order to do so, science must remain objective, without the biases, values, or attitudes of the scientist interfering with the interpretation of this data.

The most useful advantage to scientific thinking is the ability to *predict*. Of course, science can be a cumbersome way of understanding our everyday experiences. Using our example earlier, if you are lugging a couch up a stairwell, you don't have time to conduct a series of tests to determine the best course of action; you just need to move the couch. If your hard drive crashes, you probably don't want to conduct a series of tests of different procedures that may fix the problem; you just want it fixed immediately! If a conclusion drawn from tenacity or authority accomplishes this task, then so be it.

Science is, however, very useful in the understanding of more complex social phenomena. The repeated testing of hypotheses in an academic or applied research environment may lead to the basic goal of science: the development of **theory**. Accumulating these statements over time may lead to the formation of a theory, otherwise known as "a set of interrelated constructs, definitions, and propositions that present a systematic view of phenomena by specifying relations among variables, with the purpose of explaining and predicting the phenomena" (Kerlinger, 1992, p. 9). In plain terms, this is to say that systematically seeking to answer questions and understand phenomena can lead to useful heuristics (techniques to answer questions and address problems) and allow us to make informed predictions and understandings about social behavior under different circumstances. Theoretical work derived from academic research can then serve to inform everyday problems and issues.

theory
A set of interrelated constructs, definitions, and propositions that present a systematic view of phenomena by specifying relations among variables, with the purpose of explaining and predicting the phenomena.

Scholarly Research

Generally speaking, researchers draw a distinction between *scholarly research* and *applied research*. When we speak of **scholarly research**, this usually refers to primary research conducted by professors and academics and distributed through academic publications. As stated above, scholarly research is often driven by the desire to build or explain theory. Those conducting scholarly research are typically concerned with the theoretical implications of their findings and building or contributing to theories.

scholarly research
Primary research conducted by academic researchers and distributed through academic publications with the desire to build theory.

Let's take one well-known example of the development of a theory that is widely used in communication and psychology research: the Theory of Reasoned Action (Ajzen & Fishbein, 1980). Frustrated with past research in persuasion, Ajzen and Fishbein began conducting a series of experiments during the 1970s and 1980s looking at other things they thought might be important in the process of compliance. Through numerous studies, they came to the conclusion that while there is a link between attitude change and actual behaviors, there are other things that are important as well. Most notably, they identified people's intentions as a critical factor that had been overlooked. The Theory of Reasoned Action argues (to put it in the simplest terms possible) that attitudes don't directly affect people's behavior; they affect people's intentions to behave in a certain way, which then may or may not result in a change of behavior.

For example, a commercial advocating that people stop smoking might be effective in changing a person's attitude toward smoking (e.g., "Okay, now we see that smoking is a bad idea"), but this does not necessarily mean she will quit. Instead, the Theory of Reasoned Action would argue that not only does she have to realize that it is a bad idea, but also actually *decide* that she is going to quit before doing so. Of course, there are a number of reasons why things might break down; the person in question may or may not actually decide to quit, and then may or may not actually do it.

Still, something was missing. Adding a person's intentions into the equation did a better job of explaining persuasion, but did not explain it completely. As Ajzen and Fishbein continued these experiments throughout the 1980s and 1990s, they came to the conclusion that an important consideration might be people's belief that they could actually get it done. They (and others) have called this "behavioral control." In fact, they found that attitudes were more likely to drive intentions, and intentions were more likely to drive behavior, if people actually believed that they could successfully perform the behavior in question. To tie it in to our smoking example above, a person may experience a shift in her attitude toward smoking; this attitude shift is much more likely to lead her to attempting to quit if she *believes* that she can quit. Likewise, if she tries to quit, she is more likely to actually do so if she believes she can. The committed smoker, who has been doing it for years and years and has given up on the idea of ever quitting, may form an increasingly negative view of the habit, but she will not likely try to quit, and if she does try, she will likely fail.

By adding in a person's behavioral control to the theory, Ajzen and Fishbein modified their original theory and gave it a new title: Theory of Planned Behavior (TPB) (Ajzen, 1995). Through decades of fine tuning and adjustment, the results of their studies led to a well-informed and commonly applied theory that has been used to explain persuasion in a variety of contexts, including smoking, drinking, signing up for treatment programs, using contraceptives, dieting, wearing seatbelts or safety helmets, exercising regularly, voting, and breast-feeding (Fishbein, Middlestadt, & Hitchcock, 1994).

Applied Research

Fishbein and Ajzen's work has proved to be a major contribution to thinking. Developing their framework through scholarly research has helped inform not only theoretical development on the topic of persuasion, but also numerous studies evaluating the utility of the theory in real-world contexts.

Such research is often labeled *applied research*. Scholars take the theoretical lessons learned in their academic studies and further apply them to varying real-life contexts. **Applied research** is typically concerned with investigating whether theoretical developments can be taken outside of the academic setting and used to solve more tangible social problems. While applied research can often be found in the same journals and texts as theoretical research, the goal of applied research is quite different—to test theory in the field to see if it can be used to solve problems.

Often, applied research addresses very specific concerns. For example, Roberto, Krieger, Katz, Goei, and Jain (2011) tested the Theory of Reasoned Action, as described above, to see if it could be applied to pediatricians' likelihood to encourage parents to get their daughters vaccinated for the HPV virus. After mailing out a survey measuring attitudes, norms, perceived control, intentions, and behaviors, the authors analyzed the links between these data points to see if TPB held in this context. They report that it did, and that positive attitudes toward the vaccine, subjective norms regarding its use, and perceptions of behavioral control all combined to predict the likelihood that the subjects would encourage parents to get their daughters the vaccine. Thus, the authors offered evidence that this theory was effective in explaining one highly specific, real-life problem.

applied research
Research that takes the theoretical lessons learned in academic studies and applies them to varying real-life contexts.

Types of Research

As we have considered the metatheoretical foundations, research perspectives, and possible paradigms guiding scholarly research, we have yet to consider the characteristics of research. In other words, how do we conduct research? Research involves disciplined inquiry. We take a scientific approach to research, no matter our metatheoretical considerations, our paradigm, or our method. We work to avoid the problems we encounter in our everyday ways of acquiring knowledge. There are two types of research: proprietary and scholarly. Most of you at one point or another will be responsible for or involved in both types of research.

Proprietary Research

Proprietary research is conducted for a specific audience, which is not shared beyond the intended audience. Many corporations and businesses conduct research to examine anything from their business practices, to satisfaction with employee benefits programs, to marketing new products and services within potential client or consumer groups. Many of you may end up doing this type of research for your career.

Scholarly Research

Scholarly research is conducted for the goal of contributing to knowledge for public consumption. While most research methods courses focus on scholarly research, it is important to realize that the steps, methods, and/or approaches for how to conduct research don't change, regardless of what type of research you are conducting.

Characteristics of Scholarly Research.
Research is question-oriented. Academic scholarship is always interested in answering interesting questions. Questions come in all forms, from a variety of places. Sometimes we come up with questions through our experience and other everyday ways of knowing, recognizing the limitations of this type of knowledge. This is often a good way to come up with questions, but is only a starting point. Other questions come about from reading scholarly work and recognizing questions left unanswered from previous research.

- Research is methodological. As we suggested earlier, research involves planning and following a systematic approach for data collection and analysis. Regardless of the research questions, research follows rules. These rules may differ depending upon the research methodology we choose; yet, there are rules nonetheless.
- Research is creative. This is often a characteristic of research that many students fail to recognize. We are in the process of creating new knowledge or adding to existing knowledge, and there are a variety of ways we can do this. Selecting (or inventing) the best ways to know is a delightfully creative process.
- Research is self-critical. As researchers, we are obligated to examine our own work from a critical vantage point. We should always be the first critic of our own work, fairly assessing the strengths and weaknesses of our scholarship. It is imperative that we remember there is no *perfect* research study; there is always more to learn. Good scholarship acknowledges the limitations of the work as a method of advancing our understanding. This self-critical view also suggests areas of future research.
- Research is public. As we discussed earlier, academic research is conducted for public consumption. Researchers typically view scholarship as a mechanism for serving useful social purposes. If you ask

most scholars what they most love about conducting research, it is the idea that they can work toward scholarship that may be useful to someone.

- Research is both cumulative and self-correcting. All research is built upon previous scholarship. Good scholarship begins with the ability to gather scholarly research and critically assess the results of the work. This provides researchers the opportunity to correct mistakes made in other work. While we often think of correcting others' research, scholars often have the opportunity to improve upon their own previous research.

- Research is cyclical. All research occurs in stages. The stages are determined first and foremost by the type of research question(s) we ask. The research question(s) determine the methodological design of the research project and the way we analyze the data we gather. Ultimately, while research answers questions, it also generates new questions that need to be answered.

Two Logical Systems

The purpose of social science is to build knowledge that contributes to our understanding of behaviors. There are two logical systems that allow social scientists to do just that. It is important to remember that the type of question determines which logical system we use. Neither is better than the other; in fact, they are merely different entry points into the same system.

Inductive Model

One system is the **inductive model**. This approach to research is often referred to as grounded theory, and it is often appropriate when we know little about a topic. Inductive methods can help create theory that can be tested with deduction (our second system). With inductive methods, instead of starting out with a theory and testing the theory, scholars begin the research process by gathering data, observing patterns and idiosyncrasies within the data, and developing theory based upon that data. Most scholars who prefer this method of inquiry use qualitative research methods. It is said that inductive reasoning moves us from the specific (the research study) to the general (the theory), while deductive reasoning moves us from the general (the theory) to the specific (the research study).

One interesting example of induction comes from a study on physicians' disclosure of confidential patient information. Maria Brann (2006) wondered how physicians balanced families' caregiving needs for information with patients' confidentiality rights. Using grounded theory, she interviewed physicians and used a detailed thematic coding process. Her findings theorized that the nature and severity of the patient's impairment influenced physician disclosures. She determined that federal privacy laws (HIPAA regulations)

inductive model
This approach to research is often referred to as grounded theory. Scholars begin the research process by gathering data, observing patterns and idiosyncrasies within the data, and developing theory based upon that data. Most scholars who prefer this method of inquiry use qualitative research methods.

did not seem to discourage physicians from disclosing information, primarily because they were motivated by concern for the patient and belief in their own judgment. In other words, she developed a theoretical conclusion based on her research findings, which is an inductive approach.

Deductive Model

deductive model
This model is typically referred to as theory driven. Scholars preferring a deductive approach begin with a theory and gather evidence to evaluate that theory. Most scholars who prefer this method of inquiry use quantitative research methods.

The other system is the **deductive model**. This model is typically referred to as theory driven. Scholars preferring a deductive approach begin with a theory and gather evidence to evaluate that theory. Most scholars who prefer this method of inquiry use quantitative research methods.

One example of a deductive approach is Geddes' 2001 study on the impact of speech style such as gender/power on the perception of employee satisfaction and speaker effectiveness. She created both male- and female-delivered messages with one of three speech styles: powerless, powerful, and a mix of powerless and powerful. Union members were asked to evaluate one of these speech styles reporting on the effectiveness of the manager's speech style, as well as the employee satisfaction they experienced viewing the message. Geddes (2001) found that both male and female managers using the mixed speech style were rated both most effective and elicited the most satisfaction. This study demonstrates a deductive approach.

An interesting example of a deductive approach using qualitative methods is Alexander Lyon's research (2007) on Merck's marketing of the pain medication Vioxx. Building on Deetz's theory about systematically distorted communication, Lyon used a multiple case study approach to analyze Merck's corporate communication. He determined that Merck used neutralization, topic avoidance, and disqualification to reduce the amount of open information patients and physicians received about the drug, and to thus stifle their decision-making ability. Lyon used a deductive approach—starting with Deetz's theory, developing a study to apply that theory, then evaluating the theory in the context of Merck's communication.

▼ . . . .

Qualitative and Quantitative Research

Finally, to conclude our discussion of research perspectives and paradigms, we must consider the overarching concepts of qualitative and quantitative research. It is paramount that you understand what the differences are, as well as understand that the research question we ask must always drive our methodological decision making. Therefore, if we ask a question best suited to qualitative methods, even though we prefer quantitative methods, we have to consider whether we are both able and willing to step outside our comfort zone to answer the question appropriately. We suggest to our students that a good scholar will, despite her own individual preferences, come to appreciate and understand the utility of both qualitative and quantitative methods. Neither method is a better method; they just address different questions using different methods, all contributing to our understanding of the world around us.

One way to distinguish between qualitative and quantitative research is to think: Is the research what you might call *art-based* or is it *science-based?* Qualitative research is sometimes thought of more like art, while quantitative research is more like science.

Qualitative Research

Qualitative research methods embrace a naturalistic, interpretive paradigm typically conducting research from an inductive discovery based point of view. Here scholars often seek to answer research questions that consider how our reality is constructed in interaction. They are less concerned with generalizing to a wider population or other cases; rather they tend to focus on studying the way in which their research participants understand, describe, and see the world. Qualitative research methods are best used when there is not much previously known about the topic, when the topic is personal, and when you want to know more in great detail about a small unit or event. Some of the research tools that qualitative researchers make use of include: observation, participation, interviews, focus groups, reviewing documents, gathering life histories, exploring one's own life, field notes, transcripts, and narrative forms of coding data. Qualitative research strives toward the goals of preserving human behavior, analyzing its qualities, and representing different worldviews and experiences. Qualitative researchers see themselves as part of the process of creating knowledge and meaning through understanding what's going on.

qualitative research Research, usually studying words or texts, that uses methods which embrace a naturalistic, interpretive paradigm typically from an inductive discovery based point of view.

Quantitative Research

Quantitative research methods embrace a postpositivist paradigm, typically conducting research from a deductive explanatory based point of view. Here they often seek to answer research questions based on the premise that reality is knowable and measurable. Scholars taking the quantitative approach are most interested in generalizing to a wider audience, and they believe that knowledge is something objective that is found and measured. Quantitative methods are best used when you seek to learn something about a lot of people and/or when you are interested in generalizing from your sample to a larger group of people; or when you seek to generalize to a similar situation. Some of the research tools that qualitative researchers make use of include experiments, questionnaires, surveys, interviews, statistical methods, theory testing, secondary data analysis, and numerical coding. The primary goals of quantitative research include representing and explaining objective reality with the overarching goal of simplifying, organizing, predicting, and controlling human behavior.

quantitative research Research, usually studying numerical data (or reducing words to numerical data), that uses methods which embrace a postpositivist paradigm typically from a deductive explanatory based point of view.

Table 1.2 is a summary of the basic differences between qualitative and quantitative research:

Table 1.2. Basic Characteristics of Qualitative and Quantitative Research

Qualitative	Quantitative
Impressionist	Realist
Inductive	Deductive
Goal is to discover, preserve form and content of human behavior, represent different world views, create knowledge and meaning, understand what's going on.	Goal is to explain, subject the world to statistical transformations, predict and control, represent and explain objective reality.
Assumption is that reality is constructed in interaction.	Assumption that reality is objective and measureable.
Believes that knowledge is created.	Believes that knowledge is found and received.
Generalizes research findings to other cases or similar phenomena.	Generalizes research findings as widely as possible.
The purpose is to understand, describe, get close to those studied, to understand how participants see the world.	The purpose is to measure relationships among variables, test hypotheses, predict, and control.
Is appropriate when you want to know a lot about a small unit, where not much is known about the topic, when the topic is something you can be immersed in, when you have a desire to make the strange familiar or the familiar strange.	Is appropriate when you want to know something about a lot of people, when you want to generalize from your sample to a large group.

Using our previous language on ontology, epistemology, and axiology, quantitative researchers tend toward the realist end of the spectrum, while qualitative researchers tend toward the nominalist or social constructionist end of the spectrum (Table 1.2).

As we've said several times, the method you choose depends entirely on your research question—different methods are most appropriate for answering different research questions. However, as you've seen, because qualitative and quantitative research methods represent different ontologies, epistemologies, and axiologies, researchers tend toward one or the other. In other words, since how you see the world determines the type of research questions you ask, this influences the type of research methods you tend to use. So, for fun, let's see where you fall on the spectrum of beliefs and methods.

You might be a qualitative researcher if you:

Like ambiguity and complexity.
Like to ask questions.
Like to interact/be with people.

Like to analyze immediate experience.
Fantasize about what goes on behind people's windows/phone calls.
Concentrate on episodic, emotional aspects of social life.
Question authority.

You might be a quantitative researcher if you:

Like to simplify, organize, manage the world, categorize the world.
Like math and formulas.
Usually think there's a separate, objective reality to be captured.
Concentrate on rational, patterned order of social life.
Write in authoritative, declarative sentences.

		Ontological Assumptions (What do we believe about reality?)	Epistemological Assumptions (What can we know and study?)	Axiological Assumptions (What do we value in research and knowledge?)
Realist QUANTITATIVE	Positivism/ Postpositivism	Reality is orderly, fixed, and measurable.	We can know and study objective reality.	We value research that is objective and researchers who are expert authorities.
	Critical/ Cultural	May believe reality is orderly, measurable, objective. May believe reality is subjective.	We can know and study reality that is either objective or subjective. We can know and study reality that is interpreted or observed as is.	We value research that includes marginalized voices. We value research in which the researcher shares power with participants.
Nominalist/Social Constructionist QUALITATIVE	Interpretivism	Reality is both orderly and chaotic. Reality is subjective.	We can know and study subjective reality as it is constructed, mediated, and biased.	We value research in which all participants are equal authorities and in which all perspectives are represented.

Quick Reference

Worldviews might seem ambiguous and unimportant (mostly because worldview isn't your focus of attention right now), but those beliefs that you hold DIRECTLY affect research. How? Because the approach you take toward research, the questions you choose to ask and the methods you use to seek out the answers, are all based off of your worldview. For example, you'll see that later in the book, quantitative and qualitative researchers begin with different foundational beliefs about the world around them. So, they are then looking through different lenses and that changes their research.

—Kristen Hark

▼ ....

How Is Research Knowledge Distributed?

Academic Publishing

Of course, answering these questions is not a particularly useful endeavor if no one knows about it. In both the natural sciences and in social research, the most common way of distributing the answers to the questions asked by researchers is through academic publishing. There are a number of scholarly journals that provide an outlet for the distribution of these findings. Scholars often publish books and volumes of selected studies that report the findings of their research. They are also known to publish their work in journals and volumes outside the field, or in collaboration with scholars from other disciplines.

One common misconception surrounding academic publishing is the notion of the ivory tower. People often think that social researchers, sit around mulling over grand ideas that have little bearing on the real world. Many people would also say no one outside of academia reads scholarly research, or places much value in its findings and conclusions.

Social Dialogue and Public Policy

Social researchers in particular, have a long history of contributing to social dialogue on the relevant issues of the day. Government agencies, policy-makers, and businesses frequently look to research published in academic journals to inform their decision making.

Take this example: A hotly contested social issue is the unrealistic portrayal of body image on television. Public health officials, psychologists, and communication researchers have become increasingly concerned with the abundance of dangerously thin people in mainstream media, and in particular, what impact this may have on self-esteem and eating disorders among adolescents. Further, they have become concerned with the ways in which television may influence our perceptions of people of varying sizes and how this may contribute to various forms of stereotyping. In 1999, a team of communication researchers led by Bradley S. Greenberg decided to examine television characters in terms of both their body sizes and the ways in which they were portrayed. Generally speaking, they found that a little less than a third of the women on television can be classified as dangerously underweight, while larger characters on television are often ridiculed or presented in other unflattering ways.

The article was presented at an academic convention in Quebec and was eventually published in the *American Journal of Public Health* (Greenberg, Eastin, Hofshire, Lachlan, & Brownell, 2003). However, realizing that there may be a wider market that could use this information, Greenberg's research team created a press release and distributed it to varying media outlets. This press release caught the attention of *USA Today*, which promptly ran a story on the findings. Thus the findings of the study were made available not just to other scholars interested in the subject matter, but to the general public, policymakers, parents, and activists.

There are numerous examples of research being disseminated not only to those in academic circles, but also to the general public and to those in positions of authority. Researchers have even *testified before Congress* regarding the implications of their findings. Notably, a large number of researchers played a pivotal role in the 1972 Surgeon General's Commission Report (U. S. Surgeon General's Scientific Advisory Committee on Television and Social Behavior, 1972), on television violence and aggressive behavior. Researchers have presented testimonies on the influence and impact of alcohol advertising on young consumers, tobacco advertising, violence in video games, sexual television content, and numerous others.

Here's another, very different example. The May 26, 2009, edition of the *Charlotte Observer* reported on a play put on by a writing company, a university professor, and staff and residents of a residential maternity home. The play, performed for the public, depicts—through the use of drama and performance—stories and experiences of the home's clients—pregnant women, children in foster care, and at-risk adolescents. The purpose of the play is to inspire empathy (Toppman, 2009, p. 5D), and it's a great example of performance studies being used for social dialogue.

The Popular Press

Scholars often release the results of their academic work to the popular press in hopes that it will draw the attention of those in business and government. Other scholars have published books based on their research that made their way to the popular press. H. L. Goodall, for example, conducted an autoethnographic exploration of his father's work for the CIA and published a novel titled *A Need to Know: The Clandestine History of a CIA Family* (Goodall, 2006).

. . . . ▼

So What?

As you can see, both quantitative and qualitative research methods answer interesting questions and help us come closer to understanding both the world around us and the people within it. And while some researchers claim that one method is better than another, there are benefits to both methods. It is our goal to objectively consider the strengths and limitations with all types of research practices. Remember that the research question and/or hypotheses drive our decision about how to pursue our research and the research methods we follow.

. . . . ▼

Glossary

A priori
This form of reasoning is based on personal reasoning or logic, or the fact that there are some things you just simply know to be true.

Applied research
Research that takes the theoretical lessons learned in academic studies and applies them to varying real-life contexts.

Authority

The reliance upon someone in a position of power to determine what is factual. This power may be derived from a variety of places, such as expertise, political power, religious authority, or interpersonal trust.

Cognitive conservatism

The idea that how someone views the world is often based upon his or her prior beliefs.

Deductive model

This model is typically referred to as theory driven. Communication scholars preferring a deductive approach begin with a theory and gather evidence to evaluate that theory. Most scholars who prefer this method of inquiry use quantitative research methods.

Epistemology

The study of knowledge.

Experience

A common way of understanding the social world.

Hypotheses

Educated guesses about a social phenomenon based on prior observations.

Inductive model

This approach to research is often referred to as grounded theory. Communication scholars begin the research process by gathering data, observing patterns and idiosyncrasies within the data, and developing theory based upon that data. Most scholars who prefer this method of inquiry use qualitative research methods.

Proprietary research

Research that is conducted for a specific audience, which is not shared beyond the intended audience.

Qualitative research

Research, usually studying words or texts, that uses methods which embrace a naturalistic, interpretive paradigm typically from an inductive discovery based point of view.

Quantitative research

Research, usually studying numerical data (or reducing words to numerical data), that uses methods which embrace a postpositivist paradigm typically from a deductive explanatory based point of view.

Scientific reasoning

A way of knowing where one has a hunch about how things ought to be, then tests that hunch by making observations.

Scholarly research

Primary research conducted by academic researchers and distributed through academic publications with the desire to build theory.

Scholarly research

Research conducted to contribute to generalizable knowledge for public consumption.

Tenacity

The assumption that something is true because it has always been said to be true.

Theory

A set of interrelated constructs, definitions, and propositions that present a systematic view of phenomena by specifying relations among variables, with the purpose of explaining and predicting the phenomena.

▼ ....

References

Ajzen, I. (1995). Attitudes and behavior. Beliefs. Theory of reasoned action. Theory of planned behavior. In A. S. R. Manstead & M. Hewstone (Eds.), *The Blackwell dictionary of social psychology*. Oxford, UK: Blackwell.

Ajzen, I., & Fishbein, M. (1980). *Understanding attitudes and predicting social behavior.* Englewood Cliffs, NJ: Prentice-Hall.

Allport, G. W., & Postman, L. J. (1945). The basic psychology of rumor. *Transactions of the New York Academy of Sciences, 8,* 61–81.

Babbie, E. (1995). *The practice of social research.* Belmont, CA: Wadsworth.

Bochantin, J. E., & Cowan, R. L. (2016). Acting and reeacting: Work/life accommodation and blue-collar workers. *International Journal of Business Communication, 53*(3), 306–325.

Brann, M. (2006). The influence of illness factors on physicians' likelihood of disclosing confidential health information to relatives of patients. *Communication Studies, 57*(3), 259–276.

Buchler, J. (1955). *Philosophical writings of Peirce.* New York: Dover.

Burleson, B. R., & MacGeorge, E. L. (2002). Supportive communication. In M. L. Knapp & J. A. Daly (Eds.), *Handbook of interpersonal communication* (3rd ed., pp. 374–424). Thousand Oaks, CA: Sage.

Coombs, T., & Holladay, S. J. (2004). Understanding the aggressive workplace: Development of the workplace aggression tolerance questionnaire. *Communication Studies, 55*(3), 481–497.

Daft, R. L., & Lengel, R. H. (1986). Organizational information requirements, media richness, and structural design. *Management Science, 32,* 554–571.

Davis, C. S. (2008). Dueling narratives: How peer leaders use narrative to frame meaning in community mental health care teams. *Small Group Research, 39*(6), 706–727.

Davis, C. S., & Crane, J. L. (2015). A dialogue with (un)death: Horror films as a discursive attempt to construct a relationship with the dead. *Journal of Loss and Trauma, 20*(5), 417–429. doi: 10.1080/15325024.2014.935215

Davis, C. S., & Salkin, K. A. (2005). Sisters and friends: Dialogue and multivocality in a relational model of sibling disability. *Journal of Contemporary Ethnography, 34*(2), 206–234.

Deveaux, M. (1994). Feminism and empowerment: A critical reading of Foucault. *Feminist Studies, 20,* 223–248.

Dillard, J. P., Plotnick, C. A., Godbold, L. C., Freimuth, V. S., & Edgar, T. (1996). The multiple affective consequences of AIDS PSAs: Fear appeals do more than scare people. *Communication Research, 23,* 44–72.

Dixon, T. L., & Linz, D. (2000). Overrepresentation and underrepresentation of African Americans and Latinos as lawbreakers on television news. *Journal of Communication, 50,* 131–154.

Dunleavy, K. N., Chory, R. M., & Goodboy, A. K. (2010). Responses to deception in the workplace: Perceptions of credibility, power, and trustworthiness. *Communication Studies, 61,* 239–255.

Ehrlich, N., & Shami, S. (2010). Microblogging inside and outside the workplace. USA Proceedings of the Fourth International AAAI Conference on Weblogs and Social Media. May 23–26, 2010. Washington DC. Association for the Advancement of Artificial Intelligence.

Ellingson, L. L. (2005). *Communicating in the clinic: Negotiating frontstage and backstage teamwork.* Cresskill, NJ: Hampton Press.

Ellis, C. (1995). *Final negotiations: A story of love, loss, and chronic illness.* Philadelphia: Temple University Press.

Foucault, M. (1965). *Madness and civilization: A history of insanity in the age of reason.* New York: Random House.

Foucault, M. (1972). *The archaeology of knowledge and the discourse on language.* New York: Pantheon Books.

Foucault, M. (1973). *The birth of the clinic: An archaeology of medical perception* (A. M. S. Smith, Trans.). New York: Pantheon Books.

Foucault, M. (1995). *Discipline and punish: The birth of the prison* (A. Sheridan, Trans.). New York: Random House.

Fishbein, M., Middlestadt, S. E., & Hitchcock, P. J. (1994). Using information to change sexually transmitted disease-related behaviors. In R. J. DiClemente & J. L. Peterson (Eds.), *Preventing AIDS: Theories and methods of behavioral interventions.* New York: Plenum Press.

Geddes, D. (2001). Sex roles in management: The impact of varying power of speech style on union members' perception of satisfaction and effectiveness. *The Journal of Psychology, 126,* 589–607.

Gerbner, G., Gross, L., Morgan, M., & Signorielli, N. (1986). Living with television: The dynamics of the cultivation process. In J. Bryant & D. Zillman (Eds.), *Perspectives on media effects* (pp. 17–40). Hillsdale, NJ: Lawrence Erlbaum Associates.

Goodall, H. L. (2006). *A need to know: The clandestine history of a CIA family.* Walnut Creek, CA: Left Coast Press.

Greenberg, B. S., Eastin, M. S., Hofshire, L., Lachlan, K. A., & Brownell, K. (2003). Portrayals of overweight and obese individuals in commercial television. *American Journal of Public Health, 93*(8), 1342–1348.

Greenhow, C., & Robelia, E. (2009). Old communication, new literacies: Social network sites as social learning resources. *Journal of Computer-Mediated Communication, 14,* 1130–1161.

Habermas, J. (1968). The idea of the theory of knowledge as social theory. In J. Habermas, *Knowledge & Human Interest.* Cambridge, UK: Polity Press.

James, C.H., & Minnis, W.C. (2004). Organizational storytelling: It makes sense. *Business Horizons, 3,* 23–32.

Katz, E., Blumler, J. G., & Gurevitch, M. (1973). Uses and gratifications research. *Public Opinion Quarterly, 37*(4), 509–523.

Kerlinger, F. (1992). *Foundations of behavioral research*. Fort Worth, TX: Harcourt Brace.

Krauss, S. E. (2005). Research paradigms and meaning making: A primer. *The Qualitative Report*, 10, 758–770.

Ledbetter, A. M., Mazer, J. P., DeGroot, J. M., Meyer, K. R., Mao, Y., & Swafford, B. (2011). Attitudes toward online social connection and self-disclosure as predictors of Facebook communication and relational closeness. *Communication Research*, *38*, 27–53.

Lowry, D. T., Nio, T. C., & Leitner, D.W. (2003). Setting the public fear agenda: A longitudinal analysis of network TV crime reporting, public perceptions of crime, and FBI crime statistics. *Journal of Communication*, *53*, 61–73.

Lyon, A. (2007). "Putting patients first": Systematically distorted communication and Merck's marketing of Vioxx. *Journal of Applied Communication Research*, *35*(4), 376–398.

McCombs, M., & Shaw, D. (1972). The agenda-setting function of mass media. *Public Opinion Quarterly*, *36*(2), 176–187.

Meyer, G., Roberto, A. J., & Atkin, C. K. (2003). A radio-based approach to promoting gun safety: Process and outcome evaluation implications and insights. *Health Communication*, *15*(3), 299–318.

Mignerey, J.T., Rubin, R.B., & Gorden, W.I. (2005). Organizational entry: An investigation of newcomer communication behavior and uncertainty. *Communication Research*, *22*, 54–85.

Miller, K. (2005). *Organizational communication: Approaches and processes*. Boston: Thomson Wadsworth.

Miller, T. G. (1986). Goffman, positivism, and the self. *Philosophy of the Social Sciences*, 16, 177–195.

Morman, M. T. (2000). The influence of fear appeals, message design, and masculinity on men's motivation to perform the testicular self-exam. *Journal of Applied Communication Research*, *28*(2), 91–116

Nabi, R. L., Moyer-Guse, E., & Byrne, S. (2007). All joking aside: A serious investigation into the persuasive effect of funny social issue messages. *Communication Monographs*, *74*(1), 29–54.

Okoro, E., & Washington, M. (2011). Communicating in a multicultural classroom: A study of students' nonverbal behavior and attitudes toward faculty attire. *Journal of College Teaching and Learning*, *8*, 27–38.

Plotnick, R. (2015). What happens when you push this?: Toward a history of the not-so-easy button. *Information & Culture*, *50*(3), 315–338. doi: http://dx.doi.org/10.7560/IC50302

Powell, H. L. (2011). Letters to Louis: Marital dissolution through the social construction of lived experience. *Journal of Divorce & Remarriage*, *52*, 19–32.

Raney, A. A. (2002). Punishing criminals and moral judgment: The impact on enjoyment. *Media Psychology*, *7*(2), 145–163.

Real, K., & Putnam, L. L. (2005). Ironies in the discursive struggle of pilots defending the profession. *Management Communication Quarterly*, *19*(1), 91–119.

Roberto, A. J., Krieger, J. L., Katz, M., Goei, R., & Jain, P. (2011). Predicting pediatricians' communication with parents about the Human Papillomavirus (HPV) vaccine: An application of the theory of reasoned action. *Health Communicaiton*, *26*(4), 303–312.

Segrin, C., Woszidlo, A., Givertz, M., Bauer, A., & Murphy, M. T. (2012). The association between overparenting, parent-child communication, and entitlement and adaptive traits in adult children. *Family Relations*, *61*, 237–352.

Sellnow, T. L., Seeger, M. W., & Ulmer, R. R. (2002). Chaos theory, informational needs, and natural disasters. *Journal of Applied Communication Research, 30*(4), 269–292.

Silk, K. J., & Parrott, R. L. (2006). All or nothing . . . or just a hat?: Farmers' sun protection behaviors. *Health Promotion Practice, 7*(2), 180–185.

Stohl, M., & Stohl, C. (2005). Human rights, nation states, and NGOs: Structural holes and the emergence of global regimes. *Communication Monographs, 72*(4), 442–467.

Toppman, L. (2009, May 26). Mothers' bare emotions burst out in "Miracle Kick." *Charlotte Observer,* pp. 1D, 5D.

U.S. Surgeon General's Scientific Advisory Committee on Television and Social Behavior. (1972). *Television and growing up: The impact of televised violence* (DHEW Publication No. HSM 72-9086). Washington, DC.

Wilson, B. J., Kunkel, D., Linz, D., Potter, W. J., Donnerstein, E., Smith, S. L., et al. (1998). *National television violence study: Vol. 1. Violence in television programming overall: University of California–Santa Barbara study.* Thousand Oaks, CA: Sage.

Witte, K., Stokols, D., Ituarte, P., & Schnieder, M. (1993). Testing the health belief model in a field study to promote bicycle safety helmets. *Communication Research, 20,* 564–586.

Yarker, J., Munir, F., Bains, M., Kalawsky, K., & Haslam, C. (2010). The role of communication and support in return to work following cancer-related absence. *Psycho-oncology, 19,* 1078–1085.

CHAPTER 2

Reviewing and Sourcing Material: Narrowing Your Topic

This chapter addresses the purpose of reviewing the existing literature/artifacts/creative work in the research process. By explaining how researchers use existing works to frame inquiry and establish context, we learn how to craft an argument for research/study.

Upon successful completion of this chapter, you will be able to:

- Explain the purpose of the literature/artifacts/creative work in the research process.
- Identify steps inside the process of sourcing and reviewing material.
- Apply reading comprehension strategies including interpreting, evaluating, and analyzing written content.

Introduction

The key to crafting a good message or a provocative question is knowing what people are talking about. What is being said? What content is already out there? What conversations have been going on for decades, centuries, even thousands of years?

Reviewing past history, past literature, works created in the past . . . it's one small (but very important) piece of the research puzzle. You also need to be current—explore what is being written right now, find digital content that is literally going live today, delve into the world of trends . . . whether that be in the realm of food, art, health, education, the list goes on and on. But you aren't finished yet.

Research can be likened to a chess game: you study past moves, pay attention to the board and know what your AND your opponents' pieces are capable of, or else you won't know what move to make in the future. This is no different. This literature or artifact review, this getting current with what has been done, what has been said, and what is right now? You have to put it to use and figure out how to move forward. This chapter sets up the process. You'll figure it out.

▼ ·

*What Are the Purposes of Library Research?

Throughout your scholarly career (from elementary school through college), you've likely had to write a lot of research papers and conduct a lot of library research to do so. In this chapter, we'll help you understand how library research is part of the bigger process of scholarly research. We'll teach you to move from your academic research to library research and back again. We'll explain how to find and evaluate sources, and perhaps most importantly, how to actually read, understand, and use a journal article. One main purpose of this research you've been doing since possibly elementary school was to learn more about the subject you were studying. That's still one main purpose of library research and it's still one main reason that all scholars conduct library research. However, it's not the only purpose.

There are five main purposes of library research:

1. To determine what's already known about the topic and related topics.
2. To define the problem and formulate possible solutions. The assembling and analyzing of available secondary data will almost always provide a better understanding of the problem and its context, will frequently suggest solutions not considered previously, and will identify gaps in the body of knowledge for which research is needed. In addition, you don't want to duplicate what's already been done (Hart, 2001).
3. To plan the collection of primary data. You can examine the methods and techniques used by previous research efforts in similar studies, which will be useful in planning your present study. Also, this may be of value in establishing classifications that are more compatible with past studies, so that you can more readily analyze trends.
4. To define the population and select the sample in your primary information collection. This may be valuable in helping you choose areas for most productively interviewing participants if this is a part of your research project.
5. To supply background information that will fill out what you find in your primary research. You may also find information against which you can compare your own findings and experience.

body of knowledge
Research that has already been conducted.

One basic premise of academic research is that it creates, and builds upon, a **body of knowledge**. There is very little (if anything) that has not been studied in some way, by some person. Your job as a scholar is to build on the research that has already been done by contributing to it, updating it, replicating it, and/or extending it (Booth, Colomb, & Williams, 1995; Rossman, 1995). In order to find out what's already been done, you conduct library research.

*From *Straight Talk About Communication Research Methods*, Third Edition by Christine S. Davis and Kenneth A. Lachlan. Copyright © 2017 by Kendall Hunt Publishing Company. Reprinted by permission.

Types of Research

Research is the way we find answers to questions. One good way to discover what you're interested in is to listen to the voice in your head that says, "I wonder. . . ." What types of things do you find yourself wondering about? You might be sitting around your apartment talking to friends and wonder, "Why don't guys call when they say they're going to?" or "How many people my age have issues with their parents telling them what to do?" Or, perhaps, you're reading a newspaper and ask, "Why do women in abusive relationships refuse to leave the relationships?" or "What causes people to become homeless?" or "How do movies depict smoking behaviors?" Regardless of how you attempt to find the answer, your method of answering your question is research. As Booth and colleagues said, "Research is simply gathering the information you need to answer a question and thereby helping you solve a problem" (Booth et al., 1995, p. 6). Your research may be systematic and valid, or it may not be, but it's still research. If you ask a few friends if they have the same issues with their parents, you're conducting research. If you do a Google search on the Internet to identify the causes of homelessness, you're conducting research. Our purpose is to teach you how to conduct research that is considered to be valid (defensible). Defensible research is planned and conducted in an organized, orderly, methodical manner (Alberts, Hecht, Buley, & Petronio, 1993).

When you ask your friends questions, you're actually conducting what's called primary research; you are generating your own data. If you look up information on the Internet, you're conducting what's called secondary research; you're looking at other people's data.

Primary Research

If you were answering a question with **primary research**, you would be conducting a study to specifically answer that question. Primary research is research that is conducted to answer a specific problem or question. A primary source is the original, or first, published account of research findings (Galvan, 2006). Most research papers you read in journals are examples of primary research (unless it is a synthesis of the literature), so, don't get confused. When you are writing a literature review, you will be reading published articles reviewing artwork or musical compositions, or reading existing monographs, among other research activities, depending on your field of study. Those articles include a literature review section, which is secondary research (because it summarizes and reports on other people's research). Consequently, your literature review is secondary research, because it summarizes and reports on other people's research.

primary research
Research that is conducted to answer a specific problem or question and produces original data.

Secondary Research

Secondary data is information that has been collected or conducted previously. If you were answering a question with **secondary research**, you would be looking for the answer in papers or books that summarize other studies,

secondary research
Research that has been previously collected or conducted.

or you would be looking at the other studies yourself. Textbooks are classic examples of secondary research. Textbooks give you lots of information, and all of it is taken from other sources, from research previously conducted (and published) by other people. Other examples of secondary research are literature reviews. When you write the results of your library research into a paper, you're writing a literature review. By the way, if you're writing a review of the literature for a class project, you're actually conducting secondary research. When a stand-alone literature review is published in a journal, it's often called a *synthesis of the literature*, and that's another example of a secondary research report. An additional example is the literature review *section* of a research report. Or, you might see it labeled as "historiography" in historical works.

No research project should ever be conducted without first searching secondary information sources. Why? Because all scholarly research builds upon the scholarly community's body of knowledge, and you have to conduct secondary research to find out what that body of knowledge is. Think of research like a conversation. When you are conducting research, you are entering into a scholarly conversation. You'd never walk up to a conversation and just start talking without finding out what the other people are talking about, right? In the same way, to enter a scholarly conversation, you need to find out what the conversation is about.

****Carrying Out a Literature Review: Engaging with the Literature**

This section considers:

- reading and engaging with existing work;
- searching and reviewing previous work;
- keeping good notes and references;
- overcoming problems;
- good use of the existing work;
- developing critical thinking.

There is an early chapter in a dissertation, or section in an essay project, which is engaged with literature in the field and gives you a sense of theoretical perspectives. It is using the literature to establish context and argument, the perspectives of major theorists whose work informs yours – putting all of this into a dialogue with your work. It is important to remember that a literature review is a dynamic piece of work, not just a dead list of the books you have read, but an engagement with their ideas and arguments in relation to your research questions, problems or hypotheses.

▼

Reading and Engaging with Existing Work

You continue to draw on the literature throughout your work towards a project, dissertation, or long essay. From the literature, you develop the theories, themes and threads running throughout – underpinning and feeding into the conceptual findings.

You need to keep reading, but know where to stop so that you get the right stance and level of engagement from the different reading you are doing and can make sure you haven't just recorded what others say, and instead have noted arguments that have engaged your own ideas and findings and brought them into a debate about previous and current literature, as appropriate.

In order for you to make a contribution to knowledge with your research, however large or small that might be, you will need to know what has already been written in the field, what are the main debates, who the experts are, what the themes are and where your work can be positioned in relation to what's been said before and what is being said at the moment. You have probably read some of the literature that you will need for your literature review even before you developed your research question or hypothesis. Indeed, you could have thought about what your question or problem was, while reading through someone else's work and realizing there was an issue they had not covered or a disagreement between experts, or a gap in the knowledge. As you prepare for your own research you need to think about literature searching, reviewing, and engaging in a critical, conceptual dialogue with the literature.

It is a good idea to read more widely in order to identify your problem or question, the area that you're going to work on, and to narrow down your own focus. If this is in an area in which you have already read widely, look at related fields and issues and review the literature. However, you might not be fully aware of the literature in the field especially if you are moving slightly out of your own discipline or into another context, period or issue. You will need to find a wide range of literature so that you are identifying and then engaging with the key theorists, themes and debates. The work of those researchers and writers who are and have been using the key theorists in their critical research work is already engaged in the debates and provides a good start for your own engagement.

Through your reading, find out where your own work looks as though it will make a contribution, i.e. a gap in knowledge, a new angle, a different combination of ideas and area of thought, and start to engage in a discussion between the experts and the critics in your own writing. This engagement in dialogue is not undermining the authority of those who have already written; it is identifying the lively debate and joining it. It is also ensuring that your own work is not just recording what others say, or summarizing, but working at a conceptual level of idea development, ensuring that you have your own voice, something to say in the current debates, can identify the argument, the experts, what they say, and join in with the unique contribution of your work.

Searching and Reviewing Previous Work

Don't forget to involve your tutor or supervisor and any helpful librarian in helping you to identify the key words, areas and arguments through a literature search so that you get the best and the fullest detail out of it. When conducting a literature search you are:

> Discovering what the key theorists are saying in your field and in relation to your question and what they have written about the concepts and the ideas that you are using.

> Discovering what those who have been engaged in the latest work in the field are saying in order to ask questions of their particular part of the subject, or field, what their views are, how they differ, what evidence they are using, and what points they are making.

Literature Reviews/Theoretical Perspectives

Make the role of the theoretical perspectives/literature review chapter absolutely explicit. They are:

> Not a dead list of annotated comments about texts only in an early chapter

BUT

> An ongoing dialogue with the experts, theorists and theories underpinning *your* research.

Hart (p. 13) defines the literature review as 'progressive'. 'It starts with wide reading narrowing into themes and debates.' Engaging with these themes and disputes, and sharing your work, will ensure you are moving beyond a summary and into a dialogue.

Suggestions to students undertaking an existing work review:

Read widely (more than you need) for context and debates.

Talk to a librarian – they are experts in conducting existing work searches, and your subject librarian will have a good idea of where to find some of the main sources for the literature search for your literature review. Contact them early and discuss the question you're asking, the problem you're addressing and the area you're working in. They should be able to suggest online subject data bases, journals in the library, and some books.

Find out the relevant abstracting and indexing services for your subject area and look up the abstracts to journal articles. There is usually also another abstract collection which relates to people's PhD theses, some of which might be quite cutting edge for your work. If you're working in an interdisciplinary area, you might need to consult literature and abstracts in more than one subject area. Useful databases for abstracts sometimes link to the whole article.

Have a look at the references that your key books and key journal articles are using, track back through these references and then look up the sources yourself. These leads will give you the fundamental key ideas, and some further suggestions that you can look up and use.

Keep up to date with the new journal articles if you can. In undergraduate work, very few people will be going beyond some key points and sources, perhaps a journal article, and the online reading. If you really search hard and read up-to-date journal articles, you will be ahead of the game and your work will look fresh and engaged. Read them carefully and identify the arguments, and the quotations to back these up, then engage with their arguments in your own work, extract small essential quotations and properly reference your sources.

Whether you are looking at an online source, one in the library or one you have yourself or have borrowed, you need to ask yourself the following question:

How up-to-date is this? Some of the key texts from the well-established theorists and great names in the field may be quite old but because they established the main rguments in the field they are still relevant to your work. There will also be an absolutely huge range (probably) of people who have used these theorists and experts to underpin their own work, or who have done little more than represent them.

After you have skim read quite a lot of books and journal articles, you should be able to see where people are merely repeating arguments, theories and issues rather than adding to them or indicating debates and new knowledge. You do not really need to read everything. What you do need to read are the key theorists whose thoughts and work underpin the work of the critics or professional practitioner writers, those writers who have established an engagement with the debates and the themes and developed the theory or contradicted the theory, and others' work in their own work, and those who are adding new knowledge and new ideas to the ongoing debate.

For each source:

You will need to read carefully and to identify the themes and arguments made by the key players (critics, practitioners who write in the field).

Reflect and think critically about what you are reading, don't just take notes down from it; think about both the case that is being made, and the evidence to back it up. How reliable a source is this?

Does this fit with what you already know?
Does it contradict other evidence?
Have you got any evidence to back up its claim in its argument?
What is being hidden from us, any viewpoints or information?

What does not seem to be understood here?
Are the reasons for the conclusion logical and well argued?
Does the evidence back up the argument in the claims?
How can you use it in your own work?

Keeping Good Notes and References

Take not just notes of the content of the argument but also segments from what is said, using key quotations, and referencing and discussing or commenting on them.

You also need to take down publication details. When you find a source you think is useful or even one you've read that you're not sure will be useful, take down the full publication details, make some contextual and critical comments about the article, book or other source and about the issues it raises and argument it makes, and carefully reference and quote from it so that you can come back to it. You can then also use the quotes, properly referenced, i.e. noting the book, journal article, online source or whatever it is.

It is important to reflect and consider how what you're quoting relates to your own argument. In this way you select and identify the work and decide how you are going include it in your literature review.

Summarize and synthesize in order to engage in critical debate. Your arguments arise from, relate to, and are underpinned by the experts, in terms of either their content or their methods.

Common Student Issues with Reviewing Existing Works

The main point about a literature review is that it engages in a debate with the critical reading in the field and then engages your own work in this debate.

1. There are no books in my area, it is a completely new area and question.
2. My theorists are diametrically opposed – help!
3. I know nothing about this topic/area – where can I start?
4. I just need to know who are the RIGHT theorists and critics to use – please tell me (so I don't have to do all this reading).
5. It's all been said before . . . what can I add?
6. I don't want to read those writers because they might disagree with my argument.
7. I've done the literature review – now I can leave it and do all the research.
8. I'm going to do my literature review and work on my theorists after I've gathered my data.

Some Thoughts and Responses

1. The student might be right – perhaps it is a completely new area. It certainly should be a fairly new question. However, it is probable that they need to use different key words, to look more broadly, to look at work that's been done on similar issues but perhaps in different contexts, and then they will find work in books or journal articles which relates to what they are looking at.

2. This looks like bad news but actually it is good news. Already there are some grounds for debate and discussion here, setting the theorists in relation to or opposition to each other. This can help generate a healthy discussion into which your work might fit.

3. The student needs some guidance about basic reading and an instructor will be able to help here, or a librarian might. However, if the student knows absolutely nothing about the topic, perhaps it's not the best one to pick. Perhaps a topic with which they are slightly familiar, or one where they are familiar with some of the books, and have an idea about what they're interested in, would be more suitable.

4. Well, there won't be 'right' theorists and critics. The issue is that there will be debate and arguments about different points of view in different readings and this student needs to find out what these different arguments are and develop their own route through them. Suggesting that there are just right critics and theorists is a bit simplistic and looks like the student is taking short cuts. However, if we are very new to the area this is often how we respond, thinking there must be a single right way. But there rarely is. The student will have to find out what the debates are and make up their own mind on the evidence of the strength of the argument.

5. If it's really all been said before, then this is probably not a good topic to pick. However, this is probably just a response to a sense that there is an over-whelming amount of literature on the subject, shelves and shelves of books by experts. This student's question is probably quite different from anything that has been asked before, or they could focus it perhaps on a different element of the topic and so by asking something fairly new, they can direct a work by the great experts and the critics in the field to help support them in their own work.

6. If you are to develop a well argued case, you really need to know what the arguments are. It's important not to avoid authors, critics and experts who might disagree with your point of view, because their views can give you the opportunity to find out how to argue for your views and back them up with evidence.

7. Actually, you never stop doing the literature review until you hand the dissertation, project or essay in. Continuing to read in the field is import-ant as you carry out your research because you might miss something that comes out while you are doing the research, or that hasn't turned up from your researching so far. This can give you a new perspective, an edge over other people. So never stop reading, but you might not need to use all of it.

8. This really is not a good idea at all. The idea of reading in the literature is to establish the arguments, the theoretical approaches, ways in which people deal with these sorts of issues. You carry out your own research. If you had not done that kind of reading you might quite easily either work at a much lower level than most of the rest of the literature in the field, or miss the major arguments, deliberations and theoretical under-pinnings which would inform your own work. Either way, what you could

end up doing is producing a lot of data which doesn't really relate to a well focused question based on having read the literature. Don't do it. Start the reading and start to develop new questions and your own work alongside the reading and let them influence each other.

Reading into the Field Is Only One of the Tasks

If you are unaware of debates in the field you might merely recreate them.

You need to work out where your research engages with the debates and what it can add.

Writing and engaging with the literature follows this journey:

Summary
Synthesis
Evaluation and reflection
Engagement in critique
Argument and dialogue between the experts and critics have worked with the work, and with your own work
Contribution to meaning – something new which is your own.

Please consider:

- Who are YOUR main theorists?
- Who are you reading in relation to theory and to method?
- What are the debates in these areas?
- And how does YOUR work engage in a dialogue with these debates?

Developing Critical Thinking as Part of Dealing with the Literature

Critical thinking is crucial in research. Much of this involves questioning and problematizing accepted ideas and information. Much of it involves engaging in a dialogue with others who have developed theories or carried out research, creating a dialogue between theoretical perspectives and research activity. Critically reviewing the literature involves more than loosely listing a range of writers in support of an argument. For example,

Smith, K. (1976); Bloor, P., and Baggis, G. (1993); Snow, K., and Cream, C. (2004) all argue that universally women are more likely than men to develop a counselling function, while Orthrop, S., Kittle, P., and Lovel, H. (2004) suggest that this could be due in part to the caring functions more commonly presented by women

indicates the development of an argument, and key thinkers or critical contributors while:

Women are more likely to be counsellors than men (Smith, K. (1976); Bloor, P., and Baggis, G. (1993); Snow, K., and Cream, C. (2004); Orthrop, S., Kittle, P., and Lovel, H. (2004))

fails to develop an argument and just looks like a list.

Equally irritating and undiscriminating is the format where every writer on the subject is given the same space of a paragraph, with neither discrimination between major and minor contributors nor any sense of the development of an argument between the contributors.

Reading, Arguing and Writing in Different Ways for Different Purposes

As you read the literature in the field and start to use it in your own work, consider the different ways in which you use your reading in your writing. In this case we are considering the literature review, but this is also important when you start to discuss your methodology and your choice of methods and when you're interpreting your data or engaging with your writers in the middle section of your dissertation or long project. Here you again need to bring the reading on theory and other practice to bear on the work that you've been doing.

Where do you engage in dialogue? With what main theories and arguments. What are *your* points and arguments? How and where have you been analytical of theorists, research data, and your own findings?

In this section we have considered:

Ways of developing the literature review or theoretical perspectives chapter, to engage with dialogues in the field.

Identifying theories, themes and ways in which you can use extracts in your own arguments and so establish your contribution.

Now that you have thought about WHY it's important to understand previously existing work, whether in the field of creative arts, humanities, or the sciences, it's time to learn HOW to carry it out. In this next section you'll see what an amazing source the library (and the people working there) is . . . don't be afraid of all that knowledge. Dig into it. It will be worth it.

Quick Reference

I know that reviewing someone else's work may not seem appealing, but think of all the great trips to museums you've taken and how you love art, a good book and Spotify. You didn't create it, but you appreciate it and those pieces of "existing work" teach you something, cause you to ask questions, cause you to think about context and a foundation for an argument. Reviewing what has been written on a subject or listening to podcasts about a subject involve you understanding the content and the context, and then being able to summarize and synthesize the information. Perhaps that same podcast brings your attention to the fact that no one is talking about a certain subject in rural Ohio . . . you've just identified a "knowledge gap." Keep up the questioning and the curiosity.

—*Kristen Hark*

How to Discover Existing Works

▼ ....

Phases of Research

This section assumes that you have (or want to have) a research question for which you want to find the answer. Let's say your instructor has given you a research assignment for a class, or you want to do an independent study research project on a topic that's intrigued you. When you decide you want to conduct a research project (or when your instructor gives you a research assignment for a class), the first thing you need to do is come up with a topic. Sometimes you have a specific topic in mind, sometimes you have a vague idea of what your topic might be, and other times you have no idea of where to even begin when choosing a topic!

1. We'll come back to your research question in a minute. First, let's talk about the phases of research. The first phase is called *conceptualization*—forming an idea. Ideas are built on the body of knowledge that's already been created. Your idea builds on the research that's already been done on your topic or related topics.
2. Once you've formed an idea for your research project, you've got to plan it. You've got to determine exactly what you're looking at and decide how you're going to define your terms. This is called *operationalization*—defining your terms as you're using them in your research project. You often operationalize your data based on how other people have operationalized the same variables—you find this out based on your library research. You've got to decide how to study it and what research methodology to use to collect your data. You've got to know how you're going to analyze your data. One step in planning your research and methodology is to look at what other people have done with the same or similar projects—what worked for them, what didn't work, and what they recommended to do differently.
3. Then, when you're done planning, you've got to carry out the research. When you write up your research, you do what's called *reconceptualization*—you reconnect it back to the larger body of knowledge.

So, before conducting any type of research, there are two things you must do: determine exactly what information is already known about your topic and determine exactly what you want to know. You have to have a starting point. You have to start with knowing the assumptions the community of knowledge already has and build your information on that. You don't want to spend time, money, and energy gathering information that's already been gathered. Funding agencies won't fund research that's "so what" research, and publications won't publish it. One of the characteristics of academic research is that it builds on a *body of knowledge*—other research that has already been done on your topic or on related topics. So, the first use of library research is to determine what background information already exists about your topic.

Research Sources

Let's say you have a vague idea of a general topic area, but aren't sure how to narrow your idea from there. The first thing you might want to do is browse journals and books in your topic area to get ideas from what other people have studied. There are many sources of literature for your library research; some are more suited to academic purposes than others:

- Books—often give the original (or primary) information on a topic or theory, but typically are more out-of-date since there is a much longer lag time from writing to publication.
- Articles—in scholarly journals, tend to be up-to-date and therefore often cutting-edge; in peer-reviewed journals, have met academic standards.
- Governmental statistical data—often available online, usually up-to-date and available (Hart, 2001).
- Other sources, such as magazines, newspapers, and websites—typically not appropriate for a scholarly review of the literature.

There are several good sources of secondary research in general: handbooks, textbooks, edited books, and journals. Scholarly type books consist of monographs, anthologies or edited books, textbooks, and reference books (Hart, 2001). Books are more difficult than journals to identify as scholarly versus nonscholarly, but one good rule to evaluate books is to look at their references—if the book itself cites scholarly references, then it is likely a scholarly book.

How Do You Access Scholarly Journals? Now you've got lots of names of journals, but how do you access the journals? If you Google the journal name, you will likely be able to access a table of contents and maybe a list of abstracts. Perhaps this is all you need to begin forming ideas. For example, let's say you think you might be interested in family communication. Google the *Journal of Family Communication*. The first listing gives you the Web page for the journal.

When you click on that link, it takes you straight to the listing for the current issue of that journal. Notice that this listing gives "volumes" and "issues." The volume represents a year for the journal; for example, in the *Journal of Family Communication*, 2016 journals are all Volume 16. Within a year, each journal is represented by an issue. The *Journal of Family Communication* publishes four issues per year. Look at the current issue.

You will see a list of the articles in that issue. The first one sounds interesting. Let's see if you can get more information about it. Click the link for the abstract.

The abstract is a short description (usually 100–300 words) of the article. If you're only looking for general ideas, the abstract may be all you need for right now. But let's say you're intrigued and want to read the actual article. This is as far as you're allowed to go on the Internet without subscribing to the journal. However, you haven't really hit a dead end.

Your university library subscribes to many of these journals. Let's see if your library subscribes to this one. Go to the Web page for your university library (www.liberty.edu/library). It has an opening screen with a place to search the library.

Let's see what happens when you type in the journal title, *Journal of Family Communication*. The title of the journals should appear in the box titled "Journal Titles".

You're in luck if the library subscribes to it and it's available online.

If your library doesn't subscribe to the journal, you can order the article through Interlibrary Loan. Interlibrary Loan (sometimes called ILL) usually takes a few days to a few weeks to arrive, so you'd have to allow time for that in your schedule.

If your library does have this journal, you'll come to a listing of volumes for the journal. Remember that you were looking for an article in Volume 16, Issue 4. And remember that Volume 16 was 2016, so look at 2016, then select Issue 4. This time, when you click on the article from the list, it will open the article. For right now, you can either print it or read it online.

Finding Research Sources Using Search Strategies

Now let's say through browsing journals and the Internet, talking to friends, and reading the newspaper, you've decided on your topic: "grief communication." Your study objective is: "This research will determine how people communicate when they are bereaved over the death of a loved one." Your next step is to find out what other research has been done on this and related topics. Let's identify the key concepts in this objective: "bereavement communication" and "grief communication." Before you start searching, think of alternative or related concepts you can use if you need them. For example, you might also search for simply "bereavement" or "grief," or perhaps "death," or "death of loved ones."

databases
Sources that search through many journals at a time.

You would use your library Web page to search for journal articles on the topic. You conduct this search through **databases**—sources that search through many journals at a time. There are many databases you can use. Some of our favorites are "Academic Search Complete" and "Web of Science." While Google is an inappropriate search engine to use for academic research, Google Scholar might yield useful information because it includes peer-reviewed papers and articles (Munger & Campbell, 2007).

Google Scholar also might include some sites that aren't appropriate for academic research, so you'll need to be a bit more discerning if you search through that source.

You can start your search in a specific database or in all databases. You would start by choosing a search term. If you combine "bereavement" and "communication," you would type in: "bereavement AND communication." The word "AND" is in all caps because it is a **Boolean search** term, and you are using it to connect the two concepts. You are telling the search engine that you want only articles that have both of your terms in the keywords. It's really important to make sure you also check the box for "scholarly (peer-reviewed) journals" because you are only interested in scholarly or **academic journals** for this research project.

Your search should yield a list of articles that relate to your term. If you have too few "hits," you can broaden your search by eliminating one or part of your terms or by choosing a different search term. If you have too many "hits," you can narrow your search by adding additional search terms or choosing a different one.

Once you've found an article you think might fit your research needs, you click the title of the article to access the record. On the article record page, you will see options to access the PDF full text to pull up the article just as you would see it in a print journal.

Evaluating Research Sources

Not all sources are created equal. As Booth and colleagues (1995) said, "One good source is worth more than a score of mediocre ones, and one accurate summary of a good source is sometimes worth more than the source itself" (p. 71). The first step in evaluating your source is to read it—all of it. And read it slowly and carefully (Booth et al., 1995).

First of all, make sure it really is an article in a scholarly journal. You selected that check box, but databases sometimes make errors, so you need to make sure it's really a scholarly journal you're reading. The reason that this is an important distinction is because scholarly research falls under the practice of **peer review**—a "self regulatory practice designed to protect against the publication of flawed research or unsound scholarship, and to recognize and promote innovative and cutting-edge studies," says Art Bochner, NCA President (Bochner, 2008, p. 3). In other words, peer review is the way a scholarly field determines which research is acceptable, sound, and valid, and which is not. Make sure you understand the requirements of your assignment, but for most literature reviews or library research assignments for college classes, your professor will either prefer or require that you use scholarly sources. If you don't recognize the name of the journal, how else can you tell? Simply put, many journals have the word "journal" in their name. Many will state that they are published by a scholarly association. It's sad to say, but you can also use this general rule: If it looks as if it's fun to read, it might not be a scholarly journal. If it looks like a

Boolean search
A search function that is used to connect two or more concepts in a search engine. Common Boolean search operators are "and" (narrows the search) and "or" (expands the search).

academic journals
Collections of published, peer-reviewed scholarly research that are often consulted by academic scholars, government agencies, policy makers, and businesses to inform their decision making.

peer review
The way in which a scholarly field determines which research is acceptable, sound, and valid, and which is not.

magazine article with lots of glossy pages, color pictures, and white space, it's probably a magazine article, and not a journal. If it is more dense, with more complex language, usually with footnotes, endnotes, references, and citations, it's more likely to be a scholarly journal. Some people publish what look like scholarly articles on websites that are not peer reviewed and are not in scholarly journals. Don't be fooled. You want to use articles that are in recognized peer-reviewed journals, unless otherwise instructed by your professor.

In some cases, you might need additional information that is not available from academic sources. For example, suppose you are doing library research on domestic violence and you want to provide statistics on the number of people who were killed by spouses last year. An academic journal would not likely have up-to-date information on that subject, but the Internet very likely might (Munger & Campbell, 2007). You have to be careful with Internet sources, however. Anyone can create a website or post to a blog, and the Internet has no standards under which posted messages must fall. Look at who the sponsor of the site is and try to determine where the information came from (Munger & Campbell, 2007).

Just like not all sources are equal, not all journals are equal either. As a general rule, international journals are rated more highly than national journals, which are rated more highly than regional journals, which are rated more highly than state journals.

There are several other criteria to evaluate sources. The most straightforward is the year of publication. How current is the research? In most cases, the more recent, the better. For some reason, certain topics have peaks and valleys; some years there is a lot published on a topic, and in other years, not so much (Rossman, 1995). You may find this to be the case. Notice how the research has evolved in each peak—the topic likely has a slightly (or largely) different focus from one peak to another. Make sure you know which focus you're interested in. Knowing when the study was done will help determine if replicability is needed or warranted. Maybe the research you're looking at is old—does it need to be updated? If you're suggesting updating outdated research, then you should go ahead and cite the research you're updating. The exception would be if you are citing a source, that is considered a *classic* in your field.

Another consideration is the reputation of the author. How well known is this person? How much has this person published? How prestigious are the journals or publishers of this person's work? How often have the author and this article been cited? You may not have been in this field long enough to know the answers to all of these questions, but you may have heard some names related to some of the key theories or concepts in your field. If they're in your textbook, and if you're studying them in a general survey class, they're important names.

Other evaluation variables concern how the research was conducted. Is it relevant to you? How does the research topic relate to your topic? How was the population sampled? How does this population relate to your objectives?

Is the perspective of the article local, regional, national, or international? Why was the study conducted? What problem was the researcher addressing?

Finally, is this a primary or secondary source? For most of the literature reviews you are writing, you will be synthesizing primary sources, that is, you will be reporting on primary research reports that describe actual research studies. Occasionally, however, you might, in the course of your library research, find that someone has published a synthesis of the literature on your topic. Feel free to use this, but use it properly. If the synthesis says anything new, such as commenting on, critiquing, or extending the literature they're reviewing, cite that source. Otherwise, to cite the sources they are citing, you must go to the primary source. In other words, if someone named Smith cites Blumer, you must go directly to Blumer to cite Blumer. You cannot count on Smith properly explaining and summarizing Blumer. It is very bad form and lazy research to stop at the secondary source. Booth and colleagues (1995) suggest that you cite both the primary and secondary sources and reiterate that you must go to the primary source and read it before you use it. Booth and colleagues (1995) also say, "You will soon discover that you cannot trust researchers to quote reliably. It is intellectually lazy not to look up an important quotation in its original context if that source is easily available" (p. 75). Instead of relying only on the secondary source, use it to point you in the right direction. Feel free to look up references, and once you've read them yourself, then you can use them.

. . . . ▼

How to Read a Journal Article

We've said that you need to read the journal article thoroughly. But how do you read a journal article? If you start reading at the beginning and move through it, for most articles, you'll get bogged down in the "Findings" section before figuring out what you're reading.

Papers differ slightly in their headings and organization, but most articles have the following sections in roughly this order: Abstract, Introduction, Literature Review, Findings, Discussion, Limitations, and Conclusion. Note that this structure and format varies depending on your field, but the basic components are similar. We suggest you read them out of order. We know this may feel odd, but we have a good reason to suggest this. We generally read research articles in this order:

1. Abstract
2. Introduction
3. Conclusion
4. Discussion
5. Literature Review
6. Method
7. Findings
8. Limitations
9. References

Read to gather the following information, in this order:

1. What is the *research topic*?
2. What are the *main points* and *findings*?
3. What *claim* is this article making?
4. What is the *evidence* for that claim?
5. Is this *basic* or *applied* research?
6. Does this have a *research question* or a *hypothesis*? What is it?
7. How highly *regarded* is the journal?
8. How *recent* is the research?
9. What is the *methodology*? Is it clearly detailed?
10. How *in-depth* was the research?
11. How recent are the *sources*?
12. What *relevant quotes* might you use from this in your own literature review?
13. What other *sources* should you look up from the article's literature review?

If, at any point answering these questions, you find that the article is not appropriate for your library research, move on to another article; don't waste any more time on one that's not relevant to your needs.

Let's consider the article we found above in the *Journal of Family Communication* by Erin D. Basinger, Erin C. Wehrman, and Kelly G. McAninch (2016) called "Grief Communication and Privacy Rules: Examining the Communication of Individuals Bereaved by the Death of a Family Member." Under the title and names of the authors, the first thing you see is the abstract. The abstract is always found directly after the title, before the body of the paper begins. It is often in italics, centered, or otherwise set apart from the rest of the text. Perusing the abstract tells you that the article is about communication about grief, communication privacy management theory, and how people who are bereaved navigate discussions about death and the deceased. Sounds interesting so far.

From the abstract, this appears to be **applied research**, although you don't yet know the research question or hypothesis. You also know that this is a highly regarded journal, and that it is a recent article.

To find out more, you'll have to read further. Jump to the Introduction. The paper starts off with these two sentences:

> *The loss of a loved one can be a life-altering experience, and grief can have devastating effects, including increased levels of anxiety, anger, and depression (Asai et al., 2010; Holland & Neimeyer, 2010). Due to its complex nature, grief can continue for long periods of time as the bereaved work through stages of grief toward accepting their loss (Kübler-Ross & Kessler, 2005) (p. 285).*

Right up front, you know that this is a significant problem for society because grief can be life-altering, devastation, complex, and long-lasting.

The Conclusion section tells you:

The goal of this investigation was to examine grief communication through the lens of three processes identified in communication privacy management theory: privacy ownership, privacy control, and privacy turbulence (Petronio, 2013). Bereaved individuals indicated that they think of their grief as something that they own (RQ1), and they described three types of rules that govern how they interact with others about their loved one: selectivity rules, avoidance rules, and positivity rules (RQ2). In spite of their rules, however, participants also indicated that they had some turbulent exchanges with family members, friends, and romantic partners (RQ3). The types of turbulence they experienced were primarily boundary rule mistakes, dissimilar privacy orientations, and intentional rule violations (Petronio, 2002). The results of the study support assumptions in CPM about the processes that regulate the sharing or withholding of private information, and they resonate with extant research on grief communication that describes the complexity of losing a loved one (pp. 299–300).

The Conclusion summarizes the study. From the conclusion, you now know that grief feels very personal and private to people who are experiencing it; that people communicate their grief with others while following very specific social rules related to with whom they do and do not share their grief and preferences for focusing on positive aspects of the deceased; and, finally, grief communication can be turbulent.

You will want to move to the Discussion section and here you can find additional information about, for example, privacy rules and turbulence. From the Discussion section, you know that turbulent communication involved violations of privacy expectations and information sharing, and occurred over many interactions.

Now that you know what Basinger, Wehrman, and McAninch found in their research, you might decide that this paper is relevant to your own research. Take a step back and look at the first three paragraphs of their "Literature Review" to begin to get a sense about what's known thus far (before Basinger, Wehrman, and McAninch's research) on these topics:

As we observed before, loss and grief can be life-altering and devastating (according to Asai et al., 2010, and Holland and Neimeyer, 2010). Grief is complex and long-lasting (according to Kübler-Ross and Kessler, 2005). The second paragraph of the literature review also tells us that communicating about grief can be helpful in that it can help ease the emotional distress of grief (according to Rosenblatt and Elde, 1990 and Sedney, Baker, and Gross, 1994); strengthen relationships (according to Hooghe, Neimeyer, and Rober, 2011, and Shapiro, 2008); obtain social support (according to Golish and Powell, 2003, and Kübler-Ross and Kessler, 2005); help the survivors renegotiate their identities and roles in light of their loss (according to Gilbert, 1989); and lower depression and stress (according to Calvete and De Arroyabe, 2012, and Kaunonen, Tarkka, Paunonen, and Laippala, 1999). The downside of sharing about grief is that some experiences are difficult to share because of discomfort or fear of stigma (according to Brierley-Jones, Crawley, Loman, and Ayers, 2014–2015, and Maguire et al., 2015); and because of responses from others that are not helpful (according to Breen and O'Conner, 2011).

As you keep reading through the Literature Review, you'll see that it also provides the different concepts, theories, and definitions the authors are using to design this study, and you'll note that Basinger, Wehrman, and McAninch use the literature to inform their Research Questions.

Next, take a look at the Methods section and see how Basinger, Wehrman, and McAninch did what they did. "Participants" tells who they interviewed, where and how they found the people to interview, and describes the participants:

> **Method**. *We conducted individual interviews with college students who had lost a parent or a sibling. We used analytic techniques from grounded theory methodology (Charmaz, 2006; Corbin & Strauss, 2008), guided by concepts from CPM theory. Our analyses centered on how the bereaved conceptualized ownership of information about their grief, how they enacted privacy rules surrounding information about the death of their family member and their grief, and how they experienced turbulence when their privacy rules were breached.*
>
> **Participants**. *We interviewed 21 individuals whose father (n = 11, 52.4%), mother (n = 4, 19.0%), brother (n = 4, 19.0%), or sister (n = 2, 9.5%) had died. All participants were college students from a variety of majors at a large Midwestern university. Participants' ages ranged from 19–28 years (M = 21.24), and a majority were female (n = 15, 71.4%). Over half of the interviewees identified their race/ethnicity as European American/White (n = 13, 61.9%), and other participants were African American/Black (n = 6, 28.6%), Asian American (n = 1, 4.8%), and Pakistani (n = 1, 4.8%). Most family members died from health-related issues (n = 17, 81.0%), whereas others died because of accidents (n = 2, 9.5%) or were murdered (n = 2, 9.5%). Family members' deaths occurred an average of 7.17 years prior to the interview (SD = 6.06), ranging from 1 month to 20 years (pp. 288–289).*

As Basinger, Wehrman, and McAninch move through the Methods section, they describe their study procedures, consent process, and analysis process.

Finally, in the Results section, Basinger, Wehrman, and McAninch tell how they came up with their findings—how they analyzed their data and drew their conclusions. While you may not yet be familiar with the procedures they use in this paper, you can still begin to form opinions as to whether their methods seem appropriate, or if they make sense to you.

The last thing to look at is their references. You are looking for two things in the "Reference" section. First, how old are their sources? They range from 1984 to 2016, but most are from the past five years. Some of the oldest ones are classics. So, while a few of their references are older, the older ones are the classic sources, and this tells you that they are extending and applying these concepts and theories. You have to evaluate the age of their sources with the rest of their research—was it conceptually, methodologically, and analytically sound? Perhaps you could discuss your opinions of that in class. You'll learn more specifics about how to critique research throughout this textbook.

The second reason you want to look at the reference list is to *mine* their sources. Perhaps from the Literature Review, you find the concept of social support particularly useful for your study. Basinger, Wehrman, and McAninch cite Golish and Powell's 2003 article about social support, but if you want to cite Golish and Powell, you'll need to read it yourself. Think of the reference list as an additional database of potential sources for you to look up.

Taking Notes on Research

You've read an article and have begun to critique it. You've gotten to the point where you think this article will be a great one to include in your library research and literature review. Now you have to take notes on it. You're taking notes for two purposes: to make sure you have the information you need to use in your paper (to make sure you have it down thoroughly and accurately) and to make sure you have the information you need to properly cite your source.

In order to make sure your notes give you enough information to understand and remember what you've read, Booth and colleagues (1995) suggest that you write down not only the single idea you want to use, but also the paragraph or several paragraphs around it so you can fully understand the concept or argument the author is making.

Many students find it helpful to use "old-fashioned" bibliography notes written on index cards. There is also software available to categorize information, such as Endnotes, and Munger and Campbell (2007) suggest creating a personal blog (blogger.com or livejournal.com) to capture your information. However you capture the information, it's a good idea to put the information for each citation on separate pages or index cards so you can sort and resort through them later as you're organizing your synthesis. At a minimum, you want to put down your citation information, the abstract, a summary of the findings, and the key points from the discussion. To avoid unintentional plagiarism, make sure you are clear about summarizing, paraphrasing, or quoting (Booth et al., 1995). If you're using quotes, make sure you put down the page number for the quote, and make sure you put the quote in quotation marks so you remember it's a direct quote. You need to know that you must cite your sources accurately to avoid charges of plagiarism. Plagiarism can ruin careers, derail graduations, and cause students to fail courses.

Take a look at the APA, MLA, or Chicago Manual of Style citation requirements to make sure you're getting all the information you need for your citation. There's nothing worse than wanting to use a source, but not being able to because you left off an important piece of citation information and can no longer find the article or book to get it again. When you put down the citation information for a book, for example, you'll need first and last names of all the authors (in the same order listed on the book cover), year of publication, exact name, publication location, and publishing company. When you put down the citation information for a journal article, you'll need the first and last names of all the authors (in order), year of publication, name of journal, volume number, issue number, and page numbers of the article. If you've accessed the article via the Web, it would also be helpful to put the URL so you can find it again, if necessary (Munger & Campbell, 2007).

When you're taking notes on the findings or main points, make sure you get the exact quotes and page numbers for direct quotations. Make sure you correctly read the article so that you understand it and are getting the context and claim right. If you used a source to go to one of their sources, make sure you are properly differentiating between primary and secondary sources.

When taking notes, you might find it helpful to follow this format, answering each question:

- What is the correct citation for the article?
- What is the purpose statement?
- What is the research question or hypothesis?
- What are the key concepts or variables under study?
- What is the method of data collection?
- What are the key findings or conclusions?
- What are other key pieces of information you found in the article that might be relevant to your research?

Glossary

Academic journals
Collections of published, peer-reviewed scholarly research that are often consulted by academic scholars, government agencies, policy makers, and businesses to inform their decision making.

Body of knowledge
Research that has already been conducted.

Boolean search
A search function that is used to connect two or more concepts in a search engine. Common Boolean search operators are "and" (narrows the search) and "or" (expands the search).

Databases
Sources that search through many journals at a time.

Peer review
The way in which a scholarly field determines which research is acceptable, sound, and valid, and which is not.

Primary research
Research that is conducted to answer a specific problem or question and produces original data.

Secondary research
Research that has been previously collected or conducted.

References

Alberts, J., Hecht, M., Buley, J., & Petronio, S. (1993). Methods for studying interpersonal communication research. In S. Petronio, J. Alberts, M. Hecht, & J. Buley (Eds.), *Contemporary perspectives on interpersonal communication* (pp. 18–24). Dubuque, IA: Wm. C. Brown.

Argyle, M., & Henderson, M. (1984). The rules of friendship. *Journal of Social and Personal Relationships, 1,* 211–237. doi:10.1177/0265407584012005

Asai, M., Fujimori, M., Akizuki, N., Inagaki, M., Matsui, Y., & Uchitomi, Y. (2010). Psychological states and coping strategies after bereavement among the spouses of cancer patients: A qualitative study. *Psycho-Oncology, 19,* 38–45. doi:10.1002/pon.1444

Basinger, E. D., Wehrman, E. C., & McAninch, K. G. (2016). Grief communication and privacy rules: Examining the communication of individuals bereaved by the death of a family member. *Journal of Family Communication, 16*(4), 285–302. doi: 10.1080/15267432.2016.1182534

Bochner, A. (2008, May). The case against the anonymous culture of peer review. *Spectra, 44*(5), 3.

Booth, W. C., Colomb, G. G., & Williams, J. M. (1995). *The craft of research.* Chicago: University of Chicago Press.

Breen, L. J., & O'Connor, M. (2011). Family and social networks after bereavement: Experiences of support, change and isolation. *Journal of Family Therapy, 33*, 98–120. doi:10.1111/j.1467-6427.2010.00495.x

Calvete, E., & De Arroyabe, E. L. (2012). Depression and grief in Spanish family caregivers of people with traumatic brain injury: The roles of social support and coping. *Brain Injury, 26*, 834–843. doi:10.3109/02699052.2012.655363

Galvan, J. L. (2006). *Writing literature reviews: A guide for students of the social and behavioral sciences.* Glendale, CA: Pyrczak.

Golish, T. D., & Powell, K. A. (2003). Ambiguous loss: Managing the dialectics of grief associated with premature birth. *Journal of Social and Personal Relationships, 20*, 309–334. doi:10.1177/0265407503020003003

Hart, C. (2001). *Doing a literature search: A comprehensive guide for the social sciences.* London: Sage.

Holland, J. M., & Neimeyer, R. A. (2010). An examination of stage theory of grief among individuals bereaved by natural and violent causes: A meaning-oriented contribution. *Omega: Journal of Death & Dying, 61*, 103–120. doi:10.2190/OM.61.2.b

Hooghe, A., Neimeyer, R. A., & Rober, P. (2011). The complexity of couple communication in bereavement: An illustrative case study. *Death Studies, 35*, 905–924. doi:10.1080/07481187.2011.553335

Kaunonen, M., Tarkka, M., Paunonen, M., & Laippala, P. (1999). Grief and social support after the death of a spouse. *Journal of Advanced Nursing, 30*, 1304–1311. doi:10.1046/j.1365-2648.1999.01220

Kübler-Ross, E., & Kessler, D. (2005). *On grief and grieving: Finding the meaning of grief through the five stages of loss.* New York, NY: Scribner

Munger, D., & Campbell, S. (2007). *What every student should know about . . . researching online.* New York: Pearson Longman.

Rosenblatt, P. C., & Elde, C. (1990). Shared reminiscence about a deceased parent: Implications for grief education and grief counseling. *Family Relations, 39*, 206–210. doi:10.2307/585725

Ross, R. S. (1977). *Speech communication: Fundamentals and practice.* Englewood Cliffs, NJ: Prentice-Hall.

Rossman, M. H. (1995). *Negotiating graduate school: A guide for graduate students.* Thousand Oaks, CA: Sage.

Sedney, M. A., Baker, J. E., & Gross, E. (1994). "The story" of a death: Therapeutic considerations with bereaved families. *Journal of Marital and Family Therapy, 20*, 287–296. doi:10.1111/j.1752-0606.1994.tb00116.x

Shapiro, E. R. (2008). Whose recovery, of what? Relationships and environments promoting grief and growth. *Death Studies, 32*, 40–58. doi:10.1080/07481180701741277

CHAPTER 3

Praxis: How Theory Informs Action and Research

This chapter provides students an introduction to a praxis, or theory-informed action, approach. Students will learn how to engage, apply, exercise, or practice ideas. By taking the theoretical and giving it practical application in fields of study and research, students will understand the benefits of working from solid, scholarly foundations. Numerous sections in this chapter will resonate as concepts from earlier chapters continue to tie in to the research process.

Upon successful completion of this chapter, you will be able to:

- Recognize the importance of theory, tied to practical, everyday application.
- Describe and explain how praxis components can aid in scholarly efforts.
- Discover where a praxis approach may be missing, identifying possible gaps in research literature.

. . . . ▼

Introduction

Have you ever thought about how many times you've explained yourself by using the "context" cop-out? As in, "you had to be there, it was perfect for the context" or "my gift of sarcasm just comes naturally in that context." If so, you've figured out how framing something can make it legit, acceptable. Enter theory. Not your average beach read, but theory thrives because it works to frame our behavior.

Praxis is theory-informed action. Huh? This basically means that action can be predicted by theory; theory is practical. Since practice is often depicted as the act of doing something, it is usually contrasted with theory—often described as abstract ideas about some phenomenon.

A great example is Uncertainty Reduction Theory by Berger and Calabrese (1975). It was created to explain how people try to gain information about someone they're about to meet, in order to reduce their own anxiety about the encounter. Think Facebook stalking. You're trying to reduce your uncertainty in the beginning stages of a relationship by predicting the other person's behavior or interests. Say thank you to social media.

While theory may sound abstract, it's from theory that we derive general principles or rules about something or phenomenon. This is the ah-ha moment. Theory IS applicable. If it wasn't, if theory didn't help you figure something out, it wouldn't be worth your time. So, think of theory as "real" knowledge and the practical as the application of that knowledge to solve problems.

Often, in creative arts research, production often begins with a plan or design—storyboarding or a mock-up, perhaps even a small-scale model. But for the theoretical, we often begin with a question or situation. We then start to think about this situation in the light of our understanding of what is good (remember the chapter on paradigm? This is where your framework, your research paradigm comes back into play). Now you need to cultivate some practical wisdom, what Aristotle calls phronesis. Phronesis is you being able to take what you know and then applying that knowledge in wise ways… moving between the particular, or specific instances, and the general.

"The mark of a prudent man [is] to be able to deliberate rightly about what is good and what is advantageous for himself; not in particular respects, e.g. what is good for health or physical strength, but what is conducive to the good life generally." (Aristotle 2004: 209)

Foundations of Theory

▼ ....

The Idea of Theory

Theory
A unified, or coherent, body of propositions that provide a philosophically consistent picture of a subject.

Uses of the term, **theory**, range from your theories about why the Browns should win the Super Bowl to Einstein's theory of relativity. Even scientists, writers, and philosophers use the term in a variety of ways. Stephen Littlejohn defined theory more technically as "a unified, or coherent, body of propositions that provide a philosophically consistent picture of a subject."[1] We use the term *theory* here in its broadest sense as *any organized set of concepts, explanations,*

Reprinted by permission of Waveland Press, Inc. from (Littlejohn et al.) *Theories of Human Communication*, 11/E. Long Grove, IL: Waveland Press, Inc., © 2017 all rights reserved.

and principles that depicts some aspect of human experience.[2] Theories are formulated in order to help explain and understand phenomena; they provide a conceptual framework or foundation from which scholars develop knowledge. Theories serve various roles, from providing a means for the evaluation of new research data to identifying new research problems and questions to suggesting solutions to problems.

Dimensions of Theory

Theories are typically seen as consisting of four dimensions: (1) *philosophical assumptions*, or basic beliefs that underlie the theory; (2) *concepts*, or building blocks of the theory; (3) *explanations*, or dynamic connections made by the theory; and (4) *principles*, or guidelines for action. Although some theories—usually referred to as quasi theories—include only the first two, most scholars believe that a theory worthy of the name must have at least the first three dimensions—assumptions, concepts, and explanations. Not all theories include the final piece; in fact, as we will see later, the inclusion of principles is some-what controversial. Not every theory incorporates all four of these dimensions; many do not even use the word *theory* as a label for the set of explanations offered.

The First Dimension of Theory: Philosophical Assumptions

The starting point for any theory is the philosophical assumptions underlying it. The assumptions to which a theorist subscribes determine how a particular theory will play out. Knowing the assumptions behind a theory, then, is the first step to understanding that theory. Philosophical assumptions often are divided into three major types: assumptions about *epistemology*, or questions of knowledge; assumptions about *ontology*, or questions of existence; and assumptions about *axiology*, or questions of value. Every theory, explicitly or implicitly, includes assumptions about these areas—about the nature of knowledge and how it is obtained, about what constitutes existence, and about what is valuable. Looking for these assumptions provides a foundation for understanding how a given theory positions itself in relation to other theories.[3]

Epistemology.　**Epistemology** is the branch of philosophy that studies knowledge, or how people know what they claim to know. Any good discussion of theory will inevitably come back to epistemological issues. The following five questions are among the most common questions of epistemological concern to many scholars.[4]

1. *To what extent can knowledge exist before experience?* Many believe that all knowledge arises from experience. We observe the world and thereby come to know about it. But perhaps there is something in our basic

Epistemology
The branch of philosophy that studies knowledge, or how people know what they claim to know.

nature that provides a kind of knowledge even before we experience the world. The capacity to think and to perceive is cited as evidence for such inherent mechanisms. For example, strong evidence exists that children do not learn language entirely from hearing it spoken. Rather, they may acquire language by using innate models to test what they hear. In other words, a capacity for language exists in the brain *a priori*—before a child begins to know the world through experiencing it.

2. *To what extent can knowledge be certain?* Does knowledge exist in the world as an absolute—there for the taking by whoever can discover it? Or is knowledge relative and changing? The debate over this issue has persisted for hundreds of years among philosophers. Those who take a universal stance—who believe they are seeking absolute and unchangeable knowledge—will admit to errors in their theories, but they believe that these errors are merely a result of not yet having discovered the complete truth. Relativists believe that knowledge will never be certain because universal reality simply does not exist. Instead, what we can know is filtered through our experiences and perceptions; thus, theories evolve and change as well.

Anatol Rapoport presents the following amusing anecdote about three baseball umpires, which illustrates the different positions theorists take about the nature of knowledge:

> The first umpire, who was a "realist," remarked, "Some is strikes and some is balls, and I calls them as they is." Another, with less faith in the infallibility of the professional, countered with, "Some is strikes and some is balls, and I calls them as I sees them." But the wisest umpire said, "Some is strikes and some is balls, but they ain't nothing till I calls them."[5]

The first case represents knowledge as certain or absolute and awaiting discovery. The third umpire suggests the relativist position—nothing is certain until it is labeled; the label plays a large part in determining what that something is. The second umpire represents a kind of middle ground in terms of the nature of knowledge, a position that acknowledges the role of perception and the human element in the discovery of knowledge.

3. *By what process does knowledge arise?* This question is at the heart of epistemology because the kind of process selected for discovering knowledge determines the kind of knowledge that develops from that process. There are at least four positions on the issue. *Rationalism* suggests that knowledge arises out of the sheer power of the human mind to know the truth ("I calls them as they is"). This position places ultimate faith in human reasoning to ascertain truth. In contrast, *empiricism* states that knowledge arises in perception. We experience the world and literally "see" what is going on ("I calls them as I sees them").

Constructivism, the third position, holds that people create knowledge in order to function pragmatically in the world—that phenomena can be fruitfully understood many different ways—and that knowledge is what the person has made of the world ("They ain't nothing till I calls them").

Taking constructivism one step further, *social construction* is a fourth position on how knowledge comes to be; it suggests that reality is socially constructed, a product of group and cultural life. Knowledge, then, is a product of symbolic interaction within social groups. In the case of the umpires, the knowledge of what a ball is and what a strike is only can be known or constructed within the framework of the game of baseball, and both terms—*ball* and *strike*—have many other meanings in English that are quite different from the meanings they have in baseball.

4. *Is knowledge best conceived in parts or wholes?* Those who take a holistic approach believe that phenomena are highly interrelated and operate as a system. True knowledge, in other words, cannot be divided into parts but consists of general, indivisible, gestalt understandings. Others believe that knowledge consists of understanding how parts operate separately, so they are interested in isolating, categorizing, and analyzing the various components that together comprise what can be considered knowledge.

5. *To what extent is knowledge explicit?* Many philosophers and scholars believe that you cannot know something unless you can state it. Within this view, knowledge is that which can be articulated explicitly. Others claim that much of knowledge is hidden—that people operate on the basis of sensibilities that are not conscious and that they may be unable to express. Such knowledge is said to be tacit.[6]

The way scholars conduct inquiry and construct theories depends largely on their epistemological assumptions, because what they think knowledge is and how they think it is obtained determines what they find. The same holds for the next type of philosophical assumptions—assumptions of ontology.

Ontology. Ontology is the branch of philosophy that deals with the nature of being.[7] Epistemology and ontology go hand in hand because our ideas about knowledge depend in large part on our ideas about who is doing the knowing. There are four questions to consider as you learn about ontology.[8]

Ontology
The branch of philosophy that deals with the nature of being.

1. First, *to what extent do humans make real choices?* Although all investigators probably would agree that people perceive choice, there is a long-standing philosophical debate on whether real choice is possible. On one side of the issue are the *determinists* who state that behavior is caused by a multitude of prior conditions that largely determine human behavior. Humans, according to this view, are basically reactive and passive, creatures who simply respond to the world around them. On the other side of the debate are the *pragmatists*, who claim that people intentionally plan to meet future goals. This group sees people as active, decision-making beings who affect their own destinies. Middle positions also exist, suggesting either that people make choices within a restricted range or that some behaviors are determined whereas others are a matter of free will.

2. A second ontological issue is *whether human behavior is best understood in terms of states or traits*. This question deals with whether there are fairly stable, enduring dimensions of human behavior such as introversion or passivity—*traits* that an individual generally exhibits across situations—or more temporary, situational conditions or *states* that affect how people behave. The state view argues that humans are dynamic and go through numerous states in the course of a day, year, and lifetime—from feeling elated, being anxious, being cautious—depending on what is being experienced. The trait view believes that people are mostly predictable because they display more or less consistent characteristics across time. One person is generally carefree, another is fearful, and yet another is optimistic. Traits, then, do not change easily and define an individual's way of being in the world. A trait might be thought of as a continual state. There is, of course, an in-between position, and many theorists believe that both traits and states characterize human behavior.

3. *Is human experience primarily individual or social?* This ontological question deals with whether the individual or the group carries the most weight in terms of determining human action. The unit of analysis for scholars with an individualistic perspective is the psychological dimensions of the individual—the thoughts, feelings, and behaviors that affect how that individual experiences and acts in the world. Scholars who focus on the group use social life as the primary unit of analysis. These social scientists believe that humans cannot be understood apart from their relationships with others in groups and cultures. The ontological question of individual or social is especially important to communication scholars because of their focus on interaction.

4. *To what extent is communication contextual?* The focus of this question is whether behavior is governed by universal principles or whether it depends on situational factors. Some philosophers believe that human life and action are best understood by looking at universal factors—laws, if you will—that operate generally across all situations. The theory of cognitive complexity states that those with greater cognitive complexity are better at adapting messages to audiences than those with lesser complexity. This is a universal principle that applies generally to speakers addressing audiences. Others believe that behavior is richly contextual and cannot be generalized beyond the immediate situation—that the specifics of the particular interaction must be considered.

Axiology
The branch of philosophy concerned with the study of values—the values that guide research and the implications of those values for the outcome of the research process.

Axiology. **Axiology** is the branch of philosophy concerned with the study of values—the values that guide research and the implications of those values for the outcome of the research process.

Can theory be value free? Classical science answers this first axiological concern in the affirmative—theories and research are value free, scholarship is neutral, and scholars attempt to uncover the facts as they are. According to this view, when a scientist's values intrude, the result is bad science.

But there is another position on this issue: science is not value free because the researcher's work is always influenced by particular ways of viewing the world as well as preferences about what to study and how to conduct inquiry. Furthermore, government and private organizational values as well as larger political and economic interests and ideologies determine what research is funded. Scientists' choices, then, are affected by personal as well as institutional values, making value-free inquiry impossible.

A second value issue centers on the question of whether scholars intrude on and thereby affect the process being studied. In other words, *to what extent does the process of inquiry itself affect what is being seen?* To what degree does the researcher become part of the system under examination and thus affect that system? The traditional scientific viewpoint is that scientists must observe carefully without interference so that accuracy can be achieved. Critics doubt this is possible, believing that no method of observation is completely free of distortion. Even when you look at planets through a telescope, you are automatically distorting distance because of the properties of lenses. When the doctor puts a stethoscope on your chest, your nervous system reacts, and sometimes your heart rate is affected. If you bring participants into a laboratory and ask them to talk to one another as part of an experiment, individuals do not communicate in exactly the same way as they would outside the laboratory.

Not only does inquiry potentially affect what is observed but it also can affect life outside of the study itself. This means the scholar, by virtue of scholarly work, becomes an agent of change because studying human life changes that life. For example, if you interview a married couple about their relationship, simply reflecting on and talking about some aspect of their relationship can affect it in some way. The role of the scholar as change agent, then, means at a minimum considering the ethical issues raised by the research.

A third issue of axiology concerns the ends for which scholarship is conducted. *Should scholarship be designed to achieve change, or is its function simply to generate knowledge?* Traditional scientists claim that they are not responsible for the ways scientific knowledge is used—that it can be used for good or ill. According to this perspective, the discovery of nuclear fission was in and of itself an important scientific discovery—that it was used to make atomic bombs is not the scientist's concern. Critics object, saying that scientific knowledge is, by its very nature, instrumentalist. It is control oriented and necessarily reinforces certain power arrangements in society. Therefore, scholars have a responsibility to make conscious efforts to help society change in positive ways.

The TV mini-series *Manhattan* addressed the use of the nuclear bomb and the ultimate ends for its creation. Several members of the research team were interested simply in the scientific development of the bomb; what it would be used for was not their concern. Others actually tried to sabotage the project because they knew the destruction the bomb would unleash. Yet others sought a middle ground—they wanted to detonate the bomb over an unoccupied island to show the world its potential force for destruction; they did not want it to be actually used to kill people unless the demonstration failed to convince Japan to surrender. At one end of the continuum, then, is *value-free scholarship* in which researchers believe they can seek objectivity without personal values affecting that scholarship. At the other end is *value-conscious* scholarship, in which researchers recognize the importance of values to research and theory, are careful to acknowledge their particular standpoints, and make concerted efforts to direct those values in positive ways.

We turn next to the second dimension of theories. Concepts—terms and definitions—tell us what a theorist is looking at and what is considered important.

The Second Dimension of Theory: Concepts

Humans are by nature conceptual beings and group things into conceptual categories according to observed qualities. Thomas Kuhn writes that we do not "learn to see the world piecemeal or item by item"; we "sort out whole areas together from the flux of experience." In our everyday world, we learn to consider some things to be trees, some houses, and some cars, and those categories are given to us by our experiences within a family, a community, a culture.

How one categorizes is not universal. The philosopher Michel Foucault cites a passage from a Chinese encyclopedia in which "'animals are divided into: (a) belonging to the Emperor, (b) embalmed, (c) tame, (d) suckling pigs, (e) sirens, (f) fabulous, (g) stray dogs, (h) included in the present classification, (i) frenzied, (j) innumerable, (k) drawn with a very fine camelhair brush, (l) *et cetera*, (m) having just broken the water pitcher, (n) that from a long way off look like flies.'" He concludes by noting that "the thing we apprehend in one great leap . . . [is] the stark impossibility of thinking *that*." It is not, in other words, a categorical system that makes sense to us in the United States in the 21st century.

Formulating and articulating a set of concepts is an important first step in theory building. To determine concepts, the theorist observes many variables in human interaction and classifies and labels them according to perceived patterns. The set of conceptual terms identified becomes an integral part of the theory—and is often unique to that theory.

Theories that stop at the conceptual level—theories in which the goal is to provide a list of categories for something without explaining how they relate to one another—are known as *taxonomies*. Because they do not provide an understanding of how things work, many theorists are reluctant to label them theories. The best theories, then, go beyond taxonomies to provide *explanations*—statements about how the variables relate to one another—to show how concepts are connected. Notice, for example, that the conceptual terms of expectancy violations theory listed above do not have much meaning in isolation. In order to highlight their relevance, the theory must show how one concept is related to, causes, or explains another concept or concepts. The third dimension of theory—explanations—addresses relationships.

The Third Dimension of Theory: Explanations

At the level of explanation, the theorist identifies regularities or patterns in the relationships among variables. Put simply, explanation answers the question: Why? An explanation identifies a "logical force" among variables that connect them in some way. A theorist might hypothesize, for example, that if children see a lot of television violence, they will develop violent tendencies. In the social sciences, the connection is rarely taken as absolute. Instead, we can say that one thing is "often" or "usually" associated with another and that there is a probable relationship: If children see a lot of television violence, they probably will develop violent tendencies. In the theory of expectancy violation, one important proposition is that a violation of an expected communication behavior, such as failing to maintain an appropriate physical distance, causes psychological or physiological arousal, which in turn affects whether the violation and the communicator doing the violating are viewed positively or negatively.

There are many types of explanations involved in theory construction, but two of the most common are causal and practical. In *causal explanation*, events are seen as connected causally, with one variable seen as an outcome or result of the other. In causal explanation, the consequent event is determined by some antecedent event, and the researcher seeks to determine what that causal force is. *Practical explanation*, on the other hand, explains actions as goal related, with the action designed to achieve a future state. In practical explanation, actions are chosen because a particular outcome is desired. To clarify this distinction, consider how you might explain to a friend why you failed a test. Using a causal explanation, you might say: "My professor didn't provide enough background, so I didn't have the information I needed to pass the test." On the other hand, if you did well on the test, you would probably use a practical explanation: "I want to get an A in this course, so I studied hard for this test."

The distinction between causal and practical explanation is important in the debate about what a theory should do. Many traditional theorists say that theories should stop at the level of explanation. These scholars believe that theories depict things as they are by identifying and explaining the causal mechanisms of events. There is no need to go further because they have accurately depicted how a particular communication phenomenon works. Other scholars assume there are many ways to interpret and act in a situation; they assume that people are agents who take an intentional and deliberate role in creating knowledge and meaning, and the decisions each individual makes may vary considerably from how others might approach that same situation. For practical theorists, then, theories should go beyond depiction of how the world is; they should provide a guide to practical action—principles, the final dimension of theory.

The Fourth Dimension of Theory: Principles

A *principle* is a proposition, precept, or guideline that enables someone to interpret and evaluate an event and decide how to act in the situation. A principle has three parts: (1) it identifies a situation or event; (2) it includes a set of norms or values; and (3) it asserts a connection between a range of actions and possible consequences. For example, in cross-cultural adaptation theory, the first aspect is the move to and need to adapt to an unfamiliar culture. The second aspect—values or norms—includes the notion that communication is critical to adaptation. The connection asserted between actions and consequences, the third aspect of principle, is that as long as the individual remains engaged to some degree with the host culture, some adaptation will occur. Those theorists committed to making recommendations based on the theory developed believe the construction of principles in theory building to be paramount; generating principles that can be used as the basis of action in the world is the whole purpose for engaging in the theoretical enterprise. Such researchers want to improve life in concrete ways as a result of their work. In the case of *Manhattan* and the atomic bomb described above, those scientists concerned about how the bomb would be used in the world were concerned with the development of principles as part of theorizing.

The various dimensions of theory just described—assumptions, concepts, explanations, and principles—combine in different ways to construct different kinds of theories (although they are not always explicitly identified in each theory). Each starts from a different set of philosophical assumptions and makes use of different concepts and explanations.

Quick Reference

Theory is a tricky subject for many, as it can seem dry and uninteresting, or heaven forbid, even impractical. But, theories are systematic thinking and explanation. Consistently practical. Theory changes research. How so? For some researchers, theory is a lens that shapes perceptions, but for others, theory helps craft a hypothesis and test it. Theory, practically applied, can shift for different methods of research . . . qualitative, for example, thinks of theory as a lens, which then shapes perceptions and viewpoints. But, a quantitative researcher would use theory differently, perhaps as the basis for crafting their questions. This is praxis at its finest.

—*Kristen Hark*

Foundations of Theory

A theory consists of a systematic body of ideas about a particular topic or phenomenon. Psychologists have theories relating to human behavior including learning, memory, and personality, for example. These ideas form a coherent and logically consistent structure that serves two important functions. First, theories *organize and explain* a variety of specific facts or descriptions of behavior. Such facts and descriptions are not very meaningful by themselves, and so theories are needed to impose a framework on them. This framework makes the world more comprehensible by providing a few abstract concepts around which we can organize and explain a variety of behaviors. As an example, consider how Charles Darwin's theory of evolution organized and explained a variety of facts concerning the characteristics of animal species. Similarly, in psychology one theory of memory asserts that there are separate systems of short-term memory and long-term memory. This theory accounts for a number of specific observations about learning and memory, including such phenomena as the different types of memory deficits that result from a blow to the head versus damage to the hippocampus area of the brain and the rate at which a person forgets material he or she has just read.

Second, theories *generate new knowledge* by focusing our thinking so that we notice new aspects of behavior—theories guide our observations of the world. The theory generates hypotheses about behavior, and the researcher conducts studies to test the hypotheses. If the studies confirm the hypotheses, the theory is supported. As more and more evidence accumulates that is consistent with the theory, we become more confident that the theory is correct.

Sometimes people describe a theory as "just an idea" that may or may not be true. We need to separate this use of the term from the scientific meaning of *theory*. This perspective implies that a theory is essentially the same as a hypothesis. In fact, a scientific theory consists of much more. A scientific theory is grounded in actual data from prior research as well as numerous hypotheses that are consistent with the theory. These hypotheses can be tested through further research. Such testable hypotheses are falsifiable—the data can either support or refute the hypotheses. As a theory develops with more and more evidence that supports the theory, it is wrong to say that it is "just an idea." Instead, the theory becomes well established as it enables us to explain a great deal of observable facts. It is true that research may reveal a weakness in a theory when a hypothesis generated by the theory is not supported. When this happens, the theory can be modified to account for the new data. Sometimes a new theory will emerge that accounts for both new data and the existing body of knowledge. This process defines the way that science continually develops with new data that expand our knowledge of the world around us.

How does a researcher know what theoretical framework to use? To answer that question, we must explain some of the different types of theories.

*Evaluating Theory

As you encounter theories, you will need a basis for judging one against another. All theories have limitations, so you will not find a theory for which each of the following criteria are "true." Furthermore, certain criteria will be more important to certain kinds of theories. The following criteria offer a starting point from which you can begin to assess the theories you will encounter in this text.

Theoretical Scope

A theory's scope is its comprehensiveness or inclusiveness. Theoretical scope relies on the principle of generality, or the idea that a theory's explanation must be sufficiently general to extend beyond a single observation. When generalized too narrowly, the explanation is merely speculation about a single event rather than a theoretical explanation about a range of events. The opposite is also true. A theory can fail by attempting to cover too broad a range of human behavior.

Two types of generality exist. The first concerns the extent of coverage. A theory that covers a sufficiently broad domain is considered a good theory. A communication theory that meets this test would explain a variety of communication-related behaviors usually confined to a specific context—health, media, or relationships, for example. One of the powers of a good practical theory is that it can be applied to richly different situations and still be helpful.

A theory need not cover a large number of phenomena to be judged good, however. Indeed, many fine theories are narrow in coverage. Such theories possess the second type of generality. They deal with a narrow range of events, but their explanations of these events apply to a large number of situations. Certain theories of relationship breakups illustrate this type of generality. They only cover one topic, but they are powerful because they explain many instances of relationship dissolution, whether of an intimate partnership, colleagues at work, or parents and children.

Appropriateness

Are the theory's epistemological, ontological, and axiological assumptions appropriate for the theoretical questions addressed and the research methods used? In the last section, we discussed the fact that different types of theory allow scholars to do different kinds of things. One criterion by which theories can be evaluated is whether their claims are consistent with or appropriate to their assumptions. If you assume that people make choices and plan actions to accomplish goals, it would be inappropriate to predict behavior on the basis of causal events. If you assume that the most important things affecting behavior are unconscious, it would be inappropriate to survey subjects about why they did certain things. If you believe that theory should be value free, it would be inappropriate to base your definition of communication on some standard of effectiveness or any other value.

In a way, then, appropriateness is logical consistency between a theory and its assumptions. For example, some writers from the cognitive tradition state that people actively process information and make plans to accomplish personal goals. Yet theories produced by these researchers often make law-like statements about universal behaviors, which, if true, would leave little room for purposeful action. In other words, causal explanation is not appropriate for explaining intentional, deliberate action.

Heuristic Value

Will the theory generate new ideas for research and additional theory? Does it have heuristic value? *Heuristic* literally means serving as an aid to learning, discovery, or problem solving. Theories differ significantly in their heuristic value, but they accomplish this value in different ways. At one end are theories that are heuristic in generating new research questions, new hypotheses, and new concepts or variables. At the other end are theories that are heuristic to the extent that they produce new ideas by continually exploring new situations.

Validity

Generally speaking, validity is the truth value of a theory. "Truth" is not intended to mean absolute unchanging fact; rather, there may be a variety of "truth values" in an experience. Validity as a criterion of theory has at least three meanings. One kind of validity is *value*, or worth. This kind of validity refers to the importance or utility of a theory—does the theory have value? This is the primary form of validity in practical theories. The second kind of validity is *correspondence*, or fit. Here the question is whether the concepts and relations specified by the theory actually can be observed. The third kind of validity is *generalizability*, which is exactly the same as theoretical scope, discussed above. This is the classical definition of validity and applies almost exclusively to traditional, discovery-oriented, law-like theories.

Parsimony

The test of parsimony involves *logical simplicity*. If two theories are equally valid, the one with the simplest logical explanation is better. For example, if I can explain your behavior based on one simple variable such as reward, the theory is more parsimonious than if I need three variables such as *reward*, *personality*, and *difficulty*. We need to be careful with parsimony, however, as highly parsimonious explanations may be overly simplistic and may leave out many important factors that expand our insight into what is happening. Parsimony must always be balanced with other criteria.

Openness

Finally, theories can be judged according to their *openness*. This criterion is especially important in the practical paradigm. It means that a theory is open to other possibilities. A theory is considered tentative, contextual, and qualified, and any theoretical construction is seen as a way of looking rather than a reproduction of reality. It admits to diversity and invites dialogue with other perspectives. It acknowledges its own incompleteness.

So What Makes a Good Theory?

First, they provide insights we would not ordinarily have. When you read a really good theory, you have an "aha" reaction. You realize that this makes sense, yet it is not something you necessarily would have come up with on your own. In other words, the theory introduces you to new ideas and helps you see things in new ways. Such theories are fascinating precisely because their concepts are intriguing and helpful.

At the same time, theories change constantly. The leading theories of today evolved from earlier theoretical ideas that have grown, combined, and expanded through research and careful thinking. Leading theories, then, are the product of collaboration, extension, and elaboration; rarely is a single person responsible for a major theory. Although a theory may be associated with a particular scholar, you will see many contributors to it in the literature. This means that the work has attracted a number of scholars who carry on the work because the theory remains interesting and relevant.

Another hallmark, then, of an important or significant theory is that it has staying power. It was conceptualized and proposed by a theorist; developed over time, either because of that theorist's work or the work of others; and continues to evolve as scholars grapple with and contribute to it. Such theories are so useful, insightful, or interesting that they are not easily abandoned.

▼ ....

Looking Forward

By the time you finish this chapter, you may feel that you have been assaulted by a seemingly limitless list of theories and a pile of names—or maybe you're already feeling a bit overwhelmed by what's to come. Rather than using these negative metaphors, we encourage you to take a different view, to find another metaphor that helps you put what you have read in a larger, more workable perspective.

Try thinking about any subject theory as a prism. Using this metaphor, any subject becomes a multifaceted process that is understood in terms of many contexts, some narrow and some broad. You can look at a prism from any of its sides, peer into it, and watch various reflections come off the surface as you rotate it. Like a prism, any subject theory absorbs insight and reflects it back in colorful and interesting ways. Any subject theory, then, can be a way to see many possibilities for how to think about and study any subject, to discover and understand how various theories connect with and reflect one another, and to gain insight into any subject.

Or maybe a project metaphor works for you. Instead of thinking about subject theories as discrete bits of data produced by individual scholars, think of the field as a collaborative building effort. What looks to you like a coherent structure—an edifice, a building—is in fact the result of decades of particular efforts to hammer out explanations for any subject processes. But each of these efforts builds on other pieces that connect to yet other structures, and the end result looks like a single whole. Although any subject theory may appear to be a sturdy edifice because of the ways the field is organized and presented, it is constantly under construction. It is never done. Even as you read this, scholars are contributing new ideas and these will ultimately change the shape of the edifice as the years go by.

Another metaphor you might use to frame how to think about any subject theory is the metaphor of exploration. Imagine all of the theories described as having been discovered during an expedition or journey. These trails meander in many directions, looping around, crossing one another, diverging again and again. Each trail has numerous side pathways that also link up, creating a maze of possible turns to take. Over time, some pathways eventually come to be marked by deep ruts caused by heavy traffic, while others are less traveled, perhaps overgrown, and hard to find.

Glossary

Axiology
The branch of philosophy concerned with the study of values—the values that guide research and the implications of those values for the outcome of the research process.

Epistemology
The branch of philosophy that studies knowledge, or how people know what they claim to know.

Ontology
The branch of philosophy that deals with the nature of being.

Theory
A unified, or coherent, body of propositions that provide a philosophically consistent picture of a subject.

References

1   Stephen W. Littlejohn, "Theory," in *Encyclopedia of Communication Theory*, vol. 2, ed. Stephen W. Littlejohn and Karen A. Foss (Thousand Oaks, CA: Sage, 2009), 957.

2   See Steven H. Chaffee, "Thinking About Theory," in *An Integrated Approach to Communication Theory and Research*, ed. Michael B. Salwen and Don W. Stacks (Mahwah, NJ: Lawrence Erlbaum, 1996), 15–32; Stephen W. Littlejohn, "Communication Theory," in *Encyclopedia of Rhetoric and Composition: Communication from Ancient Times to the Information Age*, ed. Theresa Enos (New York: Garland, 1996), 117–21; Karl Erik Rosengren, "Substantive Theories and Formal Models—Bourdieu Confronted," *European Journal of Communication* 10 (1995): 7–39; Fred L. Casmir, "The Role of Theory and Theory Building," in *Building Communication Theories: A Socio/Cultural Approach*, ed. Fred L. Casmir (Hillsdale, NJ: Lawrence Erlbaum, 1994), 7–45.

3   For an excellent case in favor of multiple approaches to communication, see John Waite Bowers and James J. Bradac, "Issues in Communication Theory: A Metatheoretical Analysis," in *Communication Yearbook 5*, ed. Michael Burgoon
(New Brunswick, NJ: Transaction, 1982), 1–28. For a good representative presentation of various theories, see Stephen W. Littlejohn and Karen A. Foss, eds., *Encyclopedia of Communication Theory* (Thousand Oaks, CA: Sage, 2009).

4   For a good recent treatment of the philosophy of communication, including an exploration of these philosophical assumptions, see Pat Arneson, *Perspectives on Philosophy of Communication* (West Lafayette, IN: Purdue University Press, 2007).

5   For a general discussion of epistemology, see Pat Arneson, "Epistemology," in *Encyclopedia of Communication Theory*, vol. 1, ed. Stephen W. Littlejohn and Karen A. Foss (Thousand Oaks, CA: Sage, 2009), 349–52. Many schemes have been devised to classify epistemological approaches. See, for example, Stephen Pepper, *World Hypotheses* (Berkeley: University of California Press, 1942); B. Aubrey Fisher, *Perspectives on Human Communication* (New York: Macmillan, 1978); Kenneth Williams, "Reflections on a Human Science of Communication," *Journal of Communication* 23 (1973): 239–50; Barry Brummett, "Some Implications of 'Process' or 'Intersubjectivity': Postmodern Rhetoric," *Philosophy and Rhetoric* 9 (1976): 21–51; Gerald Miller, "The Current Status of Theory and Research in Interpersonal Communication," *Human Communication Research* 4 (1978): 175.

6   Anatol Rapoport, "Strategy and Conscience," in *The Human Dialogue: Perspectives on Communication*, ed. Floyd W. Matson and Ashley Montagu (New York: Free Press, 1967), 95.

7   See Michael Polanyi, *Personal Knowledge* (London: Routledge & Kegan Paul, 1958).

8   For a discussion of ontology, see Alasdair MacIntyre, "Ontology," in *The Encyclopedia of Philosophy*, vol. 5, ed. Paul Edwards (New York: Macmillan, 1967), 542–43; and James Anderson, *Communication Theory: Epistemological Foundations* (New York: Guilford, 1996), 13–101.

CHAPTER 4

Ethics in Research: Essential Conversation

CHAPTER OUTLINE

1. Introduction
2. Why Do We Care about Human Subjects Protection?
3. How Do We Follow Research Ethics and Ethical Guidelines?
   a. Respect for Persons and Informed Consent
   b. Nonmaleficence and Beneficence
   c. Including Participants in Co-Constructed Research
4. Ethics in Reporting Findings
5. Who Oversees Research Ethics? Institutional Research Boards (IRBs)
6. How Do We Maintain Ethics through all Research Phases?
7. So What?

This chapter focuses on the ethics of research, where you will learn proper, ethical methods for sourcing material. This chapter's focus on integrity allows you to demonstrate how faith informs the inquisitive conversation. Another focus is the Institutional Review Board (IRB) and how the IRB helps guide researchers toward a more ethical inquiry.

Upon successful completion of this chapter, you will be able to:

- Distinguish between ethical and unethical ways of generating material related to inquiry and scholarship.
- Recognize the importance of personal integrity and ethical responsibility in research.

▼ ....

Introduction

Most people would answer "yes" to the question "are you an ethical person?" What this chapter aims to do is ask, "Really? Are you?" Granted, the question of what is ethical can be answered different ways. Think of world-view. Think about how you answer the question of "what is good? Or what is right?" Perhaps your definition of integrity agrees with Webster's: firm adherence to a code of especially moral or artistic values. If so, then those morals aren't defined BY integrity, they are defined by what you BELIEVE in. Research requires that same adherence to a standard.

Who sets those standards? It may be your university, the IRB, your professors, or those standards may be set by the industry you're working in or on. Why is a standard so important in the realm of research? Because research requires cooperation, coordination, public support, and moral and social values. But perhaps the most important is that norms, or standards, promote the **aims of research**, such as knowledge, truth, and avoidance of error. For example, prohibitions against fabricating, falsifying, or misrepresenting research data promote the truth and minimize error. Let's look at a few key terms to help explain the above concepts.

1. Research often involves a great deal of **cooperation and coordination** among many different people in different disciplines and institutions, ethical standards promote the values essential to collaborative work, such as trust, accountability, mutual respect, and fairness.
2. Ethical norms, or standards, in research help to build **public support** for research. People are more likely to fund a research project if they can trust the quality and integrity of research.
3. Norms and standards of research promote many other **important moral and social values**, such as social responsibility, human rights, animal welfare, and public health and safety. A lapse in ethical research can significantly harm human and animal subjects, students, and the public. For example, a researcher who fabricates false data in a clinical trial may harm or even kill patients, and a researcher who fails to abide by the rules and regulations relating to biological safety may jeopardize his or her health and safety or the health and safety of staff and students.

research ethics
The specific principles, rules, guidelines, and norms of research-related behavior that a research community has decided are proper, fair, and appropriate.

ethical research
Research that is designed and conducted validly, reliably, legitimately, and representatively, and protects a research participant's rights.

*Understanding Research Ethics

Why Do We Care about Human Subjects Protection?

Research ethics refer to the specific principles, rules, guidelines, and norms of research-related behavior that a research community has decided are proper, fair, and appropriate. In short, **ethical research** protects a participant's rights (Murphy & Dingwall, 2001), but it does more than that. Ethical researchers also design and conduct research that is valid, reliable, legitimate, and representative. We will discuss the history of research ethics and human subjects' protection, provide examples of ethics breaches, discuss some major concepts behind research ethics, explain the role of Institutional Research Boards (IRBs), and teach you how to ensure that your research follows ethical guidelines. We'll discuss ethics from the points of view of both interpretive and positivist paradigms, and address the specific applications of ethical research principles in both qualitative and quantitative research.

The research ethics codes that are adhered to by most researchers were written as a result of abuses and violations of ethical principles by many researchers over many years, worldwide. You might hear these rules referred to as **human subjects protection**, which refers to the guidelines we follow to make sure we are protecting the people we are studying.

The history of human subjects protection in research really begins with the Nazi medical war crimes during World War II. These abuses were particularly heinous, including—in the name of research and science—conducting medical experiments on concentration camp prisoners. These medical experiments included such appalling acts as injecting people with gasoline, live viruses, and poisons; forcing them to sit in ice water or freezing temperatures for hours; forced sterilization; depriving them of food and water; dissecting their brains; and burning them with bomb material. After the war, former Nazis were indicted before the War Crimes Tribunal at Nuremberg. One of the outcomes of this trial was the **Nuremberg Code**, which was the first set of principles outlining professional ethics for medical researchers, and which forms the basis for today's research ethics codes in both medicine and in the social sciences. The Nuremberg Code specifically required voluntary consent among research participants, and was the first international standard for the conduct of research (Annas & Grodin, 1995). We'll further discuss the ethical standards and principles for research shortly, but first let's take a look at some other examples of violations of rights of research participants in our own country.

The most famous violation in United States history might be the Tuskegee Syphilis Study, a long-term study of black males conducted in Tuskegee by the U.S. Public Health Services. This research began in the 1930s and continued until 1972. The researchers studied over 400 African-American men with syphilis and 200 without syphilis. They were recruited without informed consent and were misled about the nature of the study and what procedures would be done on them. Most appalling, they were not informed of the complications experienced by others in the study. (The death rate among those with syphilis was twice as high as among the control group.) In addition, in the 1940s penicillin was found to be effective in treating syphilis; the study continued and the men were not informed

human subjects protection
Ethical research rules that refer to the guidelines that are followed to ensure the protection of people (participants) being studied.

Nuremberg Code
The first set of principles outlining professional ethics for medical researchers, which forms the basis for today's research ethics codes. It specifically required voluntary consent among research participants, and was the first international standard for the conduct of research.

*From *Straight Talk About Communication Research Methods*, Third Edition by Christine S. Davis and Kenneth A. Lachlan. Copyright © 2017 by Kendall Hunt Publishing Company. Reprinted by permission.

about the possible treatment. Investigation into this research abuse led to the U.S. government's oversight of ethics for federally supported research projects (Thomas & Quinn, 1991).

In 1963, studies were conducted at New York's Jewish Chronic Disease Hospital to understand whether the body's inability to reject cancer cells was due to cancer or to debilitation. To test this, they injected live cancer cells into patients. The consent process did not inform the subjects that they were about to be injected with cancerous cells, because the researchers didn't want to "unnecessarily frighten them." The researchers were later found guilty of fraud, deceit, and unprofessional conduct (Edgar & Rothman, 1995).

From 1963 to 1966, at the Willowbrook State School in New York, an institution for "mentally defective children," researchers wanted to study the natural history of infectious hepatitis. Newly admitted children were deliberately infected with the hepatitis virus. Parents gave consent, but since the hospital was only admitting patients who were in this program, this wasn't really freedom of consent because parents didn't have an alternate choice if they wanted treatment for their children (Krugman, 1971).

Don't think all research abuses and dilemmas have taken place in medical research. There are many examples of ill-treatment of research participants in social science research as well. The most famous example may be the Milgram obedience to authority experiment, in which the researcher used bogus electric shocks to measure the extent to which people would submit to authority to inflict pain on another person. Since the shocks were not real, the ethical criticism was not about the physical pain seemingly inflicted on the recipient of the shock, but on the emotional pain and duress inflicted on the research participants, who were led to believe that they were inflicting severe pain on other people (Kelman, 1967).

In 1955 researchers in Wichita studied jury deliberations in an attempt to examine group decision making and negotiating. This study was also ethically criticized because participants were not told they were being researched, observed, and videotaped, and, as part of the social institution of the jury process, had reason to believe their communication was private and confidential (Kimmel, 1988).

Many qualitative and ethnographic social science researchers have been criticized for covertly observing people without their knowledge or consent. Humphrey's (1970) study of homosexual encounters in public restrooms and Kotarba's (1979) study of sexual activity in a public jail visiting room are two striking examples, especially given the deeply personal nature of the behaviors under observation. Even seemingly innocuous observations of people's day-to-day lives can be criticized if people don't know, or forget, they are being observed. Carolyn Ellis, for example, published her research of two Eastern Virginia fishing communities in her book *Fisher folk: Two communities on Chesapeake Bay* (Ellis, 1986). While she had obtained informed consent at the onset of her research, she spent so long in the field (several years) that many community participants claimed they had forgotten she was researching them and had begun to think of her as simply a friend. As Ellis states later in many writings on the subject (see Ellis, 2007, for example), her experience requires her, and us, to question **relational ethics**—the value placed on the relationships between the researchers and those they are researching.

In response to various research abuses in the United States, especially in medical research, in 1979 the U.S. government crafted a document titled "Ethical Principles and Guidelines for the Protection of Human Subjects," commonly known as the **Belmont Report**. The Belmont Report serves as the cornerstone of ethical principles upon which federal regulations for the protection of human research participants are based. Our human subject protection guidelines are based on the three principles of the Belmont Report: respect for persons, beneficence/nonmaleficence, and justice (Murphy & Dingwall, 2001).

relational ethics
The value placed on the relationships between researchers and the people they are researching.

Belmont Report
This document serves as the cornerstone of ethical principles upon which federal regulations for the protection of human research participants are based.

How Do We Follow Research Ethics and Ethical Guidelines?

Respect for Persons and Informed Consent

The first principle, **respect for persons**, states that research participants should be treated as autonomous agents—that means they are independent, self-governing, and capable of making decisions for themselves as long as they are given sufficient information to make those decisions. This principle forms the basis for **informed consent**. In the consent process, people are to be given full information about the research, both risks and benefits, and allowed to make the decision for themselves if they will participate.

A proper consent procedure should include the participant's right to withdraw from the study without penalty, the focus of the study and methods to be employed, statements surrounding confidentiality, and a signature of both the researcher and the participant (Creswell, 2007). The informed consent process assumes that the research participant is competent to consent—that, if he or she is given all relevant information, he or she will be able to comprehend the information and be able to agree to participate in a voluntary manner that is free from coercion. As part of the informed consent process, the researcher must disclose all relevant information to potential participants, including the purpose of the study, the nature of the research procedure, reasonable alternatives to the proposed intervention (if the intervention provides a service or treatment such as in medical research), and any risks, benefits, or uncertainties of the intervention.

The process also insists that participants can change their mind and withdraw at any time (which can be more than a little nerve-wracking in long-term ethnographic research, in which the entire research study could be compromised if the participant changes his or her mind). However, withdrawing from research is always the participant's prerogative.

respect for persons
Research participants should be treated as autonomous agents—that means they are independent, self-governing, and capable of making decisions for themselves as long as they are given sufficient information to make those decisions.

informed consent
This process assumes that the research participant is competent to consent—that, if he or she is given all relevant information, he or she will be able to comprehend the information and be able to agree to participate in a voluntary manner free from coercion.

There are a few exceptions to required informed consent, however. If the research could not possibly be carried out with informed consent, and if the risk to participants is minimal, it might be ethical to waive informed consent. An example in a communication studies project might be one in which participants are being interviewed about illegal drug use. In this case, signing a consent form (and putting their name on a legal document if their participation implies admission to drug use) would be more harmful than a waiver of consent. Typically, the researcher would obtain oral consent, but not signed consent.

Sometimes, in an ethnographic research study, researchers are observing individuals in public places in which it would be impossible to obtain consent from everyone present. If the research was being conducted in a place sufficiently public that there is no reasonable expectation of privacy, consent is usually not required or obtained. Examples of this type of research might include studying anonymous chat room communication or observing non-verbal communication (from a distance) at a shopping mall. Of course, even if consent can be waived, this doesn't mean that the researcher is exempt from treating participants in an ethical manner.

There are also other types of research that are exempt from obtaining informed consent. Informed consent is, obviously, obtained from people who are research participants, typically defined as a living individual about whom a researcher obtains information through an interaction with the person. A research participant might also need to give consent to let the researcher have access to personally identifiable private information (e.g., medical records), or to let a third-party participant give information about him or her (e.g., if you are interviewing a doctor about a patient, the patient has to give consent to let the doctor talk about him or her) (Mertens & Ginsberg, 2008).

In other words, when a scholar writes a rhetorical analysis of Barack Obama's latest speech, since Obama is a public figure, his speech is considered a public event, and if the researcher has not obtained that data through interaction with Obama, informed consent is neither possible nor necessary.

In fact, the use of online information as data is a hot button right now. A 2011 article in the *Chronicle of Higher Education* (Parry, 2011) reported on the use by Harvard sociologists of 1,700 Facebook profiles of students at their university. On the "pro" side, researchers say that the research they are doing can lead to important social information about culture and communication and that steps were taken to minimize the risk of privacy violations. On the "con" side, critics of this research say that deceptive practices were used to access the Facebook information in the first place (research assistants added in people who had set restrictive privacy settings but were their own "friends" and so were available to them), and when the researchers shared the database of information with other researchers, the students' privacy was not sufficiently protected.

Those with access to the report may have been able to figure out who some of the people were by comparing information from the Facebook profiles (hometown and major, for example) with the Harvard student database. Critics further say that the fact that people whose information was included were not informed of the project and didn't give consent is a breach of research ethics. Certainly, it's unclear whether information posted online in such settings is considered public or private information, but we suggest you always make your decision on the side of caution.

Therefore, we argue that there really is a bottom line issue here—if the information is publically available (published someplace, including online), and if there is not a reasonable expectation of confidentiality, you should obtain consent if possible, cite appropriately at all times, and maintain ethical standards when using the information. If the research participant can be identified by you, regardless of whether you keep that identification confidential, and if obtaining informed consent is possible, you should obtain it. If it's not possible to obtain consent, you must make sure risks are minimal and participants are treated ethically. Sometimes, this can be accomplished by using aliases or codenames, reporting information only in aggregate (combined with other people rather than individually), leaving out identifying information, or otherwise maintaining participant confidentiality when citing Internet-based communication. Of course, researchers must always abide by decisions on consent and exemptions from consent made by their Institutional Research Boards (IRBs). We will discuss the difference between confidentiality and anonymity shortly.

There are some potential participants who may not be fully able to decide for themselves if they want to take part in research. These people are referred to in human subjects protection terms as **vulnerable populations**, and they are defined as "persons with diminished autonomy" (NIH Office of Extramural Research, 2008). Children, people with cognitive impairments, older adults, people with severe health problems, employees, and students (yes, students) are considered vulnerable populations. Most of the characteristics are obvious, but why would employees and students be vulnerable populations? Both are susceptible to coercion—by employers or professors—to participate, and safeguards must be taken to make sure that their consent is truly optional.

Some vulnerable populations, such as children, must be given additional protections in research, such as needing permission of a legal guardian overseeing their care in order to include them in research. However, researchers must give everyone, regardless of diminished autonomy, the opportunity to choose (to the extent they are able) if they want to participate in the research. This might mean that if you want to interview a person with Alzheimer's disease, you would first obtain legal consent from his or her guardian, then obtain **assent**—the permission of the person with Alzheimer's to conduct the interview just prior to doing so.

There are specific ethical challenges in conducting ethnographic, autoethnographic, and narrative research among certain vulnerable populations. Many autoethnographers have written about relationships with friends or relatives who are deceased. Obviously, it is impossible to obtain consent

vulnerable populations
Persons with diminished autonomy; specifically, children, people with cognitive impairments, older adults, people with severe health problems, employees, and students.

assent
Permission obtained from individuals with limited capacity to consent (e.g., minors), allowing themselves to be included as participants in research studies. Assent occurs after informed consent (permission to participate) is obtained from a person who is responsible for the well-being of the participant, and should occur as near as possible in time to the research intervention.

or assent from a person who is no longer alive, and IRB rules would exempt such studies from IRB oversight since the research subjects are not living participants. However, Ellis (2007) maintains that such writing should be held to even higher ethical standards. She reminds us that the dead cannot provide consent nor be libeled, and such research incites positive and negative emotions on behalf of the writer, as well as the audience.

Nonmaleficence and Beneficence

nonmaleficience
No avoidable harm should be done to participants.

beneficence
The outcome of research should be positive and beneficial.

Nonmaleficence (no avoidable harm should be done to participants) and **beneficence** (the outcome of research should be positive and beneficial) maintain that research is ethical if the "benefits outweigh the potential for harm" (Murphy & Dingwall, 2001, p. 340). Sometimes, participants may experience emotional or psychological harm that cannot be measured or may be delayed. The greatest risk in ethnography, for example, comes after publication, as a result of what is and what is not printed (Cassell, 1978; Murphy & Dingwall, 2001; Wax & Cassell, 1979). Unlike studies in more quantitatively oriented social science research, anonymity may not be possible in ethnography. It is difficult to gauge a subject's possible feelings of shame or embarrassment due to self-disclosure. To combat this phenomenon, it has been suggested that subjects have an opportunity to share in production of a work or be able to provide a response to printed material.

The principle of beneficence refers to making efforts to secure the well-being of research participants, or to maximize the possible benefits of the research and minimize its possible harm. The key to this principle is, since all research has both risks and benefits, to make sure they balance or that benefits outweigh potential harms. Benefits to research might include a monetary incentive for participation, a relationship with the researcher or other participants, knowledge or education gleaned from participation, or the opportunity to do good for society. The community of science also believes that it is important to make sure that the research is sound, and will make a sufficient contribution to knowledge that justifies any risks that may be incurred by the study participants.

anonymity
No one, including the researcher, can connect a participant's responses with his or her identity.

The principle of beneficence says that no individual shall be intentionally injured in the course of the research. Research must always protect a participant's right to privacy through anonymity or confidentiality of responses, unless the participant gives permission to waive confidentiality. **Anonymity** means that no one, including the researcher, can connect the participant's responses with his or her identity. An example of anonymous research is a survey in which participants do not release their names or chat groups in which people don't use their real names. **Confidentiality** means that, although the researcher knows what each participant said (or can find out this information), the participant's identity is kept secret when reporting or writing up the findings.

confidentiality
The identity of participants is kept secret when researchers report or write up their findings.

Sometimes, for example, participant confidentiality is ensured by providing aliases in the final report (Creswell, 2007). By many state and federal laws, a researcher must disclose information indicating a risk of harm to others (homicidal thoughts), a risk of harm to themselves (suicidal thoughts), or child or elder abuse. There may be instances in a research setting that require the interviewer/observer to report illegal activity divulged by a participant (Creswell, 2007), particularly if the information disclosed is pertinent to an ongoing legal investigation.

There are times, especially when conducting qualitative research such as narrative or autoethnographic research, when anonymity and confidentiality are not possible or desirable. If this is the case, participants must be told this up front, and the researcher should follow two other related principles: Do no harm when publishing the results, and be attentive to causing discomfort in the study. There are times when a research finding *could* be reported but *must not* be reported if doing so could cause harm to a study participant.

Most researchers consider it highly unethical to deceive a participant for the purpose of gaining information, such as gathering information secretively (except when you are observing public behavior, as we discussed earlier) (Creswell, 2007). However, if an extreme instance makes it necessary to deceive the participants, you must lessen the adverse effects from the **deception** by, after the fact, dehoaxing them (tell them what you've done), debriefing them (discussing the research with them), and desensitizing them (if they have acquired negative information about themselves in the course of the research, make sure they know it is not true).

deception
A violation of the right to informed consent that may sometimes mislead participants as to the study purpose.

While researchers are rightly concerned about our research participants, we also might safeguard against potential harm done to researchers themselves. Researchers can be adversely affected by improper boundaries between themselves and their participants, and many qualitative researchers report ethical uneasiness with the levels of affinity they develop with study participants. These feelings of closeness to the subject of the study may lead to feelings of care and protectiveness, which may in turn bias interpretations of the behaviors under observation. Qualitative researchers must also balance their own self-disclosure to participants in interview situations. Some researchers report feelings of vulnerability, guilt, and emotional exhaustion resulting from their time in the field. Other researchers not directly involved with participants, but studying data about sensitive or disturbing topics, report experiencing emotional problems resulting from their research (Dickson-Swift, James, Kippen, & Liamputtong, 2007). Dickson-Swift and colleagues (2007) suggest that researchers vulnerable to these challenges utilize a support network of colleagues and researchers with whom to debrief their experiences.

legitimation
The question of who can represent another person in narrative writing.

Including Participants in Co-Constructed Research

Researchers, especially those following the interpretive paradigm are also concerned about issues of **legitimation** (Who can speak for these people?) and **representation** (How can you speak for these people?). Representation

representation
Fully understanding the lived experiences of research participants and including the multiple realities, interpretations, experiences, and voices emergent from all individuals and all angles.

refers to understanding fully the lived experiences of research participants and including the multiple realities, interpretations, experiences, and voices emergent from all individuals and all angles. One challenge is to ensure that the people and context studied are adequately and sufficiently represented, and that rigorous attempts are made to include their own voices and interpretations. Methods that directly include—and help researchers more fully understand—participants' voices and interpretations might include interactive techniques such as interactive interviewing, interactive focus groups, co-constructed narratives, or close observation over a long period of time, which allow study participants to give their own accounts of their own experiences. Other advantages of coauthored methods include the possible avoidance of obtaining consent (since participants are also researchers), alleviation of concerns about offending subjects, and less likelihood of research participants changing their minds about participating (Denzin, 2003; Ellis, 2007).

member checks
The process of providing study participants with the research findings, and giving them the opportunity to voice agreement or disagreement with the research as reported.

Qualitative researchers should also ensure that they are representing the voice of their participants by conducting **member checks** at the conclusion of their study. Member checks consist of a process of providing study participants with the research findings and giving them the opportunity to voice agreement or disagreement with the research as reported.

Ethics in Reporting Findings

As you will discover in coming chapters, social scientists aim to test research questions and hypotheses through their observations and oftentimes through the analysis of data. Scholars have argued over the years that academic journals tend to have a bias against non-significant findings—this is to say that when the analyses don't turn out as the researcher expects, this is sometimes interpreted as an indication that the work is deficient and the piece is deemed unpublishable by reviewers and editors. Rosenthal (1979) and others have called this the "file drawer" effect. Since non-significant findings often go unpublished, there may be a temptation to "massage" data in such a way as to suggest that they support certain positions. There may also exist the temptation to engage in "HARKing," or hypothesizing after results are known (Kerr, 1998). In such instances, researchers examine the data first, then pretend that they anticipated the results all along.

Do not do this. Both of these research practices are widely considered unethical, and can lead to serious academic and professional consequences. Readers tend to have expectations of what good data reporting looks like. Dishonest reporting also produces knowledge that is fundamentally flawed, since the data don't actually support the claims made by the researchers. Data analytic issues are largely policed by journal editors and reviewers. When it comes to ethics in research procedures, ethical practices are supervised by entities called IRBs.

Who Oversees Research Ethics?
Institutional Review Boards (IRBs)

Most academic research is overseen by university IRBs (Institutional Research Boards). Simply put, IRBs act as gatekeepers to research conducted by researchers affiliated with their university. They have a three-fold purpose: to protect the university from legal repercussions of conducting research deemed unethical, to protect the university from financial (and legal) sanctions imposed by the federal government and other funders on research deemed unethical, and to protect research participants from unethical practices in research.

IRB board members usually consist of a cross-section of university faculty, and might also include legal and administrative representatives. All faculty—and some student—research must be submitted to the IRB for approval before being conducted. Even if the IRB will consider the research to be exempt from human subjects protection, most university IRBs want to make that ruling themselves. Student research conducted as part of a class project is usually exempt from IRB oversight because the students are considered to be under the oversight of their professor. However, if the research may later be submitted for publication, since peer-reviewed journals usually require IRB oversight, IRBs usually recommend that it be submitted to them anyway. Student research conducted for thesis or dissertation purposes is usually required to be submitted to the IRB.

Even if you are not conducting research under the authority of a university, you might still be subject to IRB oversight. Hospitals, research institutes, community agencies, and other organizations that conduct research frequently have their own IRBs.

Often, IRBs approve research projects quickly and efficiently. Criticism of IRBs and the IRB process occur when they don't. IRBs, at times, require researchers to change their method or procedures, and some researchers see this as a threat to academic freedom and a form of censorship, especially since most university faculty are required to conduct and publish research (Lewis, 2008; Lincoln, 2000). Critics of IRBs and other research gatekeepers claim that such censorship serves to suppress more innovative forms of research (Lincoln, 2000; Lincoln & Cannella, 2004).

Quick Reference

When you think of this chapter, remember two things, that research needs people of integrity and a strong ethical foundation AND there are institutions in place that assure that commitment. The IRB is all about ethics, yes, but think of the IRB as protectors of human subjects and animal subjects . . . that is the MAIN focus of attention, the priority of the IRB. Make it personal, so that you don't forget—how do you feel when someone is mistreated? Don't you wish that someone had stepped in? Said something, been a voice of concern? Well, when you work through the IRB, you are using that voice.

—*Kristen Hark*

How Do We Maintain Ethics through all Research Phases?

Ethical considerations in research do not stop when you are done with data collection—ethical researchers make ethical decisions at every stage of the research process, from study design to publication of findings. Booth, Colomb, and Williams (1995, pp. 255–256) address ethical decision making in all stages of the research process in their "7-commandments" of ethical research. They say that ethical researchers:

1. Do not steal by plagiarizing or claiming the results of others.
2. Do not lie by misreporting sources or by inventing results.
3. Do not destroy sources and data for those who follow.
4. Do not submit data whose accuracy they have reason to question.
5. Do not conceal objections that they cannot rebut.
6. Do not caricature those with opposing views or deliberately state their views in a way they would reject.
7. Do not write their reports in a way that deliberately makes it difficult for readers to understand them, nor do they simplify that which is legitimately complex.

To borrow from the NRA's (National Rifle Association) familiar saying about gun control: "Research doesn't harm, researchers do." Research findings, both qualitative and quantitative, can be manipulated, misinterpreted, and misrepresented. Despite the desire of quantitative positivist researchers to remain objective, researchers of all paradigms should admit that it is impossible to remain completely objective in any research.

Quantitative researchers address this dilemma by designing studies that are as objective as possible. Qualitative researchers, in contrast, address it by admitting their subjectivity, and taking that into account when analyzing their results (Hewitt, 2007). All researchers use rigorous, acceptable, analytical methods to determine what their data means.

Quantitative researchers use appropriate statistical and systematic techniques to analyze their data. Qualitative researchers take into account interpretation and context as they acknowledge their role in the construction of knowledge (Hewitt, 2007).

Intellectual Property
A legal concept referring to who owns the work created and what they are due as a result of creating that work.

When we look at the topic of plagiarism what we are really discussing is the issue of **intellectual property**—in other words, who owns the work created and what are they due as a result of creating that work. Think of it as a patent for an original invention. A patent protects the creator or inventor. A copyright is the same . . . and a citation is your way of showing that you understand you are not the creator. Any credible scientific or academic work requires notation and citation of supporting, existing work and literature, thus credit is given to all information and scholarship contributing to new research/ creative works.

Additionally, there is an aspect of humility and integrity required for a researcher in that they must recognize that their own work is built upon the foundation laid by others in the discoveries that led to their unique contribution. Integrity requires that we be especially sensitive to the contributions made by others and desire to give credit to those who have worked hard to provide the information and that we have used to support our own studies. Researchers and academics take plagiarism seriously, as it is a form of theft, to take information and pass it off as our original thought.

There are a number of writing styles and formats that can help us ensure our work is properly attributed to the original authors. This is why differing citation formats such as APA or MLA or Turabian exist; each format represents a particular method of citing and formatting, allowing current researchers to give accurate attribution to individuals, who originated the supporting, previously existing material. This means videos, images, literature, music, memes, art, etc. Credit needs to goes where it's due.

When you cite a source, you are using an expert's ideas as proof or evidence of a new idea that you are trying to communicate to the reader. Do these three things to ensure you are avoiding plagiarism:

- Refer to your sources as you are writing; don't wait until the end of the process. This shows that you have a clear understanding of the material you've read. Improve your note-taking skills.
- Make sure to distinguish your ideas, reflection, use and/or analysis of what you've read and studied from those of the original authors and creators.
  - For example, paraphrasing—taking another person's ideas and putting those ideas in your own words—without citation is still plagiarism.
- Ask yourself if you knew the information previously, or if it came from something you've accessed. If the answer is no, you need to give credit to the original content.

There are instances where individuals might have to make decisions regarding self-plagiarism. For example, if an individual previously created a work, are they required to cite their work or is it assumed that since that individual created the work they can use it as they see fit? This is a vibrant source of discussion in research and the academy, so it's a good idea to check with your individual professors and fellow researchers for their personal preference before engaging in self plagiarism.

Remember that each discipline has a particular format that is used to establish the method in which citations and references are listed. Take the time to invest in the formatting manual that is associated with your field of study. You are in the learning phase regarding research and all of its moving parts, so don't hesitate to use the knowledge of others. Don't reinvent the wheel. Stand on the shoulders of giants (as Bernard of Chartres would say, and Isaac Newton would make popular). In other words? Discover truth by building on previous discoveries.

So What?

In summary, it is our responsibility as researchers to ensure that: our research is properly designed, scientifically sound, and yields valid results; we do what we say we're going to do; the study is approved by an IRB and conducted according to protocol; informed consent is appropriately obtained; the rights and welfare of the participants are monitored throughout the study; the risks and benefits of the research are positively balanced; participant anonymity and confidentiality are appropriately maintained; and all participants—including those from underprivileged and marginalized populations—have an opportunity to have their voices and interpretations fully represented. The bottom line: Researchers are accountable and must show respect to colleagues in their profession and society at large.

Glossary

Anonymity

No one, including the researcher, can connect a participant's responses with his or her identity.

Assent

Permission obtained from individuals with limited capacity to consent (e.g., minors), allowing themselves to be included as participants in research studies. Assent occurs after informed consent (permission to participate) is obtained from a person who is responsible for the well-being of the participant, and should occur as near as possible in time to the research intervention.

Belmont Report

This document serves as the cornerstone of ethical principles upon which federal regulations for the protection of human research participants are based.

Beneficence

The outcome of research should be positive and beneficial.

Confidentiality

The identity of participants is kept secret when researchers report or write up their findings.

Deception

A violation of the right to informed consent that may sometimes mislead participants as to the study purpose.

Ethical research

Research that is designed and conducted validly, reliably, legitimately, and representatively, and protects a research participant's rights.

Human subjects protection

Ethical research rules that refer to the guidelines that are followed to ensure the protection of people (participants) being studied.

Informed consent

This process assumes that the research participant is competent to consent—that, if he or she is given all relevant information, he or she will be able to comprehend the information and be able to agree to participate in a voluntary manner free from coercion.

Intellectual Property:

A legal concept referring to who owns the work created and what they are due as a result of creating that work.

Legitimation

The question of who can represent another person in narrative writing.

Member checks

The process of providing study participants with the research findings, and giving them the opportunity to voice agreement or disagreement with the research as reported.

Nonmaleficience

No avoidable harm should be done to participants.

Nuremberg Code

The first set of principles outlining professional ethics for medical researchers, which forms the basis for today's research ethics codes. It specifically required voluntary consent among research participants, and was the first international standard for the conduct of research.

Relational ethics

The value placed on the relationships between researchers and the people they are researching.

Representation

Fully understanding the lived experiences of research participants and including the multiple realities, interpretations, experiences, and voices emergent from all individuals and all angles.

Research ethics

The specific principles, rules, guidelines, and norms of research-related behavior that a research community has decided are proper, fair, and appropriate.

Respect for persons

Research participants should be treated as autonomous agents—that means they are independent, self-governing, and capable of making decisions for themselves as long as they are given sufficient information to make those decisions.

Vulnerable populations

Persons with diminished autonomy; specifically, children, people with cognitive impairments, older adults, people with severe health problems, employees, and students.

References

Adams, T. E. (2008). A review of narrative ethics. *Qualitative Inquiry, 14*(2), 175–194.

Annas, G. J., & Grodin, M. A. (1995). *The Nazi doctors and the Nuremberg Code: Human rights in human experimentation*. New York: Oxford University Press.

Bayer, A., & Tadd, W. (2000). Unjustified exclusion of elderly people from studies submitted to research ethics committee for approval: Descriptive study. *BMJ [British Medical Journal], 321*, 992– 993.

Becker-Blease, K. A., & Freyd, J. J. (2006). Research participants telling the truth about their lives: The ethics of asking and not asking about abuse. *American Psychologist, 61*(3), 218–226.

Booth, W. C., Colomb, G. G., & Williams, J. M. (1995). *The craft of research.* Chicago: University of Chicago Press.

Cassell, J. (1978). Risk and benefit to subjects of field-work. *American Sociologist, 13*, 134–143.

Creswell, J. W. (2007). *Qualitative inquiry & research design* (2nd ed.). Thousand Oaks, CA: Sage.

Denzin, N. (2003). *Performance ethnography: Critical pedagogy and the politics of culture.* Thousand Oaks, CA: Sage.

Dickson-Swift, V., James, E. L., Kippen, S., & Liamputtong, P. (2007). Doing sensitive research: What challenges do qualitative researchers face? *Qualitative Research, 7*(3), 327–353.

Edgar, H., & Rothman, D. J. (1995). The Institutional Review Board and beyond: Future challenges to the ethics of human experimentation. *The Milbank Quarterly, 73*(4), 489–506.

Ellis, C. (1986). *Fisher folk: Two communities on Chesapeake Bay.* Lexington, KY: University Press of Kentucky.

Ellis, C. (2007). Telling secrets, revealing lives: Relational ethics in research with intimate others. *Qualitative Inquiry, 13*, 3–29.

Guba, E.G., & Lincoln, Y. S. (1989). *Fourth generation evaluation.* Newbury Park, CA: Sage.

Hewitt, J. (2007). Ethical components of researcher-researched relationships in qualitative interviewing. *Qualitative Health Research, 27*(8), 1149–1159.

Humphrey, L. (1970). *Tearoom trade: Impersonal sex in public places.* London: Duckworth.

Kelman, H. C. (1967). Human use of human subjects: The problem of deception in social psychological experiments. *Psychological Bulletin, 67*(1), 1–11.

Kerr, N.L. (1998). HARKing: Hypothesizing after results are known. *Personality and Social Psychology Review, 2*, 196–217.

Kimmel, A. J. (1988). *Ethics and values in applied social research*. Thousand Oaks, CA: Sage.

Kotarba, J. A. (1979). The accomplishment of intimacy in the jail visiting room. *Qualitative Sociology, 2*, 80–103.

Krugman, S. (1971). Experiments at the Willowbrook State School. *Lancet, 1*(7702), 749.

Lewis, M. (2008). New strategies of control: Academic freedom and research ethics boards. *Qualitative Inquiry, 14*, 684– 699.

Lincoln, Y. S. (2000). Institutional review boards and methodological conservatism: The challenge to and from phenomenological paradigms. In N. K. Denzin & Y. S. Lincoln (Eds.), *The Sage handbook of qualitative research* (pp. 165–181). Thousand Oaks, CA: Sage.

Lincoln, Y. S., & Cannella, G. S. (2004). Qualitative research, power, and the radical right. *Qualitative Inquiry, 10*(2), 175– 201.

Marshall, C. (1985). Appropriate criteria of the trustworthiness and goodness for qualitative research on educational organizations. *Quality and Quantity, 19*, 353–373.

Mertens, D. M., & Ginsberg, P. (2008). *The handbook of social research ethics*. Thousand Oaks, CA: Sage.

Murphy, E., & Dingwall, R. (2001). The ethics of ethnography. In P. Atkinson, A. Coffey, S. Delamont, J. Lofland, & L. Lofland (Eds.), *Handbook of ethnography* (pp. 339–351). London: Sage.

NIH Office of Extramural Research. (2008). Retrieved May 25, 2009, from http://phrp.nihtraining.com/users/login.php

Ozer, E. J. & Wright, D. (2012). Beyond school spirit: The effects of youth-led participatory action research in two urban high schools. *Journal of Research on Adolescence*, doi: 10.1111/j.1532-7795.2012.00780.x

Parry, M. (2011, July 15). Harvard researchers accused of breaching students' privacy: Social-network project shows promise and peril of doing social science online. *The Chronicle of Higher Education*, pp. A1, A8–A11.

Paterson, B., & Scott-Findlay, S. (2002). Critical issues in interviewing people with traumatic brain injury. *Qualitative Health Research, 12*(3), 399–409.

Rosenthal, R. (1979). File drawer problem and tolerance for null results. *Psychological Bulletin, 86*, 638–641.

Sandelowski, M. (1986). The problem of rigor in qualitative research. *Advances in Nursing Science, 8*, 27–37.

Silverman, D. (1985). *Qualitative methodology and sociology*. Aldershot: Gower.

Thomas, S. B., & Quinn, S. C. (1991). The Tuskegee Syphilis Study, 1932 to 1972: Implications for HIV education and AIDS risk education programs in the black community. *American Journal of Public Health, 81*(11), 1498–1505.

Wax, M., & Cassell, J. (1979). Fieldwork, ethics and politics: The wider context. In M. Wax and J. Cassell (Eds.), *Federal regulations: Ethical issues and social research* (pp. 85–102). Boulder, CO: Westview.

CHAPTER 5

The Sciences: A Survey of Approaches

CHAPTER OUTLINE

This chapter addresses research paradigms and methods most applicable to research in the social, physical, and life sciences, providing a survey of research designs across the discipline.

Upon successful completion of this chapter, you will be able to:

- Know the distinctions between qualitative, quantitative, and mixed methods research.
- Recognize important missing elements in scholarship in specific, scientific fields based on literature review.
- Develop a strategy to fill knowledge gaps within the existing literature.
- Predict and interpret results of a research study.

Introduction

Could you be described as a problem-solver? Do you enjoy solving puzzles? Do you watch Sherlock and think you could be Holmes? Research in the sciences aims to solve problems, create new ways of thinking, and make puzzles solvable. Let's first look at the term "sciences"—you may have heard sciences broken down into the hard sciences or the soft sciences. Generally speaking the "hard" sciences refer to the natural sciences: Physics, Chemistry, Biology, Astronomy, Geology, etc. The social sciences are considered as the "soft" sciences: Psychology, Sociology, Political Science, etc.

Regardless of where you might see yourself—within the hard sciences, soft sciences, humanities, or creative arts—differences in philosophical perspectives matter. Those philosophical or positional differences in each paradigm combine with the aims of a research study—to generally determine the focus, approach and mode of inquiry which, in turn, determines the structural aspects of a study design.

For instance, the main focus in qualitative research is to understand, explain, explore, discover and clarify situations, feelings, perceptions, attitudes, values, beliefs, and experiences of a group of people. The study designs are therefore often based on deductive rather than inductive logic. The designs are more flexible and emergent in nature, and are often non linear and non sequential in the way that they operate.

On the other hand, quantitative research study designs are more structured, rigid, fixed, and predetermined in their use to insure accuracy in measurement and classification. . . because the measurement and classification requirements of the information that is gathered demand that structure. Again, generally speaking, in qualitative studies the distinction between study designs and methods of data collection is far less clear, while quantitative study designs have more clarity and distinction between designs and methods of data collection.

Remember that when you are looking at a study design, you are seeing the method which the researcher is using to solve the puzzle. Being able to understand the method gives you insight into what the researcher is looking for and hoping to find. So keep learning to ask why! It's all coming together as we move through the disciplines.

Research Methods

Questions and hypotheses also allow us to predict or forecast what will happen in the future, essentially telling us what we can expect to observe when certain conditions are satisfied. In terms of control, once we understand how a process works, to some extent this understanding allows us to control it. Ultimately, the primary function of research questions, hypotheses, and theory is heuristic, allowing us to generate new knowledge, learning, and understanding. Notice that under this paradigm, research questions and hypotheses are built on existing theory—either extending, testing, or explicating a theory. This type of research falls under the positivist paradigm, using deductive reasoning, and researchers who conduct research in this paradigm believe that reality is fixed, measurable, controllable, orderly, and objective.

Also recall that research can be conducted under the inductive model, in which researchers seek to answer more open-ended questions and end up with, perhaps, a theory, or a deeper understanding of an extant phenomenon. This model of research falls under the interpretive paradigm, and researchers who subscribe to this metatheory tend to believe that reality is subjective, constructed, and chaotic. Note that theory—in terms of providing an organization or framework for knowledge, or understanding of reality—has its place in both paradigms and philosophies of research.

fact pattern
A factual relationship occurring repeatedly.

Theories begin with either a **fact pattern** or a question. A fact pattern is a factual relationship occurring repeatedly. A good example of a fact pattern in communication research is what we call *divergence* or *convergence*. Have you ever noticed how when you are in a conversation with someone you like, or perhaps someone you need to impress, you adjust your style of speaking to match hers? This is an example of convergence. What about when you are in a conversation with someone you feel dissimilar to or dislike in some way? Do you tend to match him? Research suggests you will maintain your own style of communicating. This is an example of divergence.

Convergence and divergence provide the basis for Communication Accommodation Theory (CAT). Giles and his colleagues have studied CAT in a variety of contexts; for example, one study examined how we adjust our communication behaviors when interacting with the elderly (McCann & Giles, 2006). A researcher working out of the positivist philosophy might design a study to see if CAT affects the therapeutic value of medical communication. A researcher working with interpretivist assumptions might instead look at medical communication in a more open-ended sense, and might in the end use CAT to help explain what they found in their study.

Theories might also begin with a question—a search for an answer to why something happens. As Miller and Nicholson (1976) suggest, "People incessantly ask questions"(p. 10). This search for answers, via questions posed, is really at the heart of the process of inquiry, the search for understanding.

Quick Reference

Quantitative inquiry or research is characterized by a few key things: measurable, testable data, true and quasi-experimental methodology, objective instruments for measuring relationships between variables, etc. Note that quantitative inquiry can be QUANTIFIED. That means numbered, measured, proven, tested. A good example of a question requiring quantitative inquiry is something that is comparative . . . for instance, comparing anxiety and stress levels in college freshmen and seniors. Within quantitative design, the focus is often structured, defined with rigid parameters, and a more linear process of research, than qualitative design.

—*Kristen Hark*

What Are Research Objectives?

Research objectives represent the reasons you give for undertaking your own research project. They are the step between your research topic, your "I wonder if . . ." musing, and your research questions or hypothesis. When you are given an assignment to conduct a research study, the first thing you will do is determine your general area of inquiry. From your general area of inquiry, you would need to narrow your focus to a slightly more specific topic for your research. We would suggest you start with something that interests you. You should work on narrowing your topic until you have something specific enough to build a research study on it.

Next, narrow it by adding modifying words and phrases to each of your topic ideas. For example, if you are interested in the general field of health communication, you might decide you are very interested in patient-provider communication. That's good, but not specific enough. Let's add some modifiers: What types of patients? How about terminally ill patients? What types of healthcare providers? How about physicians? What types of communication? How about giving the bad news about their terminal diagnosis? Ahh, so *now* we see it . . . you're interested in studying how physicians give terminal diagnoses to people with terminal illness. Now, *that's* a research topic! Always think in terms of narrowing down to very specific questions addressing very specific variables. The need for this specificity will become even more apparent in later chapters when we discuss measurement and research procedures. Beginner social scientists often try to answer questions that are too broad to be definitively addressed in a single study. If you find yourself asking, "is this too specific?" the answer is, "probably not."

Now, let's turn your topic into a research objective. Research objectives are your statements of what you ultimately want to accomplish through this research. For many studies, your research objective can be determined by filling in the blanks of this statement: "I am studying _____, because I want to find out [who/what/when/where/whether/how] _____ is, in order to understand _____" (see Booth, Colomb, & Williams, 1995). For the example above, your research objective may be stated as, "I am studying patient-provider communication, because I want to find out how physicians give terminal diagnoses to patients, in order to understand the different ways to break bad medical news." Notice that we added a new part: "in order to understand the different ways to break bad medical news." This last section answers a significance or "so what" element.

All research studies should connect to a bigger picture in some way. In the example above, you might be developing a theory about terminal diagnosis communication, or you might be testing an existing theory within this specific context. You might be understanding something that's important to society, or you might be describing something that will have public policy implications, or you might be measuring something that will have financial ramifications. There are lots of ways your study should answer the "so what" question, but you should know—up front—the significance of your own research.

Given our arguments above considering specificity, this means that you are likely addressing or informing one small part of a much larger question or phenomenon. That's okay, and it is the nature of scientific inquiry. We take on small questions and problems one at a time, and try to replicate them in different contexts and settings, in an attempt to contribute to the answers to these larger questions. Researchers from the interpretive paradigm might tackle broader questions or issues, but even these must have defined boundaries.

▼ ··

How Do You Ask Research Questions?

research question
Questions scholars ask about the way things work.

What is a **research question**? Research questions are questions scholars ask about the way things work. Just as research can be basic or applied, research questions can be either basic or applied.

While research *objectives* are used by researchers to design open-ended research about a topic, other researchers pose research questions when they want to find out certain information about a topic without making a prediction ahead of time. Research questions are good starting points for new areas of inquiry, as opposed to formal hypotheses (which we will discuss shortly). Remember, research questions are simply questions that scholars are seeking answers to; there is not a statement or assertion of what will happen, just a question the research attempts to answer.

The research question is symbolized as the capital letters RQ, followed with a numeric subscript (RQ_1). The numeric subscript refers to the number of the research question in a particular study. In a complicated study, you may have several research questions and numbering allows us to keep track of what research question is being analyzed and discussed. Here's an example of a research question from a quantitative study conducted by Segrin, Powell, Givertz, and Brackin (2003):

> RQ_1: Do members of dating couples exhibit symptoms of depression that are indicative of emotional contagion?
>
> And, here's an example of research questions from a qualitative study conducted by Davis (2009):
>
> RQ_1: What reality does hospice construct for patients and families through communication?
>
> RQ_2: How does hospice use communication to construct this reality?

Notice that the first stated RQ, for the Segrin et al. 2003 study, reflects positivist tendencies, toward a reality that is observable and measurable, while the RQs for the Davis 2009 research reflect interpretivist tendencies, toward a reality that is constructed and subjective.

Here are two other examples of research questions—these are ones posed in a qualitative study. This research (Kramer, 2004) uses ethnography to look at the dialectical tensions in group communication in a community theater group. Kramer asks:

> RQ_1: What dialectical tensions are experienced by community theater group members as they communicate to produce a group performance?
>
> RQ_2: How do members of a community theater group manage the dialectical tensions through their communication?

Note that both of these questions are questions of fact, even though they are very much open-ended questions based in the interpretivist tradition.

Here is another way to look at research questions. How many observations are necessary to make a valid conclusion about the answer? So, again, you begin to see that the question you ask drives the research design process, including what methodology is an appropriate choice.

What Are Research Hypotheses?

A research hypothesis is used when the researcher knows enough about the topic under study to make a prediction. A **hypothesis** is a statement the researcher makes about the relationship between at least two variables (a dependent and independent variable). It is often predictive, specifying how two concepts are believed to be related. Most of you are already familiar with the common definition of a hypothesis—an educated guess. And that's exactly what a hypothesis is: an educated guess about what will happen in a relationship between variables, based on what is known from existing theory.

The research hypothesis is symbolized by a capital letter H, followed with a numeric subscript (H_1). This numeric subscript refers to the number of the hypothesis in a particular study. In a complicated study, you may have several hypotheses and numbering helps you to keep track of what hypothesis is being analyzed and discussed. Some scholars add letters to denote related hypotheses (H_{1a}, H_{1b}, etc.), though we would discourage you from doing do; simply numbering the hypotheses in order is the easiest approach for most readers to follow. The symbol and numeric subscript is then followed with a statement concerning how you think the two variables will be related.

Here are some examples from Segrin et al. (2003):

H_1: There will be a negative association between depression and relational quality in dating relationships.

H_2: The poor relational quality associated with depression will be associated with increased loneliness.

"*USA Today* has come out with a new survey—apparently, three out of every four people make up 75% of the population" (*The Quotations Page*, n.d.). No doubt about it—survey research is popular in everyday society. Next, we consider one of the most common types of research methodologies: surveys. We will consider why surveys are immensely popular; examine common survey research designs; explore survey measurement techniques, including questionnaire design; and scrutinize the pros and cons of different ways of administering surveys.

Survey Research

For most of us, **survey design** is perhaps the most familiar research method, and may be the first method that comes to mind when we think about social research. When you fill out a teacher's evaluation at the end of the semester,

hypothesis
A statement a researcher makes about the relationship between a dependent and an independent variable.

survey design
A method of asking research participants questions that provides researchers with a method of information gathering from a large number of people over a relatively short period of time.

a comment card at a restaurant, or even a profile on a dating website, you are completing a survey of one type or another. Surveys are popular in both proprietary and scholarly research for a variety of reasons. First, survey design provides researchers with a method of information gathering from a large number of people in a relatively short period of time. This allows you to gather a representative sample from a population of interest to you. Second, surveys are relatively inexpensive to administer. With Web-based applications, such as Survey Monkey (www.surveymonkey.com), Survey Share (www.surveyshare.com), and Qualtrics (www.qualtrics.com), the survey creation process has become even easier and more accessible. Third, this methodology involves a relatively straightforward research strategy. You ask people questions and analyze their answers. Fourth, surveys can include both quantitative questions and qualitative (open-ended) questions. Finally, since you can easily provide and administer identical questions to many participants, a well-written survey questionnaire is a reliable measurement technique.

political polls
One of the most common and readily available uses of surveys. They provide a detailed account of who is leading whom in the run for a particular office during an election.

Political Polls.   One of the most common and readily available uses of surveys in the world today is in the form of **political polls**. It seems that every day leading up to an election, we are bombarded with a detailed account of who is leading whom in the run for a particular office. In fact, we have become so bombarded with polling data that data aggregation sites, such as Nate Silver's 538 (www.fivethirtyeight.com), have become popular resources for summary statements about what we can glean from the polls when taken together.

Oftentimes political poll surveys are conducted over the phone. The key to political polls and the validity of their findings rests upon the basic research method strategies used, the quality of sampling and sample size, the response rate, and as we will see shortly, even the types of questions asked.

evaluation research
Research that is designed to assess the effectiveness of programs or products during development or after their completion.

Evaluation Research.   Another type of survey research that many of you are already familiar with is the use of survey data in **evaluation research**. Evaluation research is designed to assess the effectiveness of campaigns, programs, or products either before (or while) they are being developed, or after their completion. The use of evaluation research for campaigns and programs allows practitioners and managers to develop more effective communication programs. A good example of evaluation research in organizational communication would be research designed to assess a new training program put in place in the organization. If you are a participant in the training, you might be asked to fill out a survey at the conclusion of the program, so the trainer can assess his or her success. In health sciences, you might be interested in evaluating the relative success of a smoking cessation program or a new exercise regimen. You could even evaluate the success of a nutrition campaign such as the "5 a day" campaign that encourages Americans to eat five fruits and vegetables a day. This type of evaluation research is often called *summative research*, as it traditionally takes place after the program has run its course or the campaign is ending (Center & Broom, 1983).

Another type of evaluation research is known as *formative research*; this is simply evaluation research that helps the campaign or program manager develop a campaign or program, or evaluate it while it is ongoing (Atkin & Freimuth, 2000; Center & Broom, 1983).

The benefit of these types of evaluation research is that they allow you to identify ways in which the program or campaign can be refined and improved. The third type of evaluation research, *needs analysis*, is a mechanism for identifying problems experienced by a group of people by comparing what exists with what study participants want. For example, organizational employees might fill out a needs assessment survey to help management develop a new training program by comparing what existing training programs offer versus what employees want or need in a training program.

This data is often used to guide in the development of communication interventions, such as skill training. Finally, the fourth type of evaluation research, *organizational feedback*, also utilizes survey design. Here, organizational members are asked to report on practices within the organization. You might be interested in surveying national insurance companies about the communication practices within their organization. You could use surveys to ask them about the use of different channels of communication, the quality of information provided, and even their preferred method of communication. The results can then be used for organizational improvement.

Market Research.   Another common example of survey design comes in the form of **market research**. This is research designed to study consumer behavior, preferences, and opinions. The idea behind market research is that if you can determine what people consume, how often, and why, then you can predict future consumption (or at least market researchers can). Market research may question consumer reactions to a new product, interest in new products, and preferences for products and services.

market research
Research that is designed to study consumer behavior.

This type of research evaluates how satisfied consumers are with products and services, as well as explores persuasive strategies for advertising, product pricing, and even packaging. The most obvious example of market research in your world is likely to be a discount or frequent shopper card on your key ring, or the survey invitations issued to you on the receipt you receive from a local discount store. It seems marketers have many opportunities to gather data about your consumer behaviors. Did you really think the shopper card is to help you save money? What types of information do companies gather from your frequent shopper card? What marketing decisions could they make with it?

Design Concerns

Sampling. Because of the techniques used in administering surveys, researchers have the ability to conduct a truly random and representative sample if they have the necessary resources. Regardless of the type of survey you are designing, your design concerns are similar. One of your first concerns related to survey research design is selecting survey participants. To do this, you must have a sampling frame. Recall that a sampling frame is ideally a list of all members of a population, or at least it is the list you let stand in for your population. In some instances, an actual list of the population may be impossible to come by.

At one time, telephone directories might have been a good choice; in today's world, this would be an incomplete sampling frame at best, because so many people use telephone numbers—cell phones, for example—that are not listed in directories. In fact, these days, we might argue that using a list of numbers from a telephone directory is only representative of, perhaps, older, less technologically savvy people, and there is evidence that the samples derived from telephone directories tend to skew toward older audiences. This is why many survey researchers are moving to random digit dialing— letting a computer randomly generate telephone numbers within an area code and exchange.

Using random digit dialing, you're not limited to listed or land-line numbers, and, if you're looking for an overall population sample, your sample should be more representative. However you decide to sample, remember that your sample should represent your population as closely as possible. If you were interested in studying dating behaviors of college students at UCONN and UNC–Charlotte, you could likely contact the registrars of each of the schools and obtain a list of potential participants (with Institutional Research Board approval, of course). This list would be your sampling frame. If you're interested in why people voted for a particular candidate in an election, it would not make sense to poll people who didn't vote. Therefore, a sampling frame of all people—regardless of whether they voted—would not be very representative of the population you're interested in studying. You'd be better off using a list of registered voters, at least eliminating those who definitely couldn't have voted.

Many types of sampling can be used with survey design: random sampling, cluster sampling, stratified sampling, purposive samples, and even volunteer samples. What defines the best choice for a particular study? That's right, it's the research question. The question(s) and/or hypothesis(es) determine the technique you choose.

cross-sectional survey
A survey design that describes the characteristics of a sample representing a population at one point in time.

Cross-Sectional Design. Another consideration and decision you must make early in the survey research design process is whether a cross-sectional or longitudinal design is best for your study. A **cross-sectional survey** describes the characteristics of a sample representing a population at one point in time. Think of it as a picture, or a snapshot. Researchers frequently utilize cross-sectional survey research because it's easy to collect data from a large number of people, in a short period of time, at a single time point. One researcher we know has, at times, been able to sample from the local jury pool. In just one afternoon, he collected nearly 500 surveys of a very wide sample of people who were appropriate for his research question. The Salmon et al. (2003) study mentioned earlier is an example of a cross-sectional study.

A cross-sectional design is great for describing the status quo—how things are right at one particular time point. However, there are some cautions to keep in mind. First, it is important to keep in mind the particular point in time when the survey was conducted. A friend of ours went through the Institutional Research Board and was approved to collect data on her project late one September. She was interested in studying different types of messages on brochures regarding breast self-exams. As she began her project, she realized that October, when she collected the majority of her data, happens to be Breast Cancer Awareness Month. Is there any chance that this particular month for data collection affected the outcome of her study? Absolutely. Data can be misleading if the survey is conducted at an unrepresentative time.

Cross-sectional surveys assume the variables and processes being studied have reached stability, but many variables and processes are constantly changing. For example, marital satisfaction, television viewing behavior, and communication apprehension are variables that have the potential to change over time. By the same token, you can't take one measurement at one point in time and assume causality. Consider the hypothesis that video game violence leads to an increase in aggressive behavior. If you measure both of these variables and find a positive correlation between them, can you conclude that video game violence caused aggressive behavior in your sample? No, you cannot. *Causal conclusions can never be drawn from cross-sectional data*. It is a lot like the question of which came first—the chicken or the egg. Do you know whether exposure to video game violence came before or after exhibiting aggressive behavior? Not if you only measure at one point of time. While a reasonable person might likely argue that watching violence causes aggressive behavior, it is possible that individuals with aggressive tendencies could choose to play violent video games. It is also equally likely that some other variable, such as family discipline, affects both video game playing and aggressive behavior.

Longitudinal Design.　　In **longitudinal survey design**, you gather data from respondents at several points in time. This allows you to evaluate the impact of unusual or unique environmental events on a population, and assess whether a population's beliefs, attitudes, and/or behaviors are enduring or stable over time. One of the greatest strengths of longitudinal design is to allow you to examine causal relationships. You add this feature to survey research with a longitudinal design by determining whether A comes before B in time. You can only do this with a minimum of two measurements over some timeframe. There are three types of longitudinal research design: a trend study, a cohort study, and a panel study.

longitudinal survey design
A survey design that gathers data from respondents at several points in time.

trend study
Measurement occurs at two or more points in time, from different samples selected from the same population. This type of study is designed to identify changes or trends in people's beliefs about a variable of interest.

Trend Study.   In a **trend study**, measurement occurs at two or more points in time, from different samples selected from the same population. This type of study is designed to identify changes or trends (thus the name) in people's beliefs about the variable of interest, or in the correlations between variables at different time points. An example of a trend study is the Gallup polls used during a presidential election. The Gallup organization, a premier research firm in the United States, draws a sample from all eligible U.S. voters and asks whom they plan to vote for in the upcoming presidential election. Each week they poll another group of people (sample) from this population (all eligible voters). Remember, the samples Gallup is taking are not the same people; they are merely samples from the same population. Keep in mind, though, that as your goal is comparison over time, you should be sampling from the same general population, at least. What if you sample first from the Socialists of America, second from the Students for Democratic Government, and third from the Young Republicans? Clearly, you cannot compare how people's attitudes changed over time because your sample would be very different each time. To compare trends, you must have comparable representative samples.

interview
A research practice with individual participants, or groups of participants, to obtain responses to survey questions by direct questioning.

Interviews.   When the researcher asks the study participant the survey questions and records the responses, this is called an **interview**, and the researcher is called an *interviewer*. Interviewing can take place in person or over the phone. The survey instrument used in an interview is often called an *interview guide*, *interview protocol*, or *survey*. Essentially, what we are talking about here is a *quantitative* survey methodology, which differs from qualitative interviewing, and as such, utilizes a different set of rules. Macias and colleagues (2008) found that interviews conducted in person yielded on average a 79 percent response rate, the highest of all the methods they studied, and telephone interviews yielded a 61 percent response rate on average.

The first concern in this type of survey is the validity of interview data. Here, the validity of the data depends highly on how participants view the interviewer, as well as how effectively the interviewer manages the interaction. It is important to be capable of recording participants' answers unobtrusively, as well as knowing how to expand a person's answer with additional questions—also known as probing and clarifying.

The key to good quality interviews is the skill and training of the interviewers. There are, in fact, several validity threats related to interviewer issues. Interviewers can inadvertently create a personal attribute effect (when characteristics of the researcher—gender, for example—influences people's behavior) or unintentional expectancy effect (by influencing participants by letting them know the behaviors the interviewer desires, such as by smiling or frowning). When conducting an interview, it's important that you don't predispose a participant to answer in some set manner. When you write your questionnaire or survey protocol, disguise your questions so the respondent does not continually try to outguess you or anticipate the answer you want.

Unskilled interviewers can damage the validity of a well-designed survey. They can bias participants' responses, they may record responses incorrectly, and they can misrepresent the goals and questions of the survey. All of these create problems with the validity of the research at hand. Often, these types of interviews are conducted by multiple interviewers; therefore, it is necessary that all interviewers are carefully trained to follow a written protocol, which details what questions will be asked in what order and how the entire interview will be conducted. Interviewers should be knowledgeable about the research, familiar with the interview questions, practice interviewing, and be skilled at building rapport with participants.

It is important that an interview gets off to the right start. Most people decide within the first few seconds whether they are willing to participate; therefore, the tone of the initial meeting and greeting with the researcher sets the tone for the rest of the interview process. A good interview should begin when the researchers introduce themselves to potential participants and identify the research entity they represent. They should identify the general research topic, explain any selection criteria for the study, and explain the time commitment participants must make. Finally, their role in the introduction of the interview is to convince the participant that his or her contribution is important to the research.

There are both advantages and disadvantages to using interviews (researcher asking the questions and recording the answers) in place of questionnaires (in which participants fill out the instrument themselves). Interviews usually have a higher response rate than questionnaires. This is particularly true of self-administered questionnaires when the researcher is not present while the questionnaire is being completed. Another benefit of interviews, when compared to traditional survey design, is that you can minimize the number of "don't know" responses. The facilitator or interviewer can use a probe, asking the question in a different way or allowing the respondent to provide additional detail concerning their answer. Interviews also allow us to guard against misunderstandings. The interviewer or facilitator can clarify what she is asking. This provides more flexibility to your design, allowing for a deeper understanding.

What Is an Experiment?

When thinking about experiments, most people think about the hard sciences. But experiments are vital in the social sciences as well. Experimental designs have been used for decades to address how people respond to interpersonal interactions, mediated information, workplace dynamics, and interactions with computers. Of course, this raises the question of exactly what an experiment is, by definition.

social experiment
A procedure in which researchers take human subjects, do something to them, and observe the effects of what they did to them.

By definition, a **social experiment** is a procedure in which researchers take human subjects, do something to them, and observe the effects of what they did to them (Baxter & Babbie, 2004). Next, we will discuss some of the nuances associated with this seemingly simple procedure, including the use of subjects, random assignment, inductions, control groups, and multiple measures. More importantly, we will discuss how you can use these design elements to build confidence in your findings by ruling out particular validity threats.

Independent and Dependent Variables

Experimental researchers deal with independent and dependent variables. We use these terms to describe causes and effects. A variable is anything that can be measured or observed by the researcher. The independent versus dependent distinction is related to the researcher's involvement in the observation.

First, let's explain some concepts about variables in experiments. Remember that—for all research—variables can be measured through self-report, measured through other-report, or measured through observation. In an experiment, the independent variable can also be "manipulated".

So, if—in your experiment—you are measuring a variable to determine beliefs, attitudes, or opinions, or to collect retrospective information about behavior or meaning, you would measure that variable using a *survey*. If, in your experiment, you are measuring a variable to analyze the content of media messages, you would measure that variable using a *content analysis*. Finally, if you are measuring a variable to analyze the content of an interpersonal message, you would measure that variable using an *interaction analysis*. So, to recap, surveys can be used as a stand-alone method, or as a way to measure a variable during an experiment. The same is true for interaction analysis.

What Are Independent Variables?
By definition, an independent variable is any observation that is controlled by the researcher. So, for example, you may want to test the effectiveness of an antismoking public service announcement (PSA). You develop two types of PSAs, one that uses a fear appeal to attempt to scare people into compliance and one that does not. You then show the fear ad to one group of people and the non-fear ad to another group.

In this instance, the independent variable is the type of ad that is being shown. While the researcher will make the observation that a particular group saw one ad or the other, it was the researcher who decided which group would see which and what those messages would look like. Any differences in the responses of the participants might be attributable to this decision. This leads us to our next way of thinking about independent variables: they are causes. Independent variables are the things that are manipulated by the researcher in order to produce a particular outcome.

What Are Dependent Variables?   Dependent variables, on the other hand, are effects. They are observations made by the researcher that are not directly controlled by the researcher, but may be attributable to decisions surrounding the independent variable. In our example above, let's say the people who saw the fear appeal ad report that they are less willing to take up smoking. In this case, the dependent variable is willingness to take up smoking. It is the assumed result of a change in the independent variable.

Why do we call it a dependent variable? Because it is dependent on the independent variable. In short, independent variables are causes, while dependent variables are effects, or consequences.

Understanding Experimental Notation and Language

Before discussing different types of designs, it is essential that we discuss the notation that is used when describing experimental procedures. We can identify three basic elements in an experimental design: observation, induction (or manipulation), and random assignment.

Observation

If you are reading the shorthand that scientists use to describe experimental designs, you will, at the very least, see a capital "O." This symbol is used to represent an *observation*. It is the basic building block of experimental design, which is after all a series of observations.

Induction

You may also see a capital "X." This symbol is used to convey some kind of **induction**—an induction is what you *do* to the participant. In a persuasion experiment, it may be a certain kind of argument that is delivered to the participant. In a television violence study, it may be a short film clip that you show. In any case, this is what you do to the participant, the independent variable, the effect of which you are examining.

Inductions are often incorrectly labeled as *manipulations*. Technically, an induction is only a manipulation if it actually works. The act of doing something to a participant, regardless of whether it affects them in any way, is more accurately referred to as an induction. In some fields, especially health sciences, this is sometimes called an *intervention* or *treatment*.

induction
What is done to a participant in an experiment.

Random Assignment

You may also encounter a capital "R" in experimental notation. This refers to the **random assignment** of participants to different groups within your design. In a true experimental design, you would want to assign people at random to different groups. Why? Well, if we were concerned about ruling out spuriousness, you would want all the groups in your study to be as similar or comparable as possible. Similar how? It depends on your study, but

random assignment
The assignment of people at random to different groups in an experimental design.

certainly if you're studying health literacy you might want the two groups to have an equivalent distribution of education, and perhaps health status and/or experience with health-care providers.

If you're studying employee productivity, you might want to make sure both groups are equivalent in terms of work experience and training. If you're studying the politeness level of communication on e-mail versus voice mail (see Duthler, 2006), you might want to make sure participants in both groups have equivalent distributions in terms of their relationships with the communication recipients. If you randomly assign people to groups—if everyone has an equal chance of being in a particular group, then (theoretically) they should be roughly the same. Of course, sometimes it is not logistically possible to have true random assignment. In these cases, you will sometimes see lines between conditions indicating that participants were not randomly assigned.

Terminology

There are also some key terms you should know in reading and understanding experiments. One of the groups is the group to whom you give the induction—this is called the **experimental group**. If you have more than one type of induction, you might have more than one experimental group. Ideally, you also have another group to whom you give no induction—this is called the **control group**. It's a group against which you can compare the experimental group. When you compare multiple experimental groups, this is known as a **between-subjects design**. When you only look at an experimental group, you call this a **within-subjects design**.

In many experiments, we measure the dependent variable both before and after exposure to the induction. The measurement before the induction is called a **pretest**, or **baseline** measurement. The measurement after the induction is called a **posttest**.

Designs and Validity

There are a number of *internal validity* concerns that are relevant to the research process. These include history, or when something outside of the procedure takes place that skews your observations. Subjects may change over time, a process known as maturation. Testing describes the phenomenon in which participants respond differently as they become accustomed to your measures. Instrumentation refers to problems associated with using different measures to get at the same idea, and how well they measure the same things.

Fortunately, one of the advantages of the experiment is that in addition to allowing for causal statements, you can design studies in different ways to address each of these concerns. As we will see in the following

---

experimental group
The group of participants to whom you give the induction.

control group
A group that does not receive induction in an experiment.

between-subjects design
Designs comparing multiple groups.

within-subjects design
Designs looking at the same group multiple times.

pretest
An examination of someone before you expose him or her to a stimulus in order to argue, to a certain extent, that what was done to the subject may have caused any changes that are observed. Also called baseline measurement.

baseline
An examination of someone before you expose him or her to a stimulus in order to argue, to a certain extent, that what was done to the subject may have caused any changes that are observed. Also called pretest.

posttest
An examination or measurement conducted after administration of the induction.

descriptions, you can determine which of these issues concerns you the most, and design your study accordingly to rule it out as an internal validity threat. There is even one seldom-used design that rules out all of them. While no experimental design can ever rule out all plausible alternative explanations, thinking about internal validity concerns and designing a study appropriately can at least help you have more confidence in your findings.

▼

Quasi-Experimental Designs

Quasi-experimental designs is a term used by Campbell and Stanley (1963) to describe designs that use pretests and posttests in more complicated ways, but that still lack random assignment.

quasi-experimental designs
Experimental designs that use pretests and posttests in more complicated ways, but still lack random assignment.

Time-Series Design

The first of these is the Time-Series Design:

$$O_1 \, O_2 \, O_3 \qquad X \qquad O_4 \, O_5 \, O_6$$

This design is geared primarily to rule out history and maturation as validity threats. As you can see, you have several pretests, an induction, and several posttests. In our example, we could ask a group of people how they feel about the jeans several times over the course of a few weeks. We could show them the ad, then measure their attitude several more times over the course of a few weeks. Looking at the results, we could tell if the participants' attitudes were already shifting before seeing the ad, or per-haps find evidence that something happened outside the lab that would influence the results. There isn't really a control group, but we can at least detect other threats.

Nonequivalent Control Group Design

Here is another quasi-experimental design, and one that is actually used quite commonly—the Nonequivalent Control Group Design:

$$O_1 \qquad X \qquad O_2$$
$$O_3 \qquad \qquad O_4$$

As you can see, we now have a true control group; these are people who get both the pretest and posttest, but not the induction. If we are to rule out a number of validity threats, it should be the case that people in the test group change from pretest to posttest, but those in the control group should remain exactly the same. This helps control against instrumentation, testing, and maturation as design threats. It does not do too much to address history, and there may be selection problems since there is no random assignment, but at least three major threats are controlled.

Multiple Time-Series Design

In order to improve this design to account for history, we can add multiple measures and produce the following, the Multiple Time-Series Design:

$$O_1 \; O_2 \; O_3 \qquad X \qquad O_4 \; O_5 \; O_6$$

$$O_7 \; O_8 \; O_9 \qquad\qquad O_{10} \; O_{11} \; O_{12}$$

As you can see, this design combines the advantages of the last two. We now have controls in place for testing, instrumentation, and maturation, and we have added a history safeguard by collecting pretest and posttest measures at different times. It is still not a perfect design, though. The lack of random assignment is still a concern.

True Experimental Designs

true experimental designs
Experimental designs that randomly assign participants to both experimental and control groups.

Fortunately, there is another class of design that, by definition, introduces random assignment: true experimental designs. Campbell and Stanley (1963) define **true experimental designs** as those that randomly assign participants to both experimental and control groups. Through random assignment, subject-related concerns should be pretty much avoided. If everyone in your population has an equal chance of being in any group, then problems like evaluator apprehension, Hawthorne effect, and selection problems should not be a concern. Over a large enough group, if these problems are present then they are at least equally distributed.

Causal Comparative Design

Another design that focuses on relationship between variables is causal-comparative design, also known as *ex post facto research*—because it looks for relationship between independent and dependent variables after the action or event has already occurred. The researcher's goal is to determine whether the independent variable affected the outcome, or dependent variable, by comparing two or more groups of individuals. There are similarities and differences between causal-comparative research and both correlational and experimental research. Causal comparative research is used to identify cause-effect relationships or examine the differences that already exist between two groups.

Field and Natural Experiments

As we've explained, when we talk about experimental designs, we almost immediately think of laboratory experiments. There are other kinds of experiments that can take place outside of the laboratory. A *field experiment* takes place in a naturalistic environment, but nonetheless involves the manipulation of independent variables and some of the design concerns we have already voiced. *Natural experiments* also generally take place in naturalistic environments, but they do not involve variable manipulation—they simply involve analysis of naturally occurring variables. While field and natural experiments may not be as precise as laboratory experiments in terms of control, they are nonetheless valuable in evaluating causal relationships. In fact, they both have one major advantage over laboratory experiments—they have much higher ecological validity. Thus, external validity versus control is a major consideration when deciding whether to do your experiment in the field or in a laboratory.

Here's an interesting example of a field experiment. Argo, Dahl, and Morales (2008) used a field experiment to see how attractiveness affects consumer consumption. Rather than set up a laboratory experiment (can you think of how they might have designed that?), they conducted an experiment in an actual retail shopping environment. They hypothesized that the attractiveness of a person touching a product affects the level of interest another consumer has in purchasing that product. Simply stated, the research was conducted in a university bookstore, and the researchers set up a *confederate* sales clerk (an actor who was in on the experiment) and a *confederate* shopper and had the shopper confederate only handle a T-shirt. They compared shopper attractiveness to interest in purchasing the T-shirt. Note the independent variable (shopper attractiveness) and dependent variable (purchase intent).

So What?

So what have we uncovered? We have discussed how researchers use experimental designs to answer research questions, and in particular we have discussed how micro-level, causal research problems lend themselves well to these types of designs. We then went on to discuss different types of research designs, and how you can build confidence in your findings by strategically using design to address particular internal validity threats. We have discussed the differences between laboratory and field experiments. And finally, we have discussed the ways in which the data derived from an experimental design can be analyzed and interpreted.

Of course, there is a major validity concern related to experimental designs that cannot be overlooked: the problem of external validity. While experimental designs are very useful for demonstrating causal relationships between independent and dependent variables, the extent to which these procedures mirror real-life behaviors may be problematic. This is especially the case with laboratory research. When you go home after class today, you may turn on the television. It is highly unlikely that a stranger will ask you to fill out a survey first, then ask you to fill one out again when you are done. When you talk to a friend, no one subsequently asks you to report how disclosive you found him or her to be. While experiments are very effective at establishing relationships between independent and dependent variables, the extent to which these findings generalize into real-life situations is questionable.

Introduction to Qualitative Research

interpretive
A research perspective in which understanding and interpretation of the social world is derived from one's personal intuition and perspective.

inductive reasoning
Reasoning that discovers patterns, inferences, and conclusions from studying and observing certain phenomena.

reflexivity
Acknowledgement of a researcher's positionality in relation to the study, study topic, and the study participants; addressing how one's own thoughts, feelings, and behaviors interact with his or her research site and his or her research itself.

naturalistic
Research that is conducted in the field or where participants live, work, and play.

fieldwork
Conducting observations in natural settings.

field sites
Groups, organizations, or cultures in which research is conducted.

in vivo
Research that takes place in a natural setting.

emergent design
A study design in which methods (including sampling,

Qualitative Approaches to Research

Qualitative research is **interpretive**, as opposed to the more objective approach of quantitative research (Creswell, 2007). Recall that in quantitative research, something is either statistically significant or it's not, or the null hypothesis is either accepted or rejected. Qualitative research is—by design—much more attuned to inference, impressions, and a more inductive form of reasoning. Scholars using **inductive reasoning** discover patterns, make inferences, and draw conclusions from studying and observing certain phenomena in depth.

Qualitative research is appropriate to use when something needs to be explored (when not much is known about a topic) or when we need a complex, in-depth, detailed understanding about something, especially within its environment or context. We also use qualitative research to investigate a complex or sensitive issue that cannot be reduced to a simple, objective, quantitative study (Creswell, 2007). Many qualitative researchers study patterns, symbols, norms, rules, and assumptions in a culture to understand how people create meaning and how these meanings influence what people do and why they do it.

Qualitative research methods are appropriate for researchers to use to describe or understand interaction patterns, possibly within and between texts, dyads, groups, cultures, and contexts; to understand the influence of society, relationships, environment, or interactions on behavior; to closely examine interactive events in their natural settings; and to examine **reflexivity**—how your own thoughts, feelings, and behaviors interact with your research site and your research itself (Bochner & Ellis, 1992; Gill & Maynard, 1995).

In what ways do qualitative researchers study the things they study? They ask people, watch people, observe, participate, interview, review documents, and gather life histories, among other things. Qualitative research is **naturalistic**—it's often conducted *in the field* (qualitative researchers conduct **fieldwork** *in places called* **field sites**)—where participants live, work, and play. Qualitative research is often conducted **in vivo**—in a natural setting; qualitative researchers observe interactions, talk to people, or participate in events as they are happening. The *data* for qualitative research can be word-based (transcripts, quotes, field notes, and texts), behaviorally based (observations, interactions, and actions), and emotion based (feelings, emotions, and thoughts). Qualitative researchers typically use an **emergent design**, revising the study (including sampling, data collection, data protocols, coding, and analysis) as the study emerges and progresses (Creswell, 2007).

Qualitative Research Paradigms

Previously, we discussed the basic research paradigms that represent the different metatheoretical considerations: positivitism, interpretivism, and the critical perspective. Remember that people who follow the positivist paradigm tend toward the realist end of the metatheoretical spectrum. Positivists believe that reality is orderly, fixed, measureable, and objective. Positivists typically use quantitative methods because those are the methods that allow them to measure variables objectively. Qualitative researchers tend to follow more critical and/or interpretive paradigms. The interpretive paradigm values **representation** and **multivocality**, and believes that reality is subjective and interpreted. The critical perspective—which critiques power and values social change that alleviates power imbalances—can lean toward an objective or an interpretive stance, but critical scholars most frequently follow an interpretive worldview because this allows them to share and critique power and voice in their research.

Some qualitative research takes what's called an **etic approach**; in that researchers base their research on a pre-existing concept or theory. This approach is more **deductive** and is said to move from the theory to the application, as research from an etic approach might seek to show the application of a specific theory (Montegut, 2017). Other qualitative research takes an **emic** approach. Research from this perspective is more **inductive** and the researcher bases his/her research on the participant's point of view and on the findings resulting from the study itself. This research is said to move from application to theory, because—as in grounded theory—a theory (or understanding) is grounded in the data itself (Scarduzio, 2017).

Qualitative research, *in many different areas of study*, can be further broken down into four main perspectives: the **rhetorical paradigm**, the **social science paradigm**, the **social constructionist paradigm**, and the **arts and humanities paradigm**. These approaches overlap, and many qualitative scholars follow more than one approach, sometimes in the same study. Regardless of what paradigm is being used, the method used must be the right one for the issue being studied. If there is a specific research question based on a theoretical concept, then it might be more appropriate to use a more social science or social constructionist approach. If the study is attempting to let the reader vicariously experience a phenomenon through multiple senses, then it might be most appropriate to use a more arts-based method, like poetry or performance (Davis, 2014).

Social Science Paradigm

You can see in Figure 5.1 that scholars who do focus groups, grounded theory, thematic analysis, or discourse analysis tend to follow more of a social science paradigm. Qualitative researchers in this paradigm see research as a systematic investigation. Qualitative researchers following a more social science stance, even though they fall on the interpretivist end of the metatheoretical

---

data collection, data protocols, coding, and analysis) are revised as the study emerges and progresses.

representation
In qualitative research, the concept that the qualitative sample should adequately represent the population under study to provide in-depth understanding of the experience.

multivocality
A form of writing that frequently includes multiple voices; it might be written from different points of view (including researchers and multiple stakeholders or participants).

etic
An approach to research that is more deductive and is based on a pre-existing concept or theory.

emic
An approach to research that is more inductive and based on the participants' point of view and on the findings resulting from the study itself.

inductive reasoning
Reasoning that discovers patterns, inferences, and conclusions from studying and observing certain phenomena.

rhetorical paradigm
A research paradigm that focuses upon a wide variety of texts in order

to gain a deep understanding of the message within the communication process, to connect that understanding to broader practical and theoretical concerns related to human communication and the human condition in general.

social science paradigm
A research paradigm in which researchers see research as a systematic investigation and tend to believe in a reality that is more observable and better understood objectively.

social constructionist paradigm
A research paradigm that believes that shared meaning is constructed through our cultural systems and focuses on culturally situated action and interaction through which meanings and interpretations are socially, historically, temporally, and culturally constructed. Qualitative researchers in this paradigm tend to see research as a social construction of meaning.

arts and humanities paradigm
A research paradigm in which researchers tend to see research as a performance and tend to use art or performance to understand the world in an embodied and holistic manner.

paradigms, tend to believe in a reality that is more observable and better understood objectively. People who do grounded theory or some kinds of discourse analysis are looking to identify meaning, although they realize the meaning they identify is subject to interpretation.

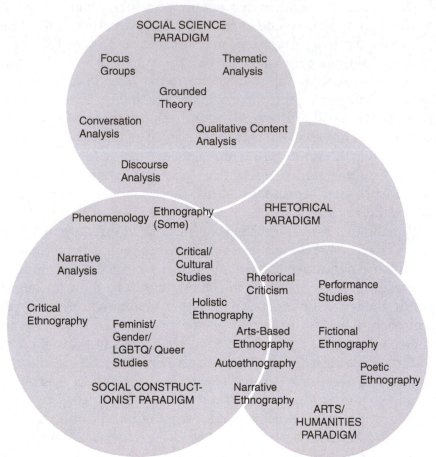

Courtesy of Christine Davis and Kenneth Lachlan. Copyright © Kendall Hunt Publishing Co.

Figure 5.1. Four Main Perspectives for Conducting Qualitative Research.

Social Constructionist Paradigm

Narrative scholars, narrative ethnographers, narrative auto-ethnographers, gender scholars, and people who do critical or cultural analysis, on the other hand, tend to follow a social constructionist paradigm, believing that shared meaning is constructed through our cultural systems and focusing on culturally situated action and interaction through which meanings and interpretations are socially, historically, temporally, and culturally constructed (Gergen, 1991). Qualitative researchers in this paradigm tend to see research as a social construction of meaning. Scholars under this perspective tend to conduct research that addresses questions about what ideas are being socially constructed; how they are being socially constructed; and what the cultural systems are that construct meaning.

Arts and Humanities Paradigm

Qualitative researchers in the Creative Arts paradigm tend to see research as a performance. Performance studies scholars or arts-based ethnographers often favor an arts-based or humanities outlook, although they might also lean toward a social constructionist mental schema. Both social constructionist and arts-based scholars end to be more upfront about actually constructing meaning within their work. They tend to be subjectivists, to believe knowledge is relative and interpretive. Social constructionist and arts-based scholars value representing multiple perspectives and sharing authority. Scholars following an arts-based model present their findings in artistic ways—dramatic compositions or poetic or creative writing, for example.

Rhetorical Paradigm

The rhetorical paradigm is used most often in the Humanities, but undergirds and interacts and overlaps in some ways with all the other qualitative epistemologies, so in this model, the rhetorical paradigm is depicted in the diagram behind and overlapping the other paradigms. Rhetorical criticism focuses upon a wide variety of texts in order to gain a deep understanding of the message, to tie that understanding to broader practical and theoretical concerns. Scholars of rhetoric take a social constructionist ontology and epistemology, and tend to have both an interpretivist and critical axiology at the heart of their work.

Of course, it is very common for scholars to overlap these paradigms in a single study—to conduct focus groups and analyze them using a feminist standpoint, for example, or to use grounded theory as a method but also employ a rhetorical concept for the analysis. Humanities scholarship typically takes a critical/cultural analytical stance.

Interpretive Research

Many qualitative researchers at least tend toward an interpretive stance. Even qualitative researchers with a more social science orientation lean toward a social constructionist bent in their ontology. Most qualitative scholars are likely to believe reality is constructed through interpersonal and cultural communication, and, as we study things, we influence those things by the act of studying them. Qualitative researchers perceive reality as not being completely objective and as being subject to interpretation. Now, how strongly a scholar believes and utilizes this determines where s/he falls on the social science-social constructionist-arts/humanities diagram. Qualitative scholars with different metatheoretical perspectives have different emphases on reflexivity, on the importance and style of writing, on being systematic, and so on.

Quick Reference

Qualitative inquiry can mean many things, but one thing you can rely on is the focus on people and their experience. That means ethnography, phenomenology (a great word that you should try to use at least one a week. Means "lived experience."), case studies, etc. The researcher's focus on a certain people group and their experiences means they are asking extremely BROAD questions. Think about it—if I want to hear a good story about your experiences in junior high, I don't ask specific questions, anything narrow, or a measurable, testable question. I ask something like, "What were the junior high years like for you?" This provides a central, broad question that invites you to tell me of your experiences.

—Kristen Hark

General Characteristics of Qualitative Research

naturalistic
Research that is conducted in the field or where participants live, work, and play.

Despite these differences, qualitative scholars have more in common than differences. Qualitative researchers conduct research that is **naturalistic**—they research in at least a somewhat natural setting. They are interested in understanding how people see, experience, and behave in the world, and they are interested in representing that understanding. And qualitative scholars use similar tools to collect data—observation, participation, interviews, focus groups, document reviews, and so on. Like all scholars, qualitative scholars conduct research to answer specific questions and solve specific problems.

Research Questions or Study Objectives in Qualitative Research

Qualitative research is goal-directed in that all scholars begin their study with at least a general sense of where they are headed with their research and—at least generally—what they want to find out. All qualitative researchers start with a specific problem or question, although sometimes it is simply to "understand x." The study objective or research question might be explicit or implicit, it might be stated or unstated, it might be broad or narrow, clear or vague, and it might change throughout the course of the research or it might stay the same.

However, all qualitative researchers start with a question or problem in mind. Qualitative research lets us understand, describe, and get close to the people or contexts we're studying. It lets us understand how people see the world. Qualitative research answers questions such as: What is going on here? How do *they* do it? What does it mean to them? How do they interpret what it means to others? How can we describe and interpret how they act, what they tell us they know, and how they justify their actions?

purposive sampling
A method of sampling in which the researcher selects participants based on their having experienced the phenomenon or issue under study.

The Role of Theory in Qualitative Research

Like scholars from all social science disciplines, qualitative scholars use theory in some way in their research. Scholars from more social science orientations reflect a specific theoretical base in their research question and study design. They use theory as a foundation for their research, and their research question, sampling, data collection, and analytical decisions all stem from that theoretical base. In contrast, a scholar from a more social constructionist or arts-based focus might take a very different view of theory.

Here is a quote from Ron Pelias, an arts-based performance studies scholar: "I don't really think about theory in the beginning. I launch into whatever interests me, which might be a detail of my life or somebody else's life or some interaction. Then once I'm in the details of the project and reading and thinking conceptually and theoretically, that's when for me the theory comes in" (Pelias, qtd. in Davis, 2014, p. 32). Like Pelias, many interpretive scholars from more social constructionistor arts-based paradigms tend to use theory as an explanation—in order to understand what they have observed in their data or in order to explain their findings at the writing stage. Other scholars might start with a foundational theory and use or develop the same or another theory as explanation. For all, theory provides a way of thinking about, seeing, and understanding the phenomena being studied.

Sampling in Qualitative Research

In qualitative research, a sample size depends on the scope and objectives of the study (Starks & Trinidad, 2007). Most qualitative methods rely on **purposive sampling** methods, looking for participants who have experienced the phenomenon or issue under study (Starks & Trinidad, 2007). Depending on the study objectives, qualitative research projects might also use other sampling methods, such as **theoretical construct sampling, maximum variation sampling, typical instance sampling,** or **extreme instance sampling**. Potential participants may be identified through **snowball** or **network sampling**.

Sampling is one area in which qualitative scholars of different meta-theoretical paradigms differ from each other. Davis (2014) describes this difference in terms of the "closeness of the relationship between the scholar and his/her research participants." Some scholars use themselves as their sample. These scholars collect data through observation, and capture it in field notes. Other scholars choose people with whom they are in a relationship as their sample, and their data consists of observation and/or informal conversations. They capture their data in field notes, and possibly via tape recording.

Other scholars choose people they don't know as their sample, and use more formal methods such as interviews or focus groups for their data collection. Their data capture consists of audio and/or videotaping" (Davis, 2014, p. 134). Sample size in qualitative research depends on a process called **data saturation**. Data saturation refers to the point in data collection at which no new information is emerging. When you have reached data saturation, you typically collect a small amount of additional data to be sure nothing new is discovered, then you can conclude it is time to complete your fieldwork.

theoretical sampling
Choosing a sample based on the people, events, groups, and so on who can shed light on a theory being investigated.

maximum variation sampling
A sampling method that selects study participants that represent a wide range of characteristics that are present in the population and are of interest to the research.

typical instance sampling
Consists of sampling units who have characteristics typical of a population.

extreme instance sampling
Consists of sampling units that have characteristics quite different from the rest of a population.

snowball or network sampling
This sampling method asks study participants to make referrals to other potential participants, who in turn make referrals to other participants, and so on.

data saturation
The collection and analysis of data until no new categories of theories are identified.

Data Collection in Qualitative Research

Data collection for qualitative researchers can be a thoroughly planned, well-thought-out endeavor for scholars on the social science end of the field, and can be more of a serendipitous emergent process for scholars taking a social constructionist or arts-based direction. Social sciences scholar Sarah Tracy takes a social scientific approach to her qualitative research and, as she says, "you have to make some decisions upfront about data collection. Am I going to work with diaries? Am I going to bring people together in focus groups? Am I going to do one-on-one interviews? . . . Doing the kind of qualitative research I do, that planning process has to be done upfront more than I might do if left to my own devices."(Tracy, qtd. in Davis, 2014, p. 35).

Carolyn Ellis and Buddy Goodall, both of whom take a more social constructionist approach to research, describe a study design that emerges as it evolves: "For me, it's a constant process of decision making. . . . I have to see what works and then I get involved in ethical considerations and what's working for the people who are my participants. Ideas keep coming to me along the way about . . . what data to collect, what's important, what isn't. I don't have a plan usually in the beginning, I kind of go in and get messy and try to figure out, . . . first, what am I looking for, next, what can we create together, then what's the best way to do it. Also taking into account I always hope my research will somehow be positive for the people I'm working with. So it has to be done in interaction with them" (Ellis, qtd in Davis, 2014, p. 34). Buddy Goodall suggests you can "write the best plan you can but you realize as soon as you're in the field it'll probably change. . . . You can't really anticipate all of the situations or questions that may come up but you can guess. You can do the best guess work you can . . . but there will be other things and probably even more interesting things that emerge in the field you probably didn't anticipate and I think that's part of it" (Goodall, qtd. in Davis, 2014, p. 35).

Chris Poulos, whose research flows between a social constructionist and an arts-based paradigm, describes his approach to data collection as "intuitive, following my instincts. Sort of decision on the spot rather than pre-planned decisions of any kind. . . . I call it a much more accidental approach; life presenting itself to me and then turning itself into a text. Sometimes I feel like I'm the channel for that" (Poulos, qtd. in Davis, 2014, p. 35). Finally, Ron Pelias who conducts creative arts-based research using an ethnodrama approach, says, "I start my initial writing process with a blank sheet of paper in front of me. I start scribbling, trying to find some kind of organizational scheme, some kind of scaffolding that might hold the subject together. The data collection for me is a way of going about the business of completing that scaffolding. So, once I have the scheme then I know what I need to go gather, whether that's interviewing or digging into my own experiences or doing additional research or whatever. I really can't proceed until I have that scaffolding in place" (Pelias, qtd. in Davis, 2014, p. 36).

Regardless of their orientation to planning ahead, qualitative scholars typically collect data through observation, interviewing (group or individual), document analysis, and/or archival or artifact analysis. Scholars frequently use multiple methods of data collection in order to achieve **crystallization**—the process of reviewing multiple sources of data to capture a full, rich, multivocal, and nuanced view of the phenomenon under study (Ellingson, 2009; Richardson, 2003).

Observations. Qualitative researchers use **observations** to gain insight into the obligations, constraints, motivations, and emotions that participants experience as they complete everyday actions. You can observe events, interactions, or phenomena. You can observe normal everyday happenings, or special, unusual, or one-time events. You might observe people shopping, or eating, or working.

Types of Observers. Observation can be formal or informal. You can, for example, simply hang out. Or you can become more involved—become a volunteer, join a group, move in. Some ethnographers take on the role of **complete observer**, in which they have little to no interaction with the people being observed. This is done rarely, however, partly due to the incompatibility of informed consent procedures with lack of interaction with participants, and partly because researchers recognize that there really is no such thing as no-interaction or true objectivity. Researchers need to be aware that the very act of observing a setting will in fact influence and change behaviors of the people being observed. Many researchers instead do **observer-as-participant**, in which the researcher interacts casually with participants, but still remains primarily an observer and does not become a member of the group being studied.

Other researchers take on the role of **peripheral-member researchers**, researchers who have some level of involvement with a group without core group involvement. **Active-member researchers** become involved with central activities of the group but do not fully commit themselves to the group. **Complete-member researchers** study settings in which they are already members or with which they are already affiliated (Angrosino & de Pérez, 2003).

Types of Observations. There are several ways to observe. In **descriptive observation**, usually done when you are first in the field, you observe everything, no matter how small. You take notes on all details and observations. In **focused observation**, conducted after you've been in the field for a while, and after you've had a chance to start ruminating on what you are finding out and thinking about the data you've been collecting, you start to narrow your focus somewhat. You still take field notes on most things you are observing, but you can ignore some phenomena you have decided (based on your emerging analysis) are irrelevant to your study. In **selective observation**, as your time in the field is winding down, you concentrate on

crystallization
The process of reviewing multiple sources of data to capture a full, rich, multivocal, and nuanced view of the phenomenon under study.

observations
A way to gain insight into the obligations, constraints, motivations, and emotions that participants experience as they complete everyday actions.

complete observer
Researchers who have little to no interaction with the people being observed.

peripheral-member researchers
Researchers who have some level of involvement with a group without core group involvement.

active-member researchers
Researchers who become involved with central activities of the group but do not fully commit themselves to the group.

complete-member researchers
Researchers who study settings in which they are already members or with which they are already affiliated.

descriptive observation
A type of observation that is usually done when the researcher is first in the field, in which the researcher observes everything, no matter how small, and takes notes on all details and observations.

focused observation
A stage in qualitative observation which occurs after the researcher has been in the field for a while and begun preliminary analysis, in which the researcher begins to narrow his/her focus and ignores some phenomena that are irrelevant to his/her study.

selective observation
A stage of observation which occurs as the researcher's time in the field is winding down, in which the researcher concentrates on certain activities and on additional analyses, interviews, coding, and so forth that correspond to the meanings emerging from the data already collected.

certain activities, again based on additional analyses, interviews, coding, and so forth (Angrosino & de Pérez, 2003).

Alternatively, in methods such as conversation analysis and discourse analysis, rather than taking field notes during the observation, researchers videotape and/or audiotape the event or interaction and then transcribe it word for word, adding information on nonverbal behavior and paralanguage.

What Observers Observe.   What specifically do you observe? People—who is involved and who is not involved; the setting, the context, or the scene; and your impressions. Some qualitative scholars focus their observations on the 5 Ws and 1 H: who, what, when, where, why, and how. In terms of what to write down, you could respond to these questions:

WHO: Who is there (and not there)?

WHAT: What are they doing? What else is going on?

WHEN: When are you there? When are things happening? How long are things taking to happen? Is there is temporal difference in when things happen and don't happen?

WHERE: Where are you? What does it look like?

WHY: What motivations are you perceiving in the people you are observing?

HOW: How are people doing what they are doing? How are people communicating?

It's also helpful to focus on your five senses (vision, hearing, smell, touch, taste) as you observe. This would take the form of responding to these questions:

VISION: What are you seeing? Who is there (not there)? What else is there (not there)? What colors do you see? Is it dull or bright? Clear or hazy? Near or far away?

HEARING: What are people saying? What other sounds do you hear? Are they loud or soft? Near or far away? Clear or garbled?

SMELL: What do you smell? Are the smells pleasant or unpleasant? Sweet or sour? What do the odors have to do with how you (and people in the field) experience the phenomena?

TOUCH: What does it feel like? It is hot or cold? Wet or dry? Hard or soft? Rough or smooth? What emotions are you experiencing? What emotions do the people around you seem to be experiencing?

TASTE: What taste is in your mouth as you are in the field? What does that say about how you (and people in the field) experience the phenomena?

Of course, what you are observing specifically depends on your research question.

field notes
A record of what was meaningful during an observation.

Field Notes.   How do you remember what you're observing? You take **field notes**. Field notes are taken in all sorts of ways: notebook, sketch pad, tape recorder, video recorder, laptop, even napkins, or, when necessary, the palm of your hand. Field notes are a record of what was meaningful. They include mental observation, note taking during or after the observation, recording during or after, and journals or diaries highlighting your impressions as you interact in the field. Write it down, record it, remember it—the only rule is to do what you need to do so that you can vividly recall it later. You'll usually write rough notes, often called **scratch notes**, then embellish those notes soon after for more detailed field notes.

scratch notes
Rough notes that are embellished upon shortly after an observation.

In-Depth Interviews.

Many qualitative researchers from all three traditions frequently use **in-depth interviews** as a method for collecting data. In qualitative research, think of the interview as an opportunity for the co-construction, exchange, and negotiation of ideas, information, and meaning. Instead of asking specific questions with pre-set responses as in quantitative surveys or interviews, qualitative interviews use an **interview guide** which typically consists of a list of topics to discuss or a topic outline. The goal of qualitative interviewing is to establish rapport with participants and to understand and learn from participants. When interviewing, qualitative researchers seek to understand participants' perspectives on an experience, because remember, in qualitative research, we want to retrieve experiences, gain insight, obtain information, obtain descriptions, foster trust, understand sensitive relationships, or create discourse to analyze (Fontana & Frey, 2003; Fontana & Prokos, 2007; Madison, 2005; Roulston, deMarrais, & Lewis, 2003; Silverman, 2003).

in-depth interviews
Opportunities for participants to describe their worlds in concert and negotiation with researchers. Such interviewing involves co-constructing a narrative with a participant—to understand his or her history and version of the story and the ways that he or she makes sense of his or her actions in the context of his or her cultural narratives.

Qualitative interviews are usually audiotaped and later transcribed, although if noticing nonverbal behaviors is also important you might prefer to videotape the interview. Word-for-word transcriptions let you analyze both what was said and how it was said (paralanguage and vocal disfluencies, for example). Alternatively, you can take notes instead of tape recording, but that does not allow you to attend to specific communication strategies in your analysis.

interview guide
An outline or list of topics or general questions to guide the in-depth interview.

Texts and Artifacts.

In ethnography, phenomenology, case study, and grounded theory, analysis of texts and other artifacts of material culture supports the interviewing and observation. In addition, rhetorical scholars, cultural ethnographers, and researchers utilizing content analysis study texts, as well as **artifacts-as-texts**. Researchers have been known to study clothing and personal adornment (hair, makeup, jewelry); architecture, buildings and grounds, and decorating; garbage bags; personal memorabilia; documents (corporate, personal); memos; logs, diaries, and journals; records (health records, driver's licenses, building contracts, bank statements, other legal or formal records); visual or audio media (songs, photographs, video); evidence of cultural rituals (wedding programs, marriage certificates) and behavior (shopping); cultural symbols (regalia, cemeteries, memorials, tombs, art); and community and social artifacts (roads, transportation) (Charmaz, 2006; Hodder, 2003). Denzin (2008) offers a critical examination of the painting *The Grand Canyon of the Yellowstone*; he explores historical documents surrounding this piece. In her piece on torch songs—songs about unrequited love—Holman-Jones (1999) explored her own experience with and about questions surrounding torch songs.

artifact
An object of study that represents material culture, such as adornment, or environmental or cultural objects.

material culture
Physical evidence of a culture; cultural artifacts.

There are many good reasons for analyzing text, documents, and artifacts—called **material culture** by Hodder (2003): Access is easy, cost to access is low, information may differ from other data collected (allowing you to triangulate or crystallize your data), they allow you to understand the perspectives of others and to pay attention to your own understandings of and experiences with those same texts, and texts endure and give historical insight and social context (Charmaz, 2006; Grbich, 2007; Hodder, 2003). Because text is written, it is an artifact that is capable of transmission, manipulation, and alteration, being used in different ways through time, and can thus acquire new and different meanings over time. Texts and artifacts are "material traces of behavior" that are left behind and give a different insight than interviews or personal communication. What people say is often very different than what people do, and texts and artifacts were constructed to *do* something. "They can be understood only as what they are— . . . produced under certain material conditions . . . embedded within social and ideological systems . . . designed specifically to be communicative and representational" (Hodder, 2003, pp. 157, 160).

Analyzing and Writing Qualitative Research

All qualitative research includes some sort of analytical interpretation. In a social sciences-based project, the analysis itself might be understated or subtly understood. Research from a social constructionist or humanities-based orientation might be written as a narrative, a poem, or a script. Narrative-based research might have explicit analytical sections or the analysis might be implied in the content, manner, and style of writing. A creative arts-based paper might let the poem or script or narrative convey the meaning and leave it to the reader to interpret the point for him/herself (letting the reader become a partner in the co-construction of the paper's message).

A social science paper, on the other hand, would be more likely to make specific claims and support those claims with exemplary pieces of data in the form of illustrative snippets from interviews or field notes. A social science based qualitative research report would look similar to its quantitative cousin—it would have clearly delineated sections similar to that of a quantitative paper (Introduction, Literature Review, Research Question, Methodology, Analysis, Discussion, Conclusion).

Regardless of the type of research project and the manner in which the analysis is undertaken, all types of research have some sort of analysis—involving some method to study the data and sort for patterns and themes. Sometimes the sorting process is explicit and systematic; other times it is intuitive. Sometimes the analysis involves separate steps and sometimes the patterns and themes become apparent in the writing process itself.

Significance Criteria

Tracy suggests that a research project should consider "a worthy topic, rich rigor, sincerity, credibility, resonance, significant contribution, . . . and meaningful coherence" (Tracy, 2010, p. 839). In other words, is the topic of significance to someone or something? Does it add to our understanding of the world (Richardson, 2000b)? Does it make a difference, or a contribution to our field (Goodall, 2008a)? Does it represent people who are marginalized; does it address critical issues of power (Denzin, 2000)? Does it move people or open up a conversation, or is it useful to somebody or something (Davis, 2014)?

RQ Criteria.   Did the researcher appropriately define the scope of the problem? Does the research have significance for society/academia? Was the research problem formally, clearly, and concisely stated? Does the research question flow from a theory if that is appropriate? Does the research question fit into the ongoing conversation in the literature? Does the study design appropriately address the research question (Davis, 2014; Tracy, 2010)?

Design/Methodology Criteria.   Was the design the most appropriate for the RQ? Is the study externally valid? What were the major limitations of the design? Were the limitations acknowledged by the researcher and taken into account in interpreting the results? If appropriate, was the study based on productive theoretical concepts (Tracy, 2010)?

Sampling Criteria.   Was the target population identified and described? Were eligibility criteria specified? Were the sampling selection procedures appropriate and clearly described? How adequate was the sampling plan in yielding a representative sample? Were there factors that affected the representativeness of the sample? Were possible sample biases identified and accounted for in the study? Was the sample size sufficient?

Data Collection Criteria.   Was the data itself productive and was the data collection rigorous (Tracy, 2010)? Did the RQ lend itself to the type of data collection? Did the data collection adequately cover the complexities of the problem under study? Who collected the data? Were data collectors qualified? How were they trained? How was the data gathered? Was it potentially distorted?

Analysis Criteria.   Was the coding sufficient, correct, and appropriate? Was an appropriate amount of quotes and supporting evidence reported? Was the information appropriately summarized and clear? Were the findings adequately supported? Were the findings appropriately tied to theory and concepts (if applicable) and does do the findings inform theory or constructs? Are the claims made appropriate for the methods used? Are the claims valid for the study reported (Davis, 2014)?

Writing Criteria.   Was the research written in a clear, concise manner? Was it well organized? If it was a narrative, was the writing action-oriented and evocative? Is it aesthetic? Did it show rather than tell? Is it evocative? Did the writing include thick description? Was the writing sufficiently reflexive? Did the writing reflect the findings, tone, and concepts you wanted to convey? Was anyone's voice left out that should have been included? Does it remind me of things in my life or does it help me better understand things in the participants' lives? Does it help me better understand certain theories or concepts? (Bochner, 2000; Davis, 2014; Denzin, 2000; Ellis, 2000).

Credibility Criteria.   Does the research make sense? Tracy asks, is it "honest, [self-reflexive], and transparent" (2010, p. 841)? Does it sound like something you can trust? Is it plausible (Tracy, 2010)? Does it have verisimilitude—does it seem to be true? In qualitative research of all kinds, the descriptions should be sufficiently rich that they are believable; the paper should offer enough description, detail, variety, evidence, and/or support so we could believe it, understand it, and see it through multiple dimensions. In other words, there should be "sufficient evidence to support the claims" (Goodall, 2008a, p. 139).

Quick Reference

The sciences require a solid framework for study, that's why understanding the steps in the research process can be really helpful. Think of it as an outline for your entire study. First, you have to read and analyze existing literature and studies to identify a problem and secondly, develop the question that you are asking. Third, you need to identify which research design will get the best answer to your question. Once you have identified the method or design, it's time to actually collect the data (this can take a long time), and then after, analyze that data. What's it telling you? Are you seeing the relationship you thought you'd see? Now, you're to the best part, presenting and discussing your findings. What good is answering a question if you don't tell anyone about what you found?

—*Kristen Hark*

Social Science Qualitative Approaches

Social Science Paradigm

Qualitative researchers under the social science paradigm see research as a systematic investigation. They believe that reality is discoverable, observable, and understandable. While they do view their research endeavors reflexively—understanding their own role in the interpretation of meaning in an experience—they also tend to focus primarily on understanding as it derives from the standpoint of other people who are the focus of their research.

Ethnography

Ethnography, simply put, is the study of a culture. Ethnography is characterized by immersion in a culture—called **fieldwork**—in order to fully understand beliefs and practices in context. This immersion usually occurs through observations, various types of participation, and formal interviewing and informal conversations. Ethnography frequently makes use of key participants, called **informants**, who can act as co-researchers and help the researcher explain and make sense of the culture (Atkinson, Coffey, Delamont, Lofland, & Lofland, 2007). Within the method called *ethnography* are many subareas, which we will explain in more detail. You may notice as you look through these descriptions that the areas sound as if they might overlap. In fact, they do, but researchers usually begin their research at one of the traditions.

Ethnomethodology. Developed by Harold Garfinkel in 1967, **ethnomethodology** focuses on understanding the lived experience and lived practices from the point of view of those within the experience (Pollner & Emerson, 2007). Researchers following this approach use participant observation to attend to what interactional participants think is important or accountable (able to be noticed and accounted for). Ethnomethodology studies interactions in everyday life and attempts to understand ordinary unnoticed interactions. Ethnomethodologists suggest that researchers "make the familiar strange," or seek to see meaning in the ordinary. They also stress reflexivity, which they refer to as the meaning constructed in an interaction while the action is taking place (Pollner & Emerson, 2007).

Appropriate Research Questions Answered by Ethnography. Ethnography in the field of Sciences Studies is appropriately used in research designed to understand, describe, or explain communication in a culture or cultural group. Ethnographic research methods allow scholars to immerse themselves in a culture in order to deeply comprehend how the culture operates. Ethnography answers "how" questions and focuses on the process rather than the outcomes or motivations.

The Role of Theory in Ethnographic Research. Theory is used in two very different ways in research projects: either as an overarching ontological position driving the project's design from its conception, or as specific explanatory theories utilized at the project's conclusion. Most ethnographic studies begin from a theoretical position which is frequently

ethnography
The study of a culture.

fieldwork
Immersion in a culture through observations, various types of participation, and formal interviewing and informal conversations.

informants
Participants who can act as co-researchers and help the researcher explain and make sense of the culture.

ethnomethodology
A type of ethnography that focuses on understanding the lived experience and lived practices from the point of view of those within the experience.

understood rather than stated, and which derives from an overarching social constructionist and/or critical ontology. In ethnographic research from the social science paradigms, other theoretical constructs are frequently pulled in during the analysis as explanatory theories to help clarify the findings and to tie the research back to the scholarly conversation.

grounded theory
A systematic approach to understanding and analyzing participants' lives.

Sampling in Ethnography.   There are as many sampling strategies in ethnographic research as there are types of ethnographic research. An ethnography that takes a **grounded theory** stance might utilize theoretical sampling, or an ethnography that has a **phenomenological** approach might sample purposively for phenomenological understanding. Other ethnographies might want people who represent different types of experiences, so they might use typical instance, maximum variation, or extreme instance sampling. Many ethnographies are methodologically **case studies** and might study only one culture or field site, but even with small samples or single site samples, all ethnographers typically conduct long periods of fieldwork (up to twelve months of observations—or more) and multiple forms of data collection of many participants in that one site.

field site
Group, organization, or culture in which research is conducted.

Selecting and Accessing a Field Site.   Ethnographic research samples within **field sites**—within groups, organizations, or cultures. The type of field site you choose will depend, again, on your research question or study objectives. Christine Davis, for example, has conducted ethnographic research at a hospice organization (Davis, 2010) and within a children's mental health system of care (Davis, 2014). If you wish to study within an organization, you might select one specific organization to study based on the same factors on which you'd base your sample selection—your initial theoretical construct, the amount of variability you want at your site, if you want an organization that is typical, or if you want an organization that is atypical.

gatekeeper
A person who controls access to a field site.

Once you've determined what type of site you wish to study, you need to gain access to the site. Most ethnographers, for example, gain access to the site through **informants**. Sometimes it's as simple as knowing someone at the site—the higher the rank, the better. Other times, you need to make an appointment with management (if it's an organization) or a respected group member or leader, then sell yourself and the project. You'll need to get past the organizational **gatekeepers**, and you may not always know who they are until after you think you have approval to conduct the research. Ironically, Christine Davis, while writing this book chapter, was attempting to collect data within a field site—a local children's mental health system of care. She thought she had permission from the people in charge of giving her referrals to potential study participants, but after she began trying to collect data, the research was blocked by a gatekeeper higher up in the site she had not known to contact. As of this writing, she is attempting to gain access to another alternative site. In naturalistic research, you have to be flexible and prepared for changes and setbacks.

Focus Groups

Focus group research is a methodology that is known by its method of data collection. Focus groups are in-depth group discussions on a specific situation or topic of interest, made up of five to twelve participants and a moderator (or two co-moderators). They provide participants a forum to discuss differing perspectives. Developed in the 1950s by sociologist Robert Merton and psychologist Paul Lazerfeld, the first focus groups were used for media testing. They have been used primarily in the marketing field for decades, but they have been more recently (re)discovered by social scientists.

Historically, focus groups are held in a small face-to-face group. Today, focus groups held via telephone, Skype, and other electronic means are more and more popular. Focus groups are either conducted with a group of people who are strangers to each other, or among a group of people who know each other (also called natural groups or bona fide groups). A group can meet one time only or regularly over a period of time. A trained facilitator leads the group session, typically follows a semi-structured moderator's guide, and asks in-depth and open-ended questions (Davis, 2016).

There are many advantages to focus groups. The foremost advantage is that you can see group interaction in action. Focus groups can be a forum to provide a voice to marginalized groups. In some ways, focus groups are more naturalistic than some other data collection methods, in that they tap into the usual *modes of communication* and *everyday social practices* that constitute people's social lives—they mirror social interchange in a relatively naturalistic way. Also, with focus groups, the relationship between the researcher and the participants is less hierarchical—the balance of power shifts from the researcher to the participants in a focus group. Of course, focus groups are inherently biased due to the interactional nature of method and this interaction should always be factored in as part of the analysis.

focus groups
Focus groups are in-depth group discussions on a specific situation or topic of interest, made up of five to twelve participants and a moderator.

Grounded Theory

The process of **grounded theory** was originally developed by Barney Glaser and Anselm Strauss (Glaser & Strauss, 1967; Strauss & Corbin, 1990), but researchers who use grounded theory use a constructivist approach to grounded theory developed by Kathy Charmaz (2000), so we will discuss Charmaz's version here.

Appropriate Research Questions Answered by Grounded Theory Research. The goal of grounded theory, says Charmaz, is to learn "what our research participants' lives are like. We study how they explain their statements and actions, and ask what analytic sense we can make of them" (2000, pp. 2–3). Grounded theory seeks to understand interaction within social practices and the resulting meaning (Starks & Trinidad, 2007). Grounded theory is appropriate for research questions that focus on experiences over time within a social context (Creswell et al., 2007).

The Role of Theory in Grounded Theory Research.

There are two main ideas incorporated into grounded theory: We are developing theories that are grounded in the data and that surface through the **theoretical saturation** of categories (we collect and analyze the data until no new categories of theories are identified); and our design is *emergent*—we analyze, collect data, reanalyze, interpret, and change our design as we go along. The process of grounded theory allows for surprises, fresh ideas, and exploration (Charmaz, 2006). The theories derived in grounded theory are explanations of social processes—grounded theory answers the question of "How does the social process of 'X' happen in the context of this environment?" (Starks & Trinidad, 2007). The focus of a grounded theory analysis is to develop a social model or theory (Creswell et al., 2007).

Sampling in Grounded Theory Research.

theoretical sampling
Choosing a sample based on the people, events, groups, and so on who can shed light on a theory being investigated.

Grounded theory typically uses a **theoretical sampling** method—you choose your sample based on the people, events, groups, and so on who can shed light on the theory you are investigating. As you collect your data, your theory may change and, as a result, your sampling design may change also. In grounded theory, you're done when you're done—when you've collected enough data to understand and explain the full complexity of the culture you're studying; when you have detailed descriptions of the ways that participants view the world; when you fully understand underlying issues, changes over time, and multiple viewpoints; when you can develop analytic categories; and when you understand differences and nuances in your data (Charmaz, 2006). Grounded theory is more interested with immersion in a culture than in sample size. In a grounded theory study, achieving understanding and rapport with our participants is more important than the number of participants we talk to. Having said that, however, grounded theory often has larger sample sizes than other qualitative methods because it uses theoretical sampling, involving participants with different experiences to compare and explore different aspects. In grounded theory, the sample size is complete when the study reaches *theoretical saturation*—when no more theories or constructs emerge by the data. Grounded theory research typically uses samples ranging from ten to sixty participants (Starks & Trinidad, 2007).

Data Collection in Grounded Theory Research.

Researchers conducting grounded theory typically use observation and in-depth interviews in which participants describe their experiences (Starks & Trinidad, 2007). Grounded theory involves a systematic process of synthesizing data throughout the course of a study (Charmaz, 2006). In grounded theory, researchers observe social processes in their natural environments, which help them see the effect of the environment on behavior and meaning (Starks & Trinidad, 2007). Since, in grounded theory, you shape and reshape your data collection and refine your study design as you try out tentative concepts, theories, and analysis throughout your study, you might return to the field to observe different things, explore additional questions or experiences, or otherwise move along your ideas as they emerge (Charmaz, 2006).

Field notes in grounded theory might include descriptions of both individual and collective behaviors, much detail including stories and observations, processes you consider to be significant, things that participants tell you they consider to be interesting or problematic, participants' language use, scenes and contexts, and analytical thoughts and ideas. Observations in a grounded theory project focus on processes—what is related to what else, what are the practices in the site, how are people organized, and what are the social networks. In grounded theory, you will be looking for data that lets you compare across time, across categories, and between concepts. In grounded theory research, think of fieldwork as an opportunity to "dig into the scene" (p. 23).

· ▼

Phenomenology

Phenomenology—developed by Max van Manen and others, and based on the philosophies of Edmund Husserl and Martin Heidegger—is the study of experience, in order to understand—in great depth—the nature, essence, and meaning of that experience. **Phenomenology** is "an encounter" with real life, says Vagle (2014, p. 12), in that phenomenologists practice their craft through embodied engagement and relationship with their experiences. Phenomenologists study an experience from within the experience as they examine "how it is to BE in the world" (Vagle, 2014, p. 21). Van Manen refers to phenomenological inquiry as "surrendering to a state of wonder" (2014, p. 15).

phenomenology
The study of experience, in order to understand—in great depth—the nature, essence, and meaning of that experience.

Appropriate Research Questions Answered by Phenomenology.

Unlike other interpretive methods that study the social construction of meaning in an experience, or that reflexively examine an experience in light of our own interpretations and experiences, the goal of phenomenology is to understand an experience as it is lived, uncontaminated by other theories or assumptions. One of the key aspects of phenomenological inquiry is to undertake a systematic identification of the researchers' preconceived ideas and thoughts, in order to be able to focus on understanding the experience with an open, blank mind (called **bracketing**). As Starks and Trinidad (2007) explain it, "phenomenology contributes to deeper understanding of lived experiences by exposing taken-for-granted assumptions about [our] ways of knowing" (p. 1373). Phenomenologists' sole focus is on the experience itself—not the people in the experience except in terms of how they live through the experience, not the construction of the experience, not the interpretation of the experience—but the pure experience, to understand how it is experienced from within. As Vagle (2014) states,

bracketing
In phenomenology, identification of the researchers' preconceived ideas and thoughts, in order to be able to focus on understanding the experience with an open, blank mind.

> *Phenomenologists . . . study how things are being and becoming. . . . The phenomenologist . . . is not studying the individual but is studying how a particular phenomenon manifests and appears in the lifeworld. . . . The "unit of analysis" in phenomenology is the phenomenon, not the individual. (pp. 22–23)*

Phenomenologists study the fundamental essence of an experience. Phenomena and experiences studied by phenomenologists might include things like "confusion, respect, despair, hope, resistance, being in love" (Vagle, 2014, p. 27), and they ask questions like, "how does someone find him/herself in a state of being in love?" Other phenomenologists might study an experience such as a healthcare experience or an educational experience, and might ask, "how is this experienced as the people are living through the experience?" The key to phenomenological understanding is to see everyday lived experience "as if we are seeing it for the first time" (van Manen, 2014, p. 43).

Sampling in Phenomenology.   The first step in phenomenology is to choose the experience you wish to study. Van Manen (2001) suggests selecting an experience that is "something you really care about and want to question" (p. 58). You then have to identify how you can enter into the experience and sample to that aim.

Phenomenological research typically has small samples, because phenomenologists are not looking to sample from a wide range of experiences—they want detailed information about a very specific experience. Phenomenological research typically uses sample sizes from one to ten participants (Starks & Trinidad, 2007); people who have experienced the phenomena under study. For that reason, phenomenological research typically uses purposive sampling or theoretical construct sampling.

Data Collection in Phenomenology.   Phenomenologists seek to understand embodied experience, to understand a phenomenon as completely as if they had experienced it themselves (Starks & Trinidad, 2007). Data collection in phenomenology seeks to identify specific concrete instances of how someone experiences the phenomenon.

Phenomenologists frequently gather data through in-depth retrospective interviews or focus groups in which participants are encouraged to relive, explain, and describe experiences in great detail. Phenomenological interviewing would include non-structured interviews that you can follow up on to understand the participant's experience. You would return to each participant multiple times to make sure you fully understand (Grbich, 2007).

▼ ·

Discourse Analysis

Discourse analysis is a methodology that is known by its method of analysis. Discourse analysis—the study of spoken or written discourse—studies speech acts—from the content of the discourse, to its delivery (paralanguage, speech, grammar), to its context, and the meaning deriving from each of these, to understand how people use language to construct ideas, meanings, and identities (Starks & Trinidad, 2007). Discourse analysis is a broad term that actually refers to a wide variety of methods of analysis (Manning & Kunkel, 2014;

Scharp & Thomas, 2017). Discourse analysis examines meaning from the level of everyday talk (speech acts) through the systemic—or social—contextual levels (Davis, 2016; Schart & Thomas, 2017; Tracy & Robles, 2013).

Discourse analysis might focus on relational roles in the interaction; language use, exchange, or persuasion strategies; conversational turns; interactional and relational history of the participants; and nonverbal strategies. Discourse analysis takes a wide view of the context of the interaction. While both **conversation analysis (CA)** and discourse analysis focus on the specific utterances (or discourse) and the meaning resulting from it, they differ in terms of their primary focus. CA focuses primarily on how people talk, while discourse analysis focuses on how that talk constructs meaning.

conversation analysis (CA)
An investigation of social interaction between humans, most especially of everyday, ordinary conversation, called in CA "talk-in-interaction."

Quick Reference

Qualitative inquiry can mean many things, but one thing you can rely on is the focus on people and their experience. That means ethnography, phenomenology (a great word that you should try to use at least one a week. Means "lived experience."), case studies, etc. The researcher's focus on a certain people group and their experiences means they are asking extremely BROAD questions. Think about it—if I want to hear a good story about your experiences in junior high, I don't ask specific questions, anything narrow, or a measurable, testable question. I ask something like, "What were the junior high years like for you?" This provides a central, broad question that invites you to tell me of your experiences.

—Kristen Hark

Mixed Methods Procedures

How would you write a mixed methods procedure section for your proposal? Up until this point, we have considered collected quantitative data and qualitative data. We have not discussed "mixing" or combining the two forms of data in a study. We can start with the assumption that both forms of data provide different types of information (open-ended data in the case of qualitative and closed-ended data in the case of quantitative). If we further assume that each type of data collection has both limitations and strengths, we can consider how the strengths can be combined to develop a stronger understanding of the research problem or questions (and, as well, overcome the limitations of each). This "mixing" or blending of data, it can be argued, provides a stronger understanding of the problem or question than either by itself. This idea is at the core of a reasonably new method called "mixed methods research."

Conveying the nature of mixed methods research and what it is begins a good mixed methods procedure. Begin with the assumption that mixed methods is a new methodology in research and that the readers need to be educated as to the basic intent and definition of the design, the reasons for choosing the procedure, and the value it will lend to a study. Then, decide on a mixed methods design to use. There are many from which to choose and consider the different possibilities and decide which one is best for the proposed study. With this choice in hand, discuss the data collection, the data analysis, and the data interpretation and validation procedures within the context of the design. Finally, end with a discussion of potential ethical issues that need to be anticipated in the study, and suggest an outline for writing the final study. These are all standard methods procedures, but they are framed in this chapter as they apply to mixed methods research. Table 5.1 shows a checklist of the mixed methods procedures.

▼ ···

Components of Mixed Methods Procedures

Mixed methods research has evolved into a set of procedures that proposal developers can use in planning a mixed methods study. In 2003, the *Handbook of Mixed Methods in the Social* and *Behavior Sciences* (Tashakkori & Teddlie, 2003) was published (and later added to in a second edition,

Table 5.1. A Checklist of Questions for Designing a Mixed Methods Procedure

_____	Is a basic definition of mixed methods research provided?
_____	Are the reasons given for using both quantitative and qualitative data?
_____	Does the reader have a sense for the potential use of mixed methods research?
_____	Are the criteria identified for choosing a mixed methods design?
_____	Is the mixed methods design identified?
_____	Is a visual model presented that illustrates the research strategy?
_____	Is the proper notation used in presenting the visual model?
_____	Are procedures of data collection and analysis mentioned as they relate to the chosen design?
_____	Are the sampling strategies for both quantitative and qualitative data collection mentioned for the design?
_____	Are specific data analysis procedures indicated for the design?
_____	Are the procedures for validation mentioned for the design and for the quantitative and qualitative research?
_____	Is the narrative structure of the final dissertation or thesis mentioned, and does it relate to the type of mixed methods design being used?

see Tashakkori & Teddlie, 2010), providing a comprehensive overview of this approach. Now several journals emphasize mixed methods research, such as the *Journal of Mixed Methods Research*, *Quality and Quantity*, *Field Methods*, and the *International Journal of Multiple Research Approaches* while numerous others actively encourage this form of inquiry (e.g., *International Journal of Social Research Methodology*, *Qualitative Health Research*, *Annals of Family Medicine*). Numerous published research studies have incorporated mixed methods research in the social and human sciences in diverse fields such as occupational therapy (Lysack & Krefting, 1994), interpersonal communication (Boneva, Kraut, & Frohlich, 2001), AIDS prevention (Janz et al., 1996), dementia caregiving (Weitzman & Levkoff, 2000), occupational health (Ames, Duke, Moore, & Cunradi, 2009), mental health (Rogers, Day, Randall, & Bentall, 2003.)

Describe Mixed Methods Research

Because mixed methods research is relatively new in the social and human sciences as a distinct research approach, it is useful to convey a basic definition and description of the approach in a method section of a proposal. This might include the following:

- Begin by defining mixed methods. Elements in this definition can now be enumerated so that a reader has a complete set of core characteristics that describe mixed methods (see a more expanded view of defining mixed methods research in Johnson, Onwuegbuzie, & Turner, 2007):
  - It involves the collection of both qualitative (open-ended) and quantitative (closed-ended) data in response to research questions or hypotheses.
  - It includes the analysis of both forms of data.
  - The procedures for both qualitative and quantitative data collection and analysis need to be conducted rigorously (e.g., adequate sampling, sources of information, data analysis steps).
  - The two forms of data are integrated in the design analysis through merging the data, connecting the data, or embedding the data.
  - These procedures are incorporated into a distinct mixed methods design that also includes the timing of the data collection (concurrent or sequential) as well as the emphasis (equal or unequal) for each database.
  - These procedures can also be informed by a philosophical worldview or a theory.
- Discuss that many different terms are used for this approach, such as *integrating, synthesis, quantitative and qualitative methods, multimethod*, and *mixed methodology* but that recent writings tend to use the term *mixed methods* (Bryman, 2006; Tashakkori & Teddlie, 2010).

■ Educate the reader about the background of mixed methods by reviewing briefly this history of this approach to research. It can be seen as a new methodology originating around the late 1980s and early 1990s based on work from individuals in diverse fields such as evaluation, education, management, sociology, and health sciences. It has gone through several periods of development including the formative stage, the philosophical debates, the procedural developments, and more recently reflective positions (noting controversies and debates) and expansion into different disciplines and into many countries throughout the world. Several texts outline these developmental phases (e.g., Creswell & Plano Clark, 2011; Teddlie & Tashakkori, 2009). This section could also include a brief discussion about the importance or rise of mixed methods today through such indicators of federal funding initiatives, through dissertations, and through the discipline-specific discussions about mixed methods found in journals across the social and health sciences (see Creswell, 2010, 2011).

■ Follow this section with statements about the value and rationale for the choice of mixed methods as an approach for the dissertation or thesis project. At a *general level*, mixed methods is chosen because of its strength of drawing on both qualitative and quantitative research and minimizing the limitations of both approaches. At a *practical level*, mixed methods provides a sophisticated, complex approach to research that appeals to those on the forefront of new research procedures. It also can be an ideal approach if the researcher has access to both quantitative and qualitative data. At a *procedural level*, it is a useful strategy to have a more complete understanding of research problems/questions, such as the following:

❑ Comparing different perspectives drawn from quantitative and qualitative data

❑ Explaining quantitative results with a qualitative follow-up data collection and analysis

❑ Developing better measurement instruments by first collecting and analyzing qualitative data and then administrating the instruments to a sample

❑ Understanding experimental results by incorporating the perspectives of individuals

❑ Developing a more complete understanding of changes needed for a marginalized group through the combination of qualitative and quantitative data

❑ Having a better understanding the need for and impact of an intervention program through collecting both quantitative and qualitative data over time

■ Indicate the type of mixed methods design that will be used in the study and the rationale for choosing it. Details of the primary strategies available will be discussed shortly. Include a figure or diagram of these procedures.

Table 5.2. Choosing a Mixed Methods Project, Expected Outcomes, Type of Design

Reasons for Choosing Mixed Methods	Expected Outcomes	Recommended Mixed Methods Design
Comparing different perspectives drawn from quantitative and qualitative data	Merging the two databases to show how the data convergent or diverge	Convergent parallel mixed methods design
Explaining quantitative results with qualitative data	A more in-depth understanding of the quantitative results (often cultural relevance)	Explanatory sequential mixed methods design
Developing better measurement instruments	A test of better measures for a sample of a population	Exploratory sequential mixed methods design
Understanding experimental results by incorporating perspectives of individuals	An understanding of participant views within the context of an experimental intervention	Embedded mixed methods design
Developing an understanding of needed changes for a marginalized group	A call for action	Transformative mixed methods design
Understanding the need for an impact of an intervention program	A formative and summative evaluation	Multiphase mixed methods design

- Note the challenges this form of research poses for the inquirer. These include the need for extensive data collection, the time-intensive nature of analyzing both qualitative and quantitative data, and the requirement for the researcher to be familiar with both quantitative and qualitative forms of research. The complexity of the design also calls for clear, visual models to understand the details and the flow of research activities in this design.

Choice Based on Type of Design Most Suited for a Field

On a practical level, the choice of a strategy depends on the inclination of fields toward certain designs. For quantitatively oriented fields, the explanatory sequential approach seems to work well because the study begins (and perhaps is driven) by the quantitative phase of the research. In qualitatively oriented fields, the exploratory sequential approach may be more appealing because it begins with an exploration using qualitative research. However, in this approach, an outcome may be a measurement instrument that is tested so that the outcome, a quantitative outcome, outweighs in importance how the study began. In some fields, the choice of approach may be dependent on collecting data efficiently, and this would argue for a convergent mixed methods study in which both quantitative and qualitative data are typically collected at roughly the same time rather than at different times that require more visits to the research site.

Summary

In designing the procedures for a mixed methods discussion, begin by defining mixed methods research and its core characteristics, briefly mentioning its historical evolution; discuss your chosen mixed methods design; and note the challenges in using the design. Convey a diagram of your procedures that includes good notation to help the reader understand the flow of activities. As you discuss your design, convey the elements that go into it, such as the procedures used in a convergent parallel, an explanatory sequential, or an exploratory sequential mixed methods study. Also consider whether you will overlay your project with a more advanced procedure that embeds the data or mixed methods within a larger design; uses a transformative framework that advocates for social justice; or strings together multiple quantitative, qualitative, or mixed methods studies into a longitudinal line of investigation, all targeted toward a single objective. Finally, consider factors that play into your choice of a mixed methods design. These involve considering what outcomes you expect from the study, the integration of the databases, the timing of them, the emphasis placed on each database, the choice of design that matches your field, and the conduct of the project either by yourself or a team of researchers.

Glossary

Active-member researchers
Researchers who become involved with central activities of the group but do not fully commit themselves to the group.

Artifact
An object of study that represents material culture, such as adornment, or environmental or cultural objects.

Arts and humanities paradigm
A research paradigm in which researchers tend to see research as a performance and tend to use art or performance to understand the world in an embodied and holistic manner.

Baseline
An examination of someone before you expose him or her to a stimulus in order to argue, to a certain extent, that what was done to the subject may have caused any changes that are observed. Also called pretest.

Between-subjects design
Designs comparing multiple groups.

Bracketing
In phenomenology, identification of the researchers' preconceived ideas and thoughts, in order to be able to focus on understanding the experience with an open, blank mind.

Complete-member researchers
Researchers who study settings in which they are already members or with which they are already affiliated.

Complete Observer
Researchers who have little to no interaction with the people being observed.

Control Group
A group that does not receive induction in an experiment.

Conversation analysis (ca)
An investigation of social interaction between humans, most especially of everyday, ordinary conversation, called in CA "talk-in-interaction."

Cross-sectional survey
A survey design that describes the characteristics of a sample representing a population at one point in time.

Crystallization
The process of reviewing multiple sources of data to capture a full, rich, multivocal, and nuanced view of the phenomenon under study.

Data saturation
The collection and analysis of data until no new categories of theories are identified.

Descriptive observation

A type of observation that is usually done when the researcher is first in the field, in which the researcher observes everything, no matter how small, and takes notes on all details and observations.

Emergent design

A study design in which methods (including sampling, data collection, data protocols, coding, and analysis) are revised as the study emerges and progresses.

Emic

An approach to research that is more inductive and based on the participants' point of view and on the findings resulting from the study itself.

Ethnography

The study of a culture.

Ethnomethodology

A type of ethnography that focuses on understanding the lived experience and lived practices from the point of view of those within the experience.

Etic

An approach to research that is more deductive and is based on a pre-existing concept or theory.

Experimental group

The group of participants to whom you give the induction.

Extreme instance sampling

Consists of sampling units that have characteristics quite different from the rest of a population.

Evaluation research

Research that is designed to assess the effectiveness of programs or products during development or after their completion.

Fact pattern

A factual relationship occurring repeatedly.

Field site

Group, organization, or culture in which research is conducted.

Field notes

A record of what was meaningful during an observation.

Fieldwork

Immersion in a culture through observations, various types of participation, and formal interviewing and informal conversations.

Fieldwork

Conducting observations in natural settings.

Focused observation

A stage in qualitative observation which occurs after the researcher has been in the field for a while and begun preliminary analysis, in which the researcher begins to narrow his/her focus and ignores some phenomena that are irrelevant to his/her study.

Focus groups

Focus groups are in-depth group discussions on a specific situation or topic of interest, made up of five to twelve participants and a moderator.

Gatekeeper

A person who controls access to a field site.

Grounded theory

A systematic approach to understanding and analyzing participants' lives.

Hypothesis

A statement a researcher makes about the relationship between a dependent and an independent variable.

In-depth interviews

Opportunities for participants to describe their worlds in concert and negotiation with researchers. Such interviewing involves co-constructing a narrative with a participant—to understand his or her history and version of the story and the ways that he or she makes sense of his or her actions in the context of his or her cultural narratives.

Induction

What is done to a participant in an experiment.

Inductive reasoning

Reasoning that discovers patterns, inferences, and conclusions from studying and observing certain phenomena.

Inductive reasoning

Reasoning that discovers patterns, inferences, and conclusions from studying and observing certain phenomena.

Informants

Participants who can act as co-researchers and help the researcher explain and make sense of the culture.

Interpretive

A research perspective in which understanding and interpretation of the social world is derived from one's personal intuition and perspective.

Interview

A research practice with individual participants, or groups of participants, to obtain responses to survey questions by direct questioning.

Interview guide

An outline or list of topics or general questions to guide the in-depth interview.

In vivo

Research that takes place in a natural setting.

Longitudinal survey design

A survey design that gathers data from respondents at several points in time.

Market research

Research that is designed to study consumer behavior.

Material culture

Physical evidence of a culture; cultural artifacts.

Maximum variation sampling

A sampling method that selects study participants that represent a wide range of characteristics that are present in the population and are of interest to the research.

Multivocality

A form of writing that frequently includes multiple voices; it might be written from different points of view (including researchers and multiple stakeholders or participants).

Naturalistic

Research that is conducted in the field or where participants live, work, and play.

Observations

A way to gain insight into the obligations, constraints, motivations, and emotions that participants experience as they complete everyday actions.

Peripheral-member researchers

Researchers who have some level of involvement with a group without core group involvement.

Phenomenology

The study of experience, in order to understand—in great depth—the nature, essence, and meaning of that experience.

Political polls

One of the most common and readily available uses of surveys. They provide a detailed account of who is leading whom in the run for a particular office during an election.

Pretest

An examination of someone before you expose him or her to a stimulus in order to argue, to a certain extent, that what was done to the subject may have caused any changes that are observed. Also called baseline measurement.

Posttest

An examination or measurement conducted after administration of the induction.

Purposive sampling

A method of sampling in which the researcher selects participants based on their having experienced the phenomenon or issue under study.

Quasi-experimental designs

Experimental designs that use pretests and posttests in more complicated ways, but still lack random assignment.

Random assignment

The assignment of people at random to different groups in an experimental design.

Reflexivity

Acknowledgement of a researcher's positionality in relation to the study, study topic, and the study participants; addressing how one's own thoughts, feelings, and behaviors interact with his or her research site and his or her research itself.

Representation

In qualitative research, the concept that the qualitative sample should adequately represent the population under study to provide in-depth understanding of the experience.

Rhetorical paradigm

A research paradigm that focuses upon a wide variety of texts in order to gain a deep understanding of the message within the communication process, to connect that understanding to broader practical and theoretical concerns related to human communication and the human condition in general.

Research question

Questions scholars ask about the way things work.

Scratch notes

Rough notes that are embellished upon shortly after an observation.

Selective observation

A stage of observation which occurs as the researcher's time in the field is winding down, in which the researcher concentrates on certain activities and on additional analyses, interviews, coding, and so forth that correspond to the meanings emerging from the data already collected.

Snowball or network sampling

This sampling method asks study participants to make referrals to other potential participants, who in turn make referrals to other participants, and so on.

Social constructionist paradigm

A research paradigm that believes that shared meaning is constructed through our cultural systems and focuses on culturally situated action and interaction through which meanings and interpretations are socially, historically, temporally, and culturally constructed. Qualitative researchers in this paradigm tend to see research as a social construction of meaning.

Social experiment

A procedure in which researchers take human subjects, do something to them, and observe the effects of what they did to them.

Social science paradigm

A research paradigm in which researchers see research as a systematic investigation and tend to believe in a reality that is more observable and better understood objectively.

Survey design

A method of asking research participants questions that provides researchers with a method of information gathering from a large number of people over a relatively short period of time.

Theoretical sampling

Choosing a sample based on the people, events, groups, and so on who can shed light on a theory being investigated.

Trend study

Measurement occurs at two or more points in time, from different samples selected from the same population. This type of study is designed to identify changes or trends in people's beliefs about a variable of interest.

True experimental designs
Experimental designs that randomly assign participants to both experimental and control groups.

Typical instance sampling
Consists of sampling units who have characteristics typical of a population.

Within-subjects design
Designs looking at the same group multiple times.

References

Creswell, J.W. (2014). *Research Design: Qualitative, Quantitative, and Mixed Methods Approaches* (4th ed.). Thousand Oaks, CA: Sage.

Davis, Christine S. and Kenneth A. Lachlan. (2017). *Straight Talk about Communication Research Methods* (3rd ed.). Dubuque, IA: Kendall Hunt.

CHAPTER 6

The Humanities: A Survey of Approaches

This chapter addresses the research paradigms and methods most applicable to research and scholarship in the humanities, with an emphasis on interdisciplinary, qualitative research questions and methods.

Upon successful completion of this chapter, you will be able to:

- Distinguish between historical, critical, and descriptive approaches to research.
- Recognize research limitations and strengths of content analysis, ethnography, and ethnomethodology.
- Understand the heuristic value of research in the Humanities.

Introduction

What comes to mind when you hear the word, "Humanities"? Is it humans? Is it the definition of humanity? The humanities study the world created by humans. Literature, architecture, government, philosophy, music, archeology . . . the list goes on and on. Research done within the Humanities is as varied as the areas that fall into it. One of the biggest misconceptions about the Humanities is that humanists read books and then write more books. Studying human culture and what it has created, and then comparing that to the world and society, attempts to give models and patterns of the "real world."

Maybe it's easier for you to understand what something is, by first understanding what it is not. At least that often works for me. A key difference between the humanities and sciences is the manner in which they each organize material: the material of their studies, how they aim to arrange and manipulate their evidence, and even the types of questions that they ask. For example, data in the Sciences are generally arranged in broad categories, widely applicable with similarities and differences between easily codified. Not so in the Humanities.

The raw, or early, material researched in the Humanities is often unique and individual . . . a human life, a work of poetry, historical records, works of fiction—and these aren't reduced to patterns or similarities or deviations from "norms." This doesn't mean things, or data, aren't organized. The fields of communication, psychology, anthropology have all had immense impact on how humans understand, organize, and explain evidence. Think traditions and cultural norms and narratives . . . these are all part of events and facts and reality can be articulated. And thus, studied.

So, be prepared to be a bit more fluid in your thinking as you go through this Humanities chapter. Don't think about data or hypotheses, per se, but rather think about **the way** you're thinking, **how** your questions are phrased, and what prompted you to ask those questions in the first place. Cheers!

Humanities

If you view research as characterized by the evidence-based exploration of a question or hypothesis, then you are correct. In a general sense, though, students, must know something about the research methods of a discipline; what constitutes "evidence" and how do you obtain it, and how do you decide if a question or line of inquiry that's interesting is also important to the discipline, fills in a gap within previous work? These questions must be answered in order to initiate a research project.

Let's look at research within the Humanities. (HINT: there is NOT a central discipline to the Humanities, it will help to remember this). Research in the Humanities takes in variety of forms and disciplines; it might include studying language, literature, philosophy, religion, culture, and many other disciplinary and interdisciplinary areas. The study of the humanities is often described as the study of the human experience.

A hallmark of study within the Humanities is that research is often **interpretive;** this is quite different than research in the Sciences (where data and hard evidence are required to draw conclusions). Because human experience cannot (and should not) be adequately captured by facts and figures alone, Humanities research employs methods that are historical, interpretive *and* analytical in nature; because of this variety research in the humanities is frequently misunderstood.

For many of us, when we think of research, we see a laboratory setting, with scientists in white-coats hunched over microscopes. This isn't incorrect, but because research in the humanities is often a rather solitary activity, it can be difficult for a research neophyte to gain a sense of what research within the scope of the Humanities looks like.

Thus, one VERY common misconception about research is thinking about it only in terms of **discovery** of things previously unknown to humanity (such as a new species or an archaeological artifact). Instead, we should see research as a process that includes the **reinterpretation or rediscovery** of known artifacts, or cultural projects, such as texts or films, photographs, or musical scores.

Reinterpretation or rediscovery requires a critical and/or creative perspective—this helps generate innovative art or new analyses. In the Humanities, this kind of discovery research might consist of literary authorship (writing a novel) or scholarly research, which adds new knowledge to the author's field of study.

Perhaps we might better understand Humanities-based research by understanding first what it is not. Unlike research in the Sciences, Humanities researchers are interested in raising questions, rather than providing absolute answers. Research within the Sciences is often narrowly thought of as an activity eventually resulting in a tangible product, aimed at solving some kind of problem. In the Humanities, however, research has many aims and outcomes and is a discipline-specific process, based upon the methods, conventions, and critical frameworks inherent in that particular academic area (literature, history, anthropology, language, et cetera). It is imperative to remember that within the Humanities, the products of research are predominantly **intellectual and intangible**, with the results contributing to an academic discipline and also informing other disciplines, a process which often effects individual or social change over time.

Methods of Humanities Research

Humanities research draws from many sources and often requires alternative methods of investigation, but it is most often characterized by **qualitative research**. You should recall that qualitative research is widely used when the goal is understanding experience. This often ties to how people perceive and make sense of their own experiences; experience is often interpretative and unobservable.

For example, a humanities-based qualitative research project might involve several professors from different universities (or professionals from differing markets) sharing information in an on-line forum, where they collaborate with colleagues in other areas of study to gain alternative perspectives on a topic. Here are a few examples to get you started:

Scenario One—In the educational setting, professors who engage in Humanities research are often posing questions about common assumptions, uncovering new meanings in artistic works, or finding new ways to understand cultural interactions. This type of inquiry can produce clearer pictures of the past, uncover the many insights that we can draw from our past, and in turn, help us better to prepare for the future. Coursework in the Humanities classroom could might look like requesting students to interpret texts, films, artworks, music, language, cultural practices, etc.

Scenario Two—In the marketplace setting, professionals engaging in Humanities research might submit in-progress research to trade publications (like *Adweek*) or an on-line journal to solicit feedback from other professionals in the field. Other projects might require gathering original information by doing fieldwork—interviewing people, unearthing previous published artifacts or documenting the history behind archived data.

Let's delve into some of the most common research methods found in the Humanities: ethnography, narrative inquiry, textual/historical analysis, and survey research.

Quick Reference

The humanities are extremely broad—history, literature, music, religion, culture, etc.—it covers a lot of ground, as you've seen in this chapter. Make a few things stand out so that you can remember how to describe research in this discipline: (1) primary sources are key, and should ALWAYS be cited properly and read ethically, (2) the questions being asked in humanities research are of the utmost importance, and (3) the goal is understanding experience. Don't get caught up in the stereotypical idea of research only involving science and cancer cells and a laboratory . . . remember that inquiry in the humanities is uncovering the intellectual and the intangible.

—Kristen Hark

Ethnography

Ethnography is interpretive approach to research and meaning-making; the goal of ethnography is to discover what things mean and where meaning comes from, by observing human behavior and activity (Geertz, 1973). The method of ethnography comes from anthropology and sociology in which the researcher needs time and space to study communication, behavior, actions and habits of a people in a natural setting. Typically, ethnographers need to rely on unobtrusive methods to blend into the background, that they might observe and not participate.

Why is this the preferred (and necessary method) for ethnographic data collection? Because the central goal of ethnography is witnessing human behavior in naturally occurring interactions and situations. Thus, the researcher should not directly participate or influence the setting, but rather be outside the research and within. For example, a professor doing ethnographic research regarding student and classroom interaction might sit quietly in the back of the classroom, observing the students as they first enter the room, watching as they choose their seat, and listen as they begin those slightly awkward first-day-of-class conversations with each other. By making herself or himself part of the classroom setting, the ethnographic researcher blends in.

A guiding principle of ethnography is discovering the behaviors of those people being studied, NOT inserting the bias or perception of the researcher onto those being studied. This can make ethnographic research difficulty, as ethnographers are *trying* not to impose their own perceptions and meanings on TV activities or behaviors of others. Note the word 'trying' here; it is impossible to be unbiased and even the best researchers bring assumptions and previous experience into their own research.

If meaning-making and observation are the hallmarks of ethnographic research, we cannot forget that the true aim is understanding meaning attached to communication and behavior. This implies then, that the researcher needs to do more than simply record fact, or data. Clifford Geertz, one of the most influential ethnographers to date, relied on what he termed 'thick description' (1973, 1983). This means that the researcher must know enough about the setting and subjects and the background to shed interpretative light on those communicative aspects and behaviors, rather than recording shallow descriptions of activities. The researcher is reaching for an in-depth understanding of a people they do not belong to; thus, it is through a delicate balance of interaction and observation with the perspectives of other cultures that enables the ethnographic researcher make meaning and attach significance to the activities being studied.

*Social Constructionist Paradigm

Characteristics of Research Under the Social Constructionist Paradigm

While all qualitative research—including research from the social science paradigm—leans toward an interpretive metatheoretical perspective and builds on some amount of a social constructionist belief system, research under the social constructionist paradigm takes the theoretical concept of social constructionism even farther. Qualitative researchers under the social constructionist paradigm specifically study how ideas, realities, and experiences are socially constructed; they recognize that their own presence in a field site in itself socially constructs its own reality; and they see their writing and reporting as itself a social construction.

Therefore, scholarship in this paradigm tends toward the critical and the narrative. **Critical scholars** (feminist, gender, LGBTQ, queer, critical, and cultural scholars) examine how power is constructed. Narrative ethnographers and **narrative scholars** look at how our personal and cultural narratives construct ideas, identities, and experiences. **Autoethnographers** study how their own personal experiences are constructed. Scholars taking a social constructionist stance toward research tend to conduct research that addresses questions about what ideas are being socially constructed; how they are being socially constructed; and what the cultural and communication systems are that construct meaning.

critical scholars
Feminist, gender, LGBTQ, queer, critical and cultural scholars, who examine how power and control are constructed through communication.

narrative scholars
Scholars who study how our personal and cultural narratives construct ideas, identities, and experiences

autoethnographers
Scholars who study how their own personal experiences are constructed through communication and interaction interpersonally and culturally.

Autoethnography and Personal Narratives

While the term itself was introduced several decades earlier, Ellis and Bochner (2000) are known for the development of **autoethnography** in the 1990s (Adams, Ellis, & Holman Jones, 2017). Recall that ethnography is the study of a culture; autoethnography is a type of ethnography in which you are an integral part of the culture you're studying. Autoethnography is to ethnography what autobiography is to biography. Autoethnographers use their own personal experiences to reflect upon, distinguish, and question cultural practices. It's a merging of the personal and the cultural (Adams, Ellis, & Holman Jones, 2017). While more traditional ethnographical research allows the researcher to observe and understand a culture at a deep level but from a distance, autoethnography lets the researcher understand a culture even more deeply, because it is an understanding that derives from within the culture. Autoethnography is usually written in the first person voice ("I"), and Ellis and Bochner (2003) identify many different forms of autoethnographic writing, including short stories, poetry, fiction, novels, and fragmented and layered writing (p. 209). Since most autoethnographic writing involves some sort of narrative writing, scholars frequently use the term **"personal narrative"** to describe autoethnography.

personal narrative
A narrative form of autoethnographic writing.

Ellis and Bochner (2000) describe five forms of autoethnography:

1. Reflexive ethnographies that provide researchers an opportunity to critique the experiences of a particular cultural community.
2. Native ethnographies in which ethnographers reflect on their own membership in a historically marginalized or mysterious culture.
3. Complete-member-researcher/ethnographies where a member of a culture reports on that culture for outside interpretation.
4. Literary autoethnographies in which writer/researchers describe their culture to those unfamiliar with the culture.
5. Personal narratives that are critical autobiographical stories of experiences. They provide the audience an opportunity to access and interpret those experiences to make sense of society.

Appropriate Research Questions Answered by Autoethnography. The appropriate research questions for autoethnography are similar to those for ethnographic research: to understand cultural practices from within the experience itself. Adams, Ellis, and Holman Jones (2017) list several purposes of autoethnographic research:

hegemonic cultural practices
Practices that create and maintain the hidden power in a society.

marginalized and silenced voices
In a culture, people who—relative to people in positions of power and privilege—do not have agency or power to participate or be heard.

1. To speak against **hegemonic cultural practices**;
2. To explain a cultural phenomenon from the point of view of someone inside the experience;
3. To take a political position in favor of **marginalized and silenced voices**;
4. To offer rich description of everyday experiences;
5. To write and publish work that is accessible to a non-academic audience.

(Adams, Ellis, & Holman Jones, 2017).

Personal narratives can provide insight into historical events and social movements. For instance, the civil rights movement sparked interest in slave narratives. The second wave of the women's movement also produced interest in women's life stories and experiences, particularly as the silenced group.

The Role of Theory in Autoethnographic Research.

Autoethnographic projects usually begin with a personal transformative experience that the scholar wants to investigate and understand (Adams, Ellis, & Holman Jones, 2017). Thus, a project idea stems from an experience rather than a theory. Theory frequently is brought in during the analysis stage when the researcher begins to connect the personal to the cultural. Of course, autoethnographers frequently use the concept of **social constructionism** as a theoretical basis for their research overall.

Ethical Concerns Specific to Autoethnography.

The most important issue related to the ethics of autoethnography is that you cannot write about your own experiences without including other people who are involved in that experience or whose own experiences overlap with yours (Ellis, 1999; Tullis, 2013). As Tullis (2013) and many other people point out, these "others" in your research may include your family members or partners, friends, colleagues, community members, and strangers. Metta (2013) talks about "the permeable self" (p. 503), a concept that addresses the fact that my story necessarily overlaps with and changes through other people. Confounding this issue is that most autoethnographic accounts are written retrospectively, using techniques to facilitate memory recall. Thus, any informed consent given by a study participant would have to be given retrospectively, and many research ethicists consider retrospective consent to be coercive (Tullis, 2013). Tullis (2013) argues, however, that this viewpoint is unrealistic and overly restrictive, and instead suggests that consent be procured as early in the process as possible. While you may not be able to obtain consent before an event occurs, you should certainly obtain consent before writing about that event, and you should—if possible—offer people included in your writing an opportunity to read and comment on what you have written.

An issue related to the inclusion of other people in your personal narrative is that frequently, anonymity cannot be promised to people who are written about in your autoethnography (for instance, if I identify someone as my spouse, it is impossible to offer him/her anonymity). Instead, scholars suggest ensuring that what you write will not harm the people about whom you are writing, and that you should check in with your participants frequently to be sure they continue to be willing to be included—what Ellis (2009b) calls "process consent" (p. 310). In fact, researchers should maintain an open dialogue about ethical concerns throughout the course of an autoethnographic project (Ellis, 2007; Tullis, 2013). Sometimes, participants' identities can be disguised by changing names, de-identifying, fictionalizing, or merging characters, and that should be decided on in conversation with participants (Davis, 2010; Tullis, 2013). Other times, it might be desirable to co-write your narrative with one or more of your participants—in effect,

social constructionism A perspective suggesting that communication is the vehicle through which reality is understood, constituted, and represented, and it is through communication that beliefs and meanings are constructed and negotiated.

relational ethics
The responsibility of a researcher who has friends and partners about whom s/he writes, or study participants with whom s/he develops a relationship throughout the course of a research project.

voice
A concept related to personal and cultural agency and repetition, referring to cultural status, embodiment, and privilege.

representation
An ethical consideration of how the voice of another person in a research project is represented in an ethical and respectful manner.

co-constructed interviewing
An in-depth interviewing technique in which the interview is collaborative, dialogic, interactive, and open-ended.

interactive interviewing
A type of interviewing that involves multiple participants and researchers who share their stories and personal experiences with the goal of co-authoring an autoethnographic project.

turning the researcher hierarchy upside down and changing the role of study participants to co-researchers.

Since other people included in autoethnographic accounts are frequently people with whom you have a relationship, there is the issue of what Carolyn Ellis (2009b) calls "relational ethics" (pp. 308–309). **Relational ethics** refers to the responsibility you as a researcher might have to friends and partners about whom you write, or to study participants with whom you develop a relationship throughout the course of a research project. Maintaining a relationship with people about whom you are writing and with whom you are critiquing your writing requires finesse and courage and takes attending to the ongoing maintenance of mutual trust and respect between you and the people about whom you are writing (Adams, Holman Jones, & Ellis, 2013). Finally, autoethnographers should consider any harm that might befall themselves in disclosure of difficult, embarrassing, or vulnerable incidents. Not all stories should be shared (Tullis, 2013).

Another issue to consider in narrative ethnography is the question of **voice**—whose voice is being privileged in the telling of a story (Tullis, 2013). Researchers often take on an authoritative voice; that is, they interpret the narration, but that is frequently not the most ethical way to present another's voice or standpoint. Related to the issue of voice is the issue of **representation**—how can we represent the voice of another person in an ethical and respectful manner? It's important to remember that when I write about another person's experience, it is not a representation of his/her experience but it is my interpretation of that experience. This is why many researchers employ autoethnography, co-constructed ethnography, or reflexive ethnography—to include the other person's own voice in the co-construction of the interpretive narrative.

Sampling and Data Collection in Autoethnography.   Autoethnographers might write about mundane everyday experiences, or they might write about turning points, traumatic events, or significant times in their lives. Autoethnographers sample from their own personal experiences by writing field notes of events of their past relying on emotional recall (Ellis, 2009a) and journaling, and taking field notes and journaling about events as they are happening. Ellis (2009a) describes emotional recall in comparison with Strasberg's method acting:

> To give a convincing and authentic performance, the actor relives in detail a situation in which she or he previously felt the emotion to the enacted. I place myself back into situations, conjuring up details until I was immersed in the event emotionally (p. 108).

As far as a personal narrative might include other people, data collection might include reflexive types of interviewing. **Co-constructed interviewing** and **interactive interviewing** are two such types of interviewing. Co-constructed interviewing is an in-depth interviewing technique in which the interview is collaborative, dialogic, interactive, and open-ended. In a co-constructed interview, the lines between researcher and researched are blurred and both are seen more as equal conversational partners who share their mutual expertise, hold equivalent power and authority, open up to a constructive conversation, blur their roles, and consider the ethical responsibilities of their relationship. This type of interview is marked by the inclusion of voice among people whose voice may not have traditionally been highlighted or counted (Patti & Ellis, 2017). Interactive interviewing similarly involves multiple participants and researchers who share their stories and personal experiences with the goal of co-authoring an autoethnographic project. Because this type of interviewing by necessity involves sharing and vulnerability, participants have to be open to the process and have to trust that it will lead to deeper understanding and respect (Phillips, 2017).

Analysis in Autoethnography.   Sometimes the autoethnographic narrative is broken up thematically, and in those cases, more traditional thematic coding (as described in previous chapters) might be used. The final result might include sections of **grounded theory** or **thematic analysis** with supporting literature. The study might make claims based on the themes and narrative snippets or excerpts might be used to illustrate the claims. However, as we've stated, frequently the organization takes a more narrative or creative bent, and the analysis is more organic and understated. In these cases, the writing itself is evocative, written much as a creative writing work might be written, usually with the addition of some sort of cultural, critical, or analytical discussion woven into the text. Some forms of autoethnographic research seek to represent the data through narrative, description, or other arts-based forms. Sometimes these narratives, poems, or works of art are based on themes derived from coding the data as we've described above; other times, the narratives are organized chronologically or for aesthetic reasons, and no formal coding scheme is used.

grounded theory
A systematic approach to understanding and analyzing participants' lives.

Thematic analysis
A method of categorizing data into thematic categories.

Many autoethnographers talk about Laurel Richardson's (2000) concept of **writing as a method of inquiry**, in which they think about the meaning of what they're studying as they're writing. Thus, the analysis and writing stages might be one and the same. In the same vein, autoethnographers often speak of interpretation, rather than analysis. Chris Poulos explains the distinction:

writing as a method of inquiry
An approach to qualitative analysis in which the researcher thinks about the meaning of what s/he is studying as s/he is writing and thus the analysis and writing stages might be one and the same.

> *If you can buy into a kind of social constructionist's view of identity, then you can understand we're always engaging our world actively in a kind of ongoing co-construction project with our peers, then you can see that every story, everything that happened, is subject to some kind of interpretation. . . . My interpretive process comes down to, organic, I'm interpreting as I'm writing . . . I also have a sense of where I'm going . . . I have a sense of the direction I'm going in, but I don't quite know how it's going to end . . . I know when I get there, this is the end* (Davis, 2014, p. 254).

Carolyn Ellis sees analysis as creating a story that creates conversations with the reader, and with which others can relate (Davis, 2014). Since autoethnography is usually written as a narrative, the analysis happens as the writer creates narrative coherence. Buddy Goodall, in Davis (2014), describes the process:

> *It's in the writing itself where I'm actually sitting down at the computer and composing a story I actually come to understand what I'm writing about . . . For me it's very much connecting the dots. It's also a narrative trajectory I'm interested in . . . For me, it's very much a story I'm after. How should this be told?* (pp. 89-90).

dramatic or scenic method of writing
A creative, nonfiction method of writing that is often written as a series of scenes connected by a series of narrative summaries.

Narrative ethnography is typically written in the first person, in an evocative, active voice. One key characteristic of this type of research is the re-storying of the researcher's and/or participants' stories into a chronological narrative with plots, time, place, and scene (Creswell, Hanson, Clark, & Morales, 2007). Autoethnographic scholars frequently use a **dramatic or scenic method of writing**, or, what Caulley (2008) calls **creative nonfiction** writing. In this style of writing, you would actually show a scene of what happened rather than describe it or tell about it. This is more compelling reading. Usually written in present tense, this style of writing is more action-oriented. It's often written as a series of scenes connected by a series of narrative summaries. Depending on the research and on your style of writing, sometimes there will be more narrative summaries than scenes, and other times there will be more scenes than narrative summaries.

In research that involves other people, the narrative writing approach blends narratives from other participants' points of view with narratives from the researcher's own point of view. Researchers using the narrative approach also include autoethnographic narratives on their own personal reflections on issues raised in the course of doing the research. Good writing of this style is an evocative narrative, reminiscent of a novel, with characters, plot, action, and movement that uses plot and character development to illustrate themes.

thick description
An immersive writing technique in which researchers include rich details, vivid language, and specific quotes to connect culture, environment, behaviors, theory, and meaning.

When you write up qualitative research findings using a dramatic or scenic method, you want to use realistic details; concrete nouns with concrete adjectives that appeal to the senses (sight, sound, smell, taste, touch); words that imply emotion; conversations to convey emotion and to pull the reader into the story; and active verbs (he ate the cake) rather than passive verbs (the cake was eaten). Narrative writing involves the use of **thick description** (Geertz, 1973), which refers to an immersive writing technique in which researchers include rich details, vivid language, and specific quotes to connect culture, environment, behaviors, theory, and meaning. In this method, your writing should include thick description about details, contexts, emotions, relationships, feelings, history, voices, actions, and meanings. Adequately describe the research participants so your reader can actually see them. Use **reflexive writing**—include yourself and your biases, frames of reference, and personal connections to the topic in the writing. How can you write such detail? By capturing it in your field notes. Write detailed notes about the environment and context. You never know what details you might want to use later. Write detailed notes about dialogue, or—even better—record the dialogue so you can use it later. Open and close the writing with a narrative, the first narrative to set the stage and the second to conclude it (Caulley, 2008; Ponterotto & Grieger, 2007).

reflexive writing
Writing that includes the researcher and his/her biases, frames of reference, and personal connections to the topic in the writing.

Examples of Autoethnography.   Carolyn Ellis, among many other scholars, is known for writing narrative autoethnographies, studies which use narratives about her own life to make critical statements about the larger culture in which she is a part. For instance, in a piece called "Katrina and the Cat: Responding to Life's Expendables" (Ellis, 2007), she used a personal story of rescuing an injured cat to relate to the situation of poor people in New Orleans, Louisiana, in the aftermath of Hurricane Katrina. The story leads to the questions of whether she adequately cared for the cat and whether we as a society adequately care for people who need our help.

Using analysis of narratives, Davis (2008), in "Final Stories: The Ultimate Sensemaking Frame," analyzed stories told by her mother prior to her death, and Montalbano-Phelps (2003) conducted an analysis of narratives of domestic violence survivors, identifying several major themes within those narratives. Using narrative ethnography in "A Family Jigsaw Puzzle: Secrets and Gaps," Davis (2009) used a narrative approach to tell a story of secrets within her family of origin. Davis (2010, pp. 75–76), for example, wrote her hospice ethnography as a narrative. The sample below gives you an example of rich, detailed narrative writing (Davis, 2010, p. 2).

2   *Chapter One*

her husband, John, died 15 years earlier. She doesn't like being in the hospital, not one bit. It brings back too many unhappy memories. Since John's death, she has tried to remain optimistic and upbeat, especially in front of her daughter, Katherine. But today she has a bad feeling. They're doing a biopsy to check out some pain she has been having. "Just a routine precaution," the doctor said. But she has a bad feeling. A really bad feeling.

"Hey, honey, what do you say we get out of here and you take me over to the mall?" Marian asks the aide who's wheeling her out of her hospital room down the hall toward the operating room.

He laughs loudly and repeats her question. "Take you to the mall!" He laughs again as he continues pushing her. She can feel her pulse quickening, her breaths becoming shallower. The blanket covering her is soft, and she feels its weight as she shivers underneath it. Cold, she feels cold, down to her bones. The cold comes from deep within her and mingles with her fear as it spreads from her toes to her stomach to her throat. They're moving quickly, and Marian looks up at the ceiling tiles as they float by. White square after white square. Row after row of tiles in a white checkerboard pattern. White checkerboard merges into the tops of white walls. People walking by are a blur of flesh-colored faces above white jackets. White. White everywhere.

"Here you are," the aide says, as he parks the stretcher in what looks like a small empty cubicle. "This is a holding room. You're going to wait here until they're ready for you." He pauses at the edge of her sight. "Good luck."

She looks around. More white tiles, more white walls on each side of her. A gray curtain, pulled back, on the wall in front of her feet. Beyond, she can see what looks like a nurse's station. The nurses' desk area is light gray, the lights are dim, and the room is empty. It looks brand new, clean, with no evidence of a person anywhere. No papers, no clutter, no coffee cups. She is in here alone, and it feels like a ghost town.

Marian takes a deep breath and closes her eyes.

Critical and Feminist Ethnography

Critical ethnography, as with all critical methodologies, is the study of power and control. Critical ethnographers, like all other ethnographers, view positivist objectivity as a myth, and acknowledge their own biased viewpoints and backgrounds inherent in their research. Critical ethnography is often an action-oriented method in which participants see the possibility of their participation resulting in changes to social problems. **Critical scholarship**

critical scholarship
A lens through which to view a research topic in order to question issues of oppression, social justice, and power—most specifically, how power is constructed and reified through cultural communication and social systems.

overlaps with other methods, in that it is a lens through which to view a research topic much more than a method in and of itself. Critical scholars may use, for instance, ethnographic or autoethnographic methods, rhetorical methods, or performative methods with the distinction that their research question, study design, analysis, and writing look at issues of oppression, social justice, and power—most specifically, how power is constructed and reified through cultural communication and social systems. Critical ethnographers and autoethnographers examine their experiences from the viewpoints of everyday life within social contexts such as stigma and privilege (Boylorn & Orbe, 2014). Critical scholars are engaged scholars, which means they have as their scholarly goal to gain social impact and facilitate social change through the study of symbolic and material discourse (Harter, Dutta, & Cole, 2009).

Appropriate Research Questions Answered by Critical Ethnography.

Critical ethnography is the practice of ethnography for the purpose of exposing and critiquing cultural intersections of power (Foley & Valenzuela, 2007; McDonald, 2017) such as race, class, gender, ethnicity, sexual identity, and dis/abilty identity (Meade, 2017), and position such as nationality, age, or spirituality (Boylorn & Orbe, 2014). Critical scholarship studies taken-for-granted social structures and symbols and dominant discourses to understand how power in a society is constructed. As critical scholars, feminist scholars, for example, look at how conceptions of gender are constructed through discourse, language, communication (verbal and nonverbal), messages, or texts. Feminist scholars critique the ways in which cultural discourses privilege gender and voice and call attention to the significance of women's ways of knowing (Breede, 2017).

How Critical Ethnography Uses/Incorporates Theory.

Critical scholarship utilizes critical traditions such as neo-Marxism, cultural studies, postmodernism, and poststructuralism, and refers to critical theorists such as philosopher Karl Marx, feminist and gender theorist Judith Butler, philosopher Michel Foucault, critical theorist Walter Benjamin, and philosopher Jacques Derrida, among too many others to name, as a framework for their research—foundational theories through which to design their study, and as explanatory theories to analyze their findings. Much feminist scholarship, for instance, commences from: "both a Foucauldian and postmodern feminist sense of power and resistance, sex and gender, agency, and passivity. Foucault's unique contribution was to question how discourses and associated practices came to be accepted as true or legitimate, and how these normalized discourses become objects for thought, to reimagine power as a productive force and to question the normalizing, long established, and societal practices associated with bias and the development of an ethic of the self (Foucault, 1972; 1973; 1995; Motion & Leitch, 2007). "Foucault's work was especially important in understanding power as it is experienced and conveyed in everyday practices and discourses, and a Foucauldian perspective examines the biopolitics that use the body as a field for power, control, and discipline (Deveaux, 1994; Foucault, 1972; 1973; 1995)" (Davis, 2014, p. 105).

Ethical Concerns Specific to Critical Ethnography. Critical scholarship is itself an ethical response to cultural and ideological positions that exploit, marginalize, and privilege certain groups and categories of people. Thus, critical scholars specifically attend to issues of **representation** and **voice** (who has the power to represent another's voice), **embodied practice** (the idea that the researcher's personal and bodily experiences are essential to understanding the culture under study), **collaboration** (research participants are co-researchers with equivalent power to the researcher), and the power positionality between the researcher and the research participants (Meade, 2017).

> **embodied practice**
> The idea that the researcher's personal and bodily experiences are essential to understanding the culture under study.

Data Collection in Critical Ethnography. Today's critical ethnographers utilize qualitative methods such as ethnography, autoethnography, arts-based research, and related methods that give them access to the understanding of voice and privilege (Breede, 2017b; Farmer & Chevrette, 2017). Critical ethnography is frequently characterized by conversational, informal interviewing; collaborating with participants; reader-friendly writing; and offering participants the opportunity to edit or give feedback on transcriptions and findings (Foley & Valenzuela, 2007).

Analysis and Writing in Critical Ethnography. Critical ethnographers write and analyze their findings with an eye for examining marginalization, resistance, and social justice. Critical scholars specifically look at the social construction of power dynamics in cultural discourse. Critical scholars frequently employ Derrida's framework of deconstruction in which they critique the hidden meanings in social discourse, cultural practices, and social structures (McDonald, 2017). Queer scholarship, for instance, critiques construction of identity; deconstructs the way language creates and reifies gender, sexual, and ethnic binaries; and questions the discursive nature of our bodily identities (Adams & Holman Jones, 2017).

Critical scholarship frequently entails co-creation of texts with participants and sometimes involves political activism activities (Meade, 2017). Critical scholarship advocates for social change (Adams & Holman Jones, 2017; Breede, 2017b; McDonald, 2017). Reporting of critical methods frequently utilizes non-traditional formats that legitimate alternative voices and forms. For example, critical autoethnography is typically written in an evocative narrative format that might or might not implicitly invoke overt analysis (Boylorn & Orbe, 2014), and other critical scholarship is frequently written in arts-based or performative formats to privilege oral forms of knowing and understanding.

Examples of Critical and Feminist Ethnography. Winkle-Wagner (2008) conducted a critical ethnography to study the way black undergraduate college women negotiated identity as they navigated issues of feminism, race, and gender. She used ethnographic methods to look at how these women constructed strength, assertiveness, and empowerment at a predominantly white college.

Generally, Foucauldian feminist scholarship (see Trethewey, 1999, for example) explores women's gendered embodiment of self within social, personal, and professional identities. Other feminist scholars, for example, see women's issues, such as anorexia, as a function of gendered discourse and power (see Moulding, 2006; Whitehead & Kurz, 2008). Feminist scholars use many methods to study these issues, including ethnography, autoethnography, and phenomenology. Trethewey, for example, used in-depth interviews to look at the ways women "discipline their bodies" as they adorn, carry, and size their bodies in socially acceptable ways.

Digital and Online Ethnography

digital ethnography
A type of ethnography used to investigate communication in digitized spaces.

A discussion of ethnographic methods would not be complete without including the rapidly growing interest in digital and online methods of ethnography. **Digital ethnography** is a method used to investigate communication in digitized spaces. Digital ethnography involves ethnography of an online or computer-mediated field site, such as a virtual space, chat room, blog, discussion forum, online gaming, or social media site, among many, many others (Kaur & Dutta, 2017).

Appropriate Research Questions for Digital Ethnography. In many ways, digital ethnographic methods are similar to those for ethnographic research in face-to-face sites. The research question, as with other ethnographic research, would be to seek to understand communication in that site. In digital ethnography, the online space is viewed as a culture within which to study social and interpersonal interactions (Kaur & Dutta, 2017). Since the researcher would typically be participating in the digital space, digital ethnography would appropriately be autoethnography or at least reflexive ethnography in many instances (Gatson, 2011).

Ethical Considerations for Digital Ethnography. The issue of public versus private space is an ethical consideration in digital ethnography. Having access to a site does not insure that site is a public space. Many of the interactions occurring in a site may be considered private and may therefore require informed consent, which may be difficult to obtain in a space in which participants' identities are anonymous. Revealing private information without consent from online sources may cross legal as well as ethical boundaries. At the least, in most cases, you should inform the online group that you are conducting research before beginning to collect data (Kaur & Dutta, 2017). Gatson (2011) points out that "the site of the online ethnography necessarily pushes the definitional boundaries of generally accepted concepts such as self, community, privacy, and text" (p. 515).

Digital ethnography involves types of data collection which should be considered private but may not obviously be so. For instance, reading online content may not feel as if you are crossing ethical boundaries, but in this type of environment it would probably be considered participant observation, and if the person posting that content had a reasonable expectation of privacy, you should obtain informed consent before using it (Gatson, 2011). Many scholars consider that if a site requires membership or passwords to access, it is considered private and informed consent must be obtained. Even in more public sites, anonymity and confidentiality must be assured before inclusion of materials, and informed consent may be required if the researcher's participation would influence or connect with other group members.

Data Collection in Digital Ethnography.

Depending on the site specifics, data collection would most likely include participant observation, but may also include interviews, focus groups, and archival research. Participant observation in digital ethnography would likely include visits to chatrooms, discussion groups, or virtual reality sites, and would involve immersion in the digital sites through visiting the sites, participating in the site activity, and writing about the experience.

Data collection in digital ethnography has its own set of challenges. Determining the boundaries of an online site may be problematic (Gatson, 2011). The anonymity of digital sites and the enactment of multiple identities must be taken into account in terms of how they interact with the discourse under study (Kaur & Dutta, 2017). As participants in the online community of study, researchers also should be reflexive about the power differentials between community members and the loss of control once posts are submitted (Gatson, 2011).

Examples of Digital Ethnography.

Kozinets (2002) discusses the use of "netnography" (p. 61), or online ethnography, for marketing research purposes. As we mentioned, ethnography of online or digital spaces has many of the same methodological considerations as face-to-face ethnographic methods. Marketing research netnography studies online communities such as message boards, Web pages, and chat rooms, for the purpose of understanding "an unprecedented level of access to the heretofore unobservable behaviors of interacting consumers" (Kozinets, 2002, p. 63). Kozinets suggests a less involved and more unobtrusive observation method than participation; he suggests lurking to simply observe (and code and analyze) online texts and messages. Kozinets gives as an example a netnography of an online community related to coffee consumption. Researchers used this method to understand the culture of coffee drinkers, their motivations for making coffee decisions, brand perceptions and preferences, and details about the practical aspects of their consumption.

Kozinets also raises the same ethical issues mentioned earlier, about the ambiguous distinctions between private and public spaces in online communities; he recommends disclosure and insuring confidentiality and anonymity to address ethics concerns.*

Narrative Inquiry

The design of narrative inquiry revolves around story-telling (Riessman, 2008), in which a researcher asks an individual, or group of individuals, to provide stories about their lives and experiences. The idea of narrative research gained traction from Walter Fisher's narrative paradigm (1984, 1987) that stated human beings are, by nature, story-telling animals and that as such, we learn to evaluate society and the behavior required for certain situations and settings by listening to those stories, rather than a reading or be trained from a manual for 'learning how to socialize'.

In narrative research, the events of the person's life are recaptured in story form, generally in a chronological format, and as that story is retold, it can often end up taking on the researcher's views and paradigms as well. This upholds the idea of reciprocity in storytelling, that the teller of the story has the potential to enter into the story and influence the listener, just as the listener is understanding and entering that story as well. The power of story doesn't only reside in who the story comes from, but who tells it and who hears it. This is a great example for rediscovery or reinterpretation within research; as Solomon said, "there is nothing new under the sun." (Ecclesiastes 1:9)

Textual Analysis

Textual analysis applies to any written or recorded message (Frey et al., 2002). And because of that immense, widely sweeping definition, textual analysis houses numerous types of critical research approaches. The three we will take a brief look at in this chapter are: historical criticism, rhetorical criticism, and content analysis.

Textual analysis, as a whole, seeks to uncover content of messaging, but evaluate the structure, or nature of messages as well. This means you could study how Shonda Rhimes' depicts masculinity and femininity in her television characters, or the power dynamics of those same character roles. You could choose a non-profit in your hometown and breakdown the strategies of persuasion to specific audiences or neighborhoods in your area.

NOTE: Remember that 'criticism', in the realm of research, isn't someone ripping on your choice of football team, but is rather a system of critique, of analyzing and evaluating. Solid critique requires an understanding of what the researcher is looking at and for. We have all been critiqued by someone who didn't know enough about the subject, and so you found yourself unable to heed their advice (i.e., parents ☺). On the other hand, you recognize that your coach for long jump in track & field has great critique for your form, and you listen. What's the difference? You recognize the knowledge and expertise of the coach. (if only it were that easy for your parents ☹).

The track example might fall flat, but I say all of that so that you might understand what you *must* do to use criticism in the right way—you'll need to work and research to comprehend and appreciate all that surrounds your subject of study. If I choose to critique a work of literature, but have no idea what was happening historically at that period of time, or even more specifically, happening in the life of the author, I miss a great deal; thus, because my research was insufficient, my critical interpretation is shallower than it should be.

*Narratives and Rhetorical Criticism

Walter Fisher (1984) dubbed our species as *Homo narrans*: that is, he defines storytelling as essential to our human nature. There is much evidence to support Fisher's view, as storytelling is indeed central to our shared human experience. We certainly use stories extensively. We use them to connect with one another. When old friends get together after being separated for a few years, they reestablish their relationship by retelling old stories about their shared past, and bring one another up to date by sharing new stories regarding what they have done since last they last met. When couples begin their relationships they use stories to get to know and bond with one another.

We also use stories to entertain ourselves and others. We enjoy telling jokes, reading novels, attending plays, viewing films and television shows, and playing video games that have a narrative structure. In addition, we use stories to advance arguments. Prosecutors tell stories intended to convince judges and juries to convict defendants, while defense lawyers use stories in the hopes of gaining an acquittal for their clients. Politicians rely upon stories to garner votes. And, we use stories to make sense of the world we inhabit and to define our place within it. The Judeo-Christian Bible, Islamic Koran, Hindu Mahabharata, and other sacred texts use narratives to offer religious adherents answers to some of life's most profound questions. Clearly, stories play a significant role in our personal and collective lives, and for that reason they are texts worthy of serious and sustained rhetorical analysis.

As a means of judging stories themselves, and in making judgments based upon them, Fisher (1984) proposes his **narrative paradigm**, which examines stories in terms of their **coherence** and fidelity. A narrative that is coherent is consistent, has characters that behave believably, and lacks puzzling gaps,

narrative paradigm
Proposed by Fisher (1984), the criteria by which to examine stories in terms of their coherence and fidelity.

narrative coherence
A narrative that is coherent is consistent, has characters that behave believably, and lacks puzzling gaps, perplexing contradictions, and gross exaggerations.

narrative fidelity
The extent to which a story rings true in confirming and conforming to our own values, beliefs, and lived experience.

perplexing contradictions, and gross exaggerations. **Narrative fidelity** is judged by the extent to which a story rings true in confirming and conforming to our own values, beliefs, and lived experience. The story might indeed be true, and it might not. As is often the case, we cannot independently verify the veracity of story via video or eyewitness testimony. But we can reject as true stories that lack fidelity.

Whether knowingly or not, television's popular Judge Judy evaluates the claims of litigants who appear on her show using criteria outlined by Fisher. In rendering her judgements, she takes into account the coherence of the stories they tell and their fidelity to probable truth. So too do police officers when interrogating suspects. And so do we in our day-to-day encounters with one another. Fisher's narrative paradigm has not proven to be particularly heuristic; that is, it hasn't inspired much original research that makes use of its theoretical lens. However, it has practical and pedagogical value, as Melissa Hobart (2013) demonstrates in a classroom exercise she developed in which she has students use Fisher's criteria for determining narrative probability to assess dubious Internet warnings, urban legends, and other suspicious stories; and in doing so, she also teaches her students the practical value of being rhetorically literate.

mythical analysis
Rhetorical analysis of myths, narratives that may or may not be literally true in terms of the details of their storylines, but which convey deeper truths about the human condition and which conserve and pass on traditional wisdom.

the hero's journey
A narrative formula described by Fisher which is characterized by a hero, a call to adventure, a supernatural gift or wise mentor, dangers and trials, and ultimate transformation.

Fisher's narrative paradigm is not the only rhetorical means of examining stories. **Mythical analysis** is another method used by rhetorical critics. Myths are narratives that may or may not be literally true in terms of the details of their storylines, but which convey deeper truths about the human condition. In doing so, myths are cultural treasures that conserve and pass on traditional wisdom. One influential method of mythic rhetorical criticism is offered by Joseph Campbell (1904–1987). Drawing upon the work of Swiss psychologist Carl Jung, Campbell (1949) identified a popular narrative monomyth that informs stories both old and new from diverse cultures across time and throughout the world. Central to this narrative pattern is a formula, which he calls **the hero's journey**, found in stories ranging from traditional fairytales and folktales from the past to popular series of Harry Potter books and films. George Lucas famously patterned the first three films of his Star Wars epic after this mythic formula.

A simplified version of the elaborated hero's journey that Campbell (1949), first outlined in *The Hero with a Thousand Faces*, begins with a call to adventure, in which a hero is summoned from the mundane world in which he or she lives and charged with accomplishing an impossible mission that involves a difficult journey. To accomplish the task, the hero is given aid in the form of supernatural gifts and/or a wise mentor. Additional help and helpers may appear later. Along the course of the journey the hero faces dangers and encounters trials, but eventually manages to accomplish the mission, after which he or she returns home transformed by the adventure. Many academic studies and popular reviews make use of Campbell's hero's journey. Wilson Koh (2009), for example, points out how that mythic pattern shaped the plot and contributed to the commercial success of the 2002 film *Spider-Man*.

Another and more distinctively American approach to mythic criticism is that of the **American monomyth** described by John Shelton Lawrence and Robert Jewett (2002), which adheres to the following formula:

> *A community in a harmonious paradise is threatened by evil; normal institutions fail to contend with this threat; a selfless superhero emerges to renounce temptations and carry out the redemptive task; aided by fate, his decisive victory restores the community to its paradisiacal condition; the superhero then recedes into obscurity. (p. 6)*

Although there are notable exceptions, the American monomyth typically celebrates lone male heroes. It what has become something of a cliché, at the end of Western films that adhere to this mythic pattern the hero "rides off," as does Alan Ladd in *Shane*, John Wayne in *True Grit*, and Clint Eastwood in the "Man with No Name" Western Trilogy. Like the hero's journey, the American monomyth has informed much rhetorical criticism. According to Mark Poindexter, (2008) the ABC documentary *The Path to 9/11* derives much of its emotional power from tapping into the American monomyth. As a contrast to the masculine radical individualism of the conventional American monomyth, Maureen Murdock (1990) points to a narrative that she refers to as **the heroine's journey**. Females who undertake a heroine's journey do so in collaboration with others. Buffy the Vampire Slayer and Xena the Warrior Queen are examples of popular culture heroines whose heroic quests are collaborative adventures.*

the American monomyth
A narrative formula described by Fisher which is characterized by celebration of lone male heroes.

the heroine's journey
A narrative formula which is characterized by females who undertake a heroine's journey in collaboration with others.

Content Analysis

Perhaps the most widely used method of criticism under textual analysis, is Content Analysis. Content analysis seeks to identify content and then categorize that content according to the purpose of the research study. There must be explicit rules (or coding) for dividing and categorizing the content to be studied, ambiguity is of no help here. To analyze an entire Harry Potter novel might prove to arduous a task, but to select how many times certain people speak or how often a certain pattern occurs, makes *The Goble of Fire* much more manageable.

The unit of content set aside to analyze could be specific words or phrases, themes, paragraphs or sentences, television programs, or certain scenes. This is why content analysis is so widely used—you could analyze the content of any message to which you have access. But remember, you have to have a research goal. . . what are you adding to the field by doing this content analysis?

To recap, content analysis has three main objectives: (1) to describe the characteristics of the content itself; (2) to make valid arguments based on the content and producers of the content; and (3) to interpret the content in order to reveal something about the nature of the audience (Berelson, 1952).

Note: Because content analysis requires a systematic method of identifying a unit of analysis and then measuring those units, it can at times fall under quantitative methods.

Historical Criticism

The method of historical criticism involves reconstructing the past, systematically and objectively, by collecting evidence and data, evaluating it, verifying it and assessing it so that informed conclusions can be reached (Soulen & Soulen, 2001; Frampton, 2006). Benedict Spinoza (1632–1677) is credited with the creation of this approach, to literary forms (most notably the Bible). Though historical criticism deals with the past, it doesn't stop with a description of what has been, but moves forward to suggest (based on careful research) serveral things: (1) why things happened as they did, (2) how comparison to similar events might help bring forth new understanding and (3) a type of value judgment (right/wrong, good/bad, effective/ineffective).

Rhetorical Criticism

The word rhetoric refers to persuasive communication; you might think of it as persuasion or argumentation, speech that affects decision-making and choice making. Frey et al. (2002) refer to rhetorical criticism as "a systematic method for describing, analyzing, interpreting, and evaluating the persuasive force of messages." So, if you, the researcher, are employing the method of rhetorical criticism, you might choose a series of television commercials for a certain company and compare those TV commercials to the same company's series of YouTube ads. Not only would you describe each, but then you would analyze and interpret the content on the ability of each to persuade their target audience.

rhetorical criticism
The study of the ways that written or spoken language (such as speeches, books, images, performances, texts, and films), in their historical and cultural context, work—to persuade, instruct, inform, entertain, arouse, engage, and convince.

texts
Any communicative message, such as an advertisement, book, film, speech, etc.

*Characteristics of Rhetorical Criticism

As a method of communication inquiry, **rhetorical criticism** focuses upon a wide variety of **texts**. These texts may be oral messages delivered by speakers in real time to live audiences, such as lectures, sermons, and political speeches. Often, rhetorical critics rely upon print and recorded versions that preserve such oral presentations after they have been delivered. Written texts also attract the attention of rhetorical critics. These include novels, poems, short stories, and all manner of fictional and nonfictional literature. In addition, the scope of rhetorical inquiry encompasses texts disseminated via the mass and social media, including advertisements, blogs, comic books, films, magazines, musical recordings, podcasts, radio talk shows, television series, videogames, websites, etc. Rhetorical critics also look at texts collected via ethnographic methods, such as the stories

*From *Straight Talk About Communication Research Methods*, Third Edition by Christine S. Davis and Kenneth A. Lachlan. Copyright © 2017 by Kendall Hunt Publishing Company. Reprinted by permission.

workers share with one another within an organization. Put simply, rhetorical critics engage a wide and diverse range of texts.

In examining texts, rhetorical criticism focuses primarily upon the message within the communication process. This is not to say, however, that such criticism ignores those who send or receive messages. They too are important but are typically treated as secondary considerations viewed primarily in relation to the shared texts they create and consume. There are some good reasons why rhetorical critics prefer to focus upon texts rather than those who produce them or the audiences to which they are directed.

One reason is that neither senders nor receivers are fully aware of the full range of rhetorical methods embedded within and informing their mutual communication, and consequently they are not able to articulate how or why they manage to influence others or be influenced. Of course, if communicators could do so there would be no purpose in producing rhetorical criticism, which would then only serve to point out the obvious. Another reason texts are privileged by rhetorical critics can be inferred from the kind of texts they traditionally study, which are typically fixed in some way like books or films. These can be more easily shared and studied by critics than such ephemeral phenomena as casual conversations. The emerging social media might serve to expand the range of texts rhetorical critics examine.

Appropriate Research Questions Answered by Rhetorical Criticism

Rhetorical criticism involves close readings of texts. These readings look beneath the surface and beyond the obvious. The goal is to obtain a deeper understanding of the text, or some important aspect of it, than one gains from a merely superficial reading; and to tie that understanding to broader practical and theoretical concerns. In examining texts, rhetorical criticism traditionally seeks to answer questions regarding influence. How is such influence exercised explicitly and implicitly? Who does that influence affect? Who benefits and who does not? And how: culturally, economically, politically, and socially? What do texts reveal and what do they conceal? How? And why?

Data in Rhetorical Criticism

The texts rhetorical critics examine are not data per se, but rather the sources from which data are drawn for analysis. Such data include narrative threads, quotations culled from dialogue, descriptions (from written and oral texts), depictions (from visual texts), and other words and images. The principal sources from which rhetorical data are derived are the **primary texts** that critics examine, the very texts listed in the first

primary texts
The principal sources from which rhetorical data that critics examine are derived.

secondary texts
Separate texts that comment upon and refer back to a primary text.

extra text
Texts made possible by contemporary technology that accompany and are sometimes embedded within primary texts, such as the extra features included in many DVDs and videogames: alternate endings, deleted scenes, promotional material, voice-over commentary, interviews with the creative team, Easter eggs (hidden features), etc.

critique
Critical analysis which is guided by rhetorical theory, which provides critics with a lens through which to view the texts they are examining.

paragraph of this section. Another important source of data is what John Fiske (1987) refers to as **secondary texts**. These are separate texts that comment upon and refer back to a primary text. For example, a rhetorical critic examining the 2012 film *The Avengers* might also look at reviews of the film or interviews with the film's creative team (its actors, director, producer, and writer) broadcast on radio or television or published in newspapers, magazines, and online websites. The rhetorical critic might also pay attention to materials that Robert Alan Brookey and Robert Westerfelhaus (2002) call **extra text**. These are texts made possible by contemporary technology that accompany and are sometimes embedded within primary texts, such as the extra features included in many DVDs and videogames: alternate endings, deleted scenes, promotional material, voice-over commentary, interviews with the creative team, Easter eggs (hidden features), etc.

In examining primary and secondary texts the goal of rhetorical criticism is not to be blandly descriptive, but rather to offer new insights regarding the text made possible through systematic analysis. Such critical analysis, also referred to as **critique**, is guided by rhetorical theory, which provides critics with a lens through which to view the texts they are examining. Theory suggests what texts to examine, which textual features should be looked at, and how best to interpret them. Several major rhetorical theories and their approaches to criticism are featured later in this section.

So What?

This chapter has briefly surveyed a few methods of research within the Humanities, and as such, focus on a humanistic approach to inquiry. Qualitative research approaches can be described as focusing on exploring meaning-making, by asking questions, interpreting the answers to those questions, asking emergent questions as follow-up.

In the Humanities, the interpretation of meaning is the central concern. Individual meaning is of the utmost importance, as is understanding the complexity of the situation or period of history being studied. The subjectivity of meaning is not a drawback in the disciplines of the Humanities; meaning is subjected to the individual, the researcher, the social processes and habits of both and the goal is better and richer understanding.

References

Fisher, W. (1984). Narration as a human communication paradigm: The case of public moral argument. *Communication Monographs, 51, pp. 1–22.*

Fisher, W. (1987). Human Communication as narration: toward a philosophy of reason, value and action. Columbia, SC: University of SC Press.

Geertz, C. (1973). The interpretation of cultures. NY: Basic Books.

Geertz, C. (1983). Local knowledge: further essays in interpretive anthropology. NY: Basic Books.

Frampton, Travis (2007). Spinoza and the Rise of Historical Criticism of the Bible. T&T Clark International. ISBN: 9780567375117

Soulen, Richard N. and Kendall R. Soulen (2001). Handbook of biblical criticism (3rd ed., rev. and expanded. ed.). Louisville, KY: Westminster. John Knox Press. ISBN 0-664-22314-1

Frey, L.R., Botan, C.H., & Kreps, G.L. (2002). Investigating communication : an introduction to research methods (2nd ed.). Boston: Allyn & Bacon. (pg.229 for quote)

Berelson, B. (1952). Content Analysis in Communication research. NYC: Free Press. (p18 for quote).

Riessman, C.K. (2008). Narrative methods for the human sciences. Thousand Oaks, CA: Sage.

CHAPTER 7

The Creative Arts: A Survey of Approaches

This chapter addresses research paradigms and methods most applicable to research inquiry in the creative arts, with an emphasis on the creative process and project development.

Upon successful completion of this chapter, you will be able to:

- Recognize current and missing elements or gaps in the creative arts field, based on creative works review.
- Know the distinctions between design process, content analysis, and mixed methods.
- Begin asking accurate, research-based questions within the field of creative arts.

Introduction

It's important to understand that research and the research process differs according to discipline; it's simply the nature of the beast. And, of course, the **results** of research vary. It may be even more important, however, to understand that these differences do not constitute one discipline being "better" or "worse" at research and the research process. These differences mean that you will need to expand your understanding of what it means to research. As you work through your education, you will be engaged in research—from finding the right topic for a class paper to understanding and arguing well your stance in debate—you WILL be sifting through what's been done before and deciding if the previous work is helpful to you. Creative Arts research is no different.

A significant part of Creative Arts research is the **process**. Often, research seems to center around results, but any researcher worth their salt understands that it is the process that brings results. In the Creative Arts, the result of research might be a book cover, a screen play, vector imaging, a painted canvas, a photography exhibit, live edge furniture . . . the list goes on and on. But this chapter wants you to focus on the process. The steps to how and why are of the utmost importance. Don't stop asking those two questions.

For instance, in graphic design, as a professional, creative work is often produced for clients. And understanding the process of the designer goes both ways. The client chooses the designer and the designer owns what kind of work they do. In wedding or event photography, a client chooses a photographer (a competitive and highly selective process that includes considerations of quality and competence). Consequently, the photographer doesn't offer to be all things to all people . . . when the photographer has her/his own design practice, showcases of previous work indicates the kind of photography, the quality of the work done, and the process used to produce the work.

This is why artists have a favorite medium, one that is their specialty, that they're KNOWN for. Think of architects, like Frank Lloyd Wright, whose buildings showcase certain features, so that people recognize a Wright building . . . those right angles? They're one of Wright's signatures. Have you ever thought about what is meant by "signature style?" If not, now you are. Let's dig into the process. As Eric Thomas says, "fall in love with the process, and the results will come."

Quick Reference

When you think creative arts, think music, think sculpture, think graphic design, theatre, photography, etc. While these areas vary, the research process is extremely similar: analysis of the artifact or area, discussion, design ideation, developing the concept, creating a prototype or sample, and then actual implementation and delivery. Let me use Bob Ross as an example. (If you haven't ever watched Bob Ross paint, I suggest you stream immediately and watch him paint 'happy trees'. Trust me, you'll see the whole process.) Here the process is laid out, but it's not quantifiable, it's all about the PROCESS—the most important consideration in Creative Arts research.

There are great examples of creative arts research everywhere—look into musicology, ethnomusicology, visual rhetoric, compositional analysis, etc. What interests you? What artist interests you? See if you can find out their creative process!

—Kristen Hark

Aiga's Designing Framework

Designing Framework, developed by AIGA (the American Institute of Graphic Arts) may also prove a useful model, either for those seeking creative structure or for those seeking to define the power of design. Created by AIGA to increase the understanding of design, this model showcases design

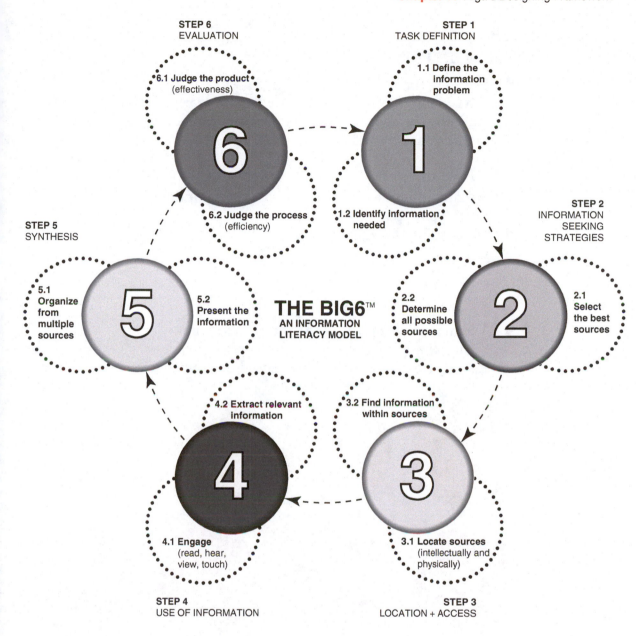

STEP 6
EVALUATION

STEP 1
TASK DEFINITION

6.1 Judge the product (effectiveness)

1.1 Define the information problem

6.2 Judge the process (efficiency)

1.2 Identify information needed

STEP 5
SYNTHESIS

THE BIG6™
AN INFORMATION
LITERACY MODEL

STEP 2
INFORMATION
SEEKING
STRATEGIES

5.1 Organize from multiple sources

5.2 Present the information

2.2 Determine all possible sources

2.1 Select the best sources

4.2 Extract relevant information

3.2 Find information within sources

4.1 Engage (read, hear, view, touch)

3.1 Locate sources (intellectually and physically)

STEP 4
USE OF INFORMATION

STEP 3
LOCATION + ACCESS

thinking and outlines its role in business strategy, creative development, and value creation.

AIGA's Designing Framework divides project development into three categories: defining the problem, innovating, and generating value. Each of these categories offers a series of steps that may be engaged in any order, depending on the size, scope, and purpose of the project at hand. The process is not intended to be linear and may be taken out of sequence to achieve project aims.

Especially helpful to individuals new to the concepts of design research or established creative processes, AIGA's Designing Framework is illustrated by a growing series of online case studies, submitted by individuals and firms that have successfully used this structure in professional practice.

AIGA's Designing Framework is outlined below.

Defining the Problem:

- Defining the problem
- Envisioning the desired end state (knowing what victory looks like)
- Defining the approach by which victory can be achieved
- Inciting support and then action

Innovating:

- Seeking insight to inform the prototyping of the solution
- Prototyping potential solutions
- Delineating the tough choices
- Enabling the team to work as a team

Generating Value:

- Choosing the best solution, then activating it
- Making sure people know about your solution
- Selling the solution
- Rapidly learning and "tacking" based on your successes and failures

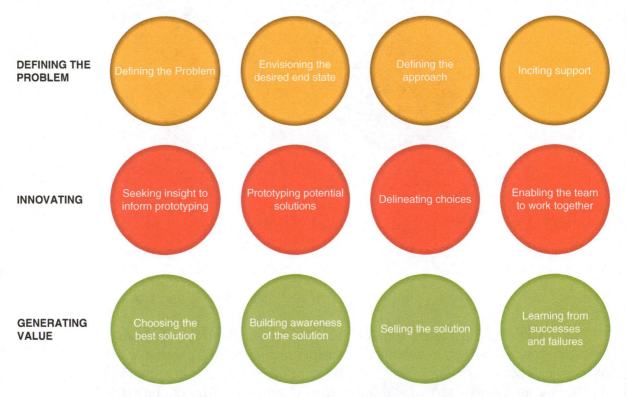

Above
AIGA's Designing Framework breaks the creative process into three distinct categories: defining the problem, innovating, and generating value. During project development, designers may engage in multiple sub-categories, using the process in a nonlinear fashion to improve not only their end results but also their ability to promote the value of the resulting artifacts and the thinking that created them.

Design Council Outlines The Design Process

Another applicable structure for creative development inclusive of research is The Design Process as outlined by the United Kingdom's Design Council, an organization created by the British government in 1994 to champion design. The Design Process outlines successful project development steps for creative professionals working in any field. It diagrams five stages that all designers must navigate when undertaking a commission. The Design Council suggests that this model is most functional when there is active collaboration between designer and client.

The Design Process is summarized below.

First steps

- Begin with a design brief that frames the project and outlines strategic objectives.
- Ask the right questions. This is essential to writing a good brief.
- Investigate why design work is needed.
- Define the problem before working toward a solution.

Research

- Carry out research both before and during the design process.
- Focus research on the user.
- Observe customer behavior. This makes it easier to create something that fulfills a need and can also provide creative inspiration.

Planning

- Account for internal resources, people, and information.

Communication

- Make the relationship between client and designer a two-way street.
- Predetermine review stages so that the project doesn't progress in the wrong direction.
- Ensure that all parts of an organization are on board with the evolving design process.

Implementation

- Don't let designers exit the scene during implementation.
- Establish assessment procedures so that the design process can be improved in the future.

Articulating Value

Cultivating an environment conducive to research investigations is an important step in every designer's professional development. Research—the key to aiming creative impulses properly—provides the designer with documentation supporting aesthetic/design decisions. Clearly articulating the relevance of research and process is essential—resulting in both time and budgetary allowances for proper investigation and project development.

Subjectivity Finds Context

By nature, designers are visual people. They have years of training dedicated to communicating with an external audience through the use of typography, color, and imagery. They often understand intuitively what it takes to create attention-grabbing artifacts that delight, inform, or inspire. However, designers speak an industry-specific language, and when working directly with clients—the majority of whom went to business school—they may not only find themselves up against a language barrier but against a difference of aesthetic principles as well. "Taste" is subjective, and no one will admit that they don't have any. Thus designers often find themselves explaining aesthetic decisions with formal design or typographic principles. Clients may well view these choices as arbitrary (remember, they don't know the difference between Helvetica and Arial). When documented research has been used to help guide the creative process, however, the designer will experience more success validating their work. For example, if the Pantone Institute was commissioned to do color choice validation as primary research, the designer could point to that expert report (read: investment) to justify their color selections.

Research for Student Designers

The goal of all design research is to empower the designer to make informed decisions and then to provide support for their aesthetic rationale. In the case of student work, project scope and limited resources often force research practices to be more informal. Students can, however, use a number of methodologies to inform their decisions from assignment to assignment—ultimately honing their professional skills for the job market. Here are a number of ways that design students can use research practices to better inform their design solutions.

Literature Review

The term "literature review" is fairly self-explanatory: gather all materials relevant to your subject. For many students, research begins and ends online. Though the Internet is a powerful tool, the academic library is one of the best places to go for books, academic journals, newspapers, magazines, and manuscripts from professional conferences. A university library also offers access to many tools that are not readily available to the general public, such as proprietary research portals, inter-university databases, and graduate dissertations. Furthermore, trained professionals are available to assist patrons with their research efforts. Starting a project is often the hardest part. But conducting a literature review will offer valuable insight into your subject matter and better prepare you for framing the problem to be solved.

Marketing Research

Though students may lack the resources to conduct their own marketing research, they can gain much by reviewing the results of previously published marketing studies relating to their current project. Most colleges and universities have business libraries with specific access to this research. Taking the time to read and understand this type of secondary data can help focus the design process and provide statistics to support aesthetic choices. There are many online resources for free market data, including those provided by state and national governments. In the United States, for instance, the U.S. Department of Labor website (www.dol.gov) offers a great deal of data on specific industries and occupations. Outside of the United States, similar information can be found though governmental labor agencies.

Visual Exploration

As we tell all of our students: sketch! The sketching phase is a critical step in the design process and can lead to truly innovative and creative solutions. Though students' design abilities mature and they develop their own methodology for visualization, pencil and paper remain highly effective tools. Sketching allows designers to prototype concepts rapidly without being influenced by technology—so they are focused on solving the problem first and fabricating the solution second. Additionally, sitting down with a sketchbook naturally allows some time for brainstorming, forcing designers to really think about what they're trying to solve.

Arts-Based Paradigm

Characteristics of Research Under the Arts-Based Paradigm

Researchers in the **Arts** paradigm tend to see research as a performance. The method of reporting (narrative, poetry, performance, artwork) the research has a three-fold purpose: to present the findings in a manner which represents and evokes the aesthetic of what you are trying to communicate; to challenge, resist, and transform the more traditional hegemonic methods of representing reality; and to bridge academic writing and lay writing (Davis, 2014; Pelias, 2014).

arts
In this type of research paradigm, scholars tend to see research as a performance.

Performance-based scholarship reflects the dramatistic paradigm—the belief that everyday life is a performance and thus must be understood through the frame of a performance. This type of scholarship also reflects a social constructionist belief system as the scholars enter into that construction themselves through their work.

As a Performance Studies scholar, you can write your work as a script and perform it in a theater. You can write poetry or create artwork. You might perform your research as radical street or public performances, such as rallies, puppet shows, marches, vigils, choruses, clown shows, or ritual performances. You might do a co-performance in which you bring the audience into the text and invite them to share the experience with you. You can advocate for a specific cause by creating an exhibition out of something that has happened; asking people to confront something that they normally don't think about or interact with; showing an idealized version of reality, or depicting traditional, culturally shared beliefs or values. You might create a documentary to depict your research. What all of these forms of scholarship have in common is an attention to the aesthetic way of knowing—to the sensorial (through the senses), intuitive, and imaginative ways in which knowledge is experienced and understood (Harter, Ellingson, Dutta, & Norander, 2009).

Performance Studies

In **performance studies**, researchers represent cultural experiences by observing and reenacting culturally situated communicative acts to reflect an interpretation of cultural practice through human expression. The communicative act performed can either be a cultural text or an ethnographic account, which is why performance studies are sometimes known as **performance ethnography** because they represent a culture through performance. Performance ethnography creates an appreciation for representation of others by enabling the actor to fully embody the others' experience. Pelias (2014) says that this type of knowledge "welcomes the body in to the mind's dwellings" (p. 11). This embodiment of cultural practice also results in a critical observation of knowledge (Alexander, 2005). In other words, when I perform your actions as if I were you, I can more fully understand your experience and your situation. In addition, when you see my performance, you can more fully understand yourself and others. In the performance, the audience is allowed to see others related to how they see themselves. For this reason, performance studies combine theory and praxis (practice or normal behavior) as they perform theory and make it alive to the audience (Holman Jones, 2000). In addition, the evocative nature of performance studies scholarship "opens up space, . . . allows me to say some things I can't quite say any other way" (Pelias, in Davis, 2014, p. 293). Performative work makes the "text alive in the present," suggests Denzin, in Davis (2014, p. 268).

Performance ethnography is considered a standpoint epistemology because it is a particular moment of knowing that allows participants and the audience to understand themselves and others through and as the other. In conducting performance studies, it is important to balance your everyday experiences with your commentary on the subjects. As a performance studies scholar, you would practice reflexivity. You would clearly define yourself in relation to the people being portrayed, your research intentions, and your prior knowledge.

Since it is impossible to separate life stories from those cultural, social, and political contexts that influence experiences; and since cultural, social,

performance studies
A method in which researchers represent cultural experiences by observing and reenacting culturally situated communicative acts to reflect an interpretation of cultural practice through human expression.

performance ethnography
Representation of a culture through performance.

and political contexts impact the performance itself (actors, setting, audience perspectives) (Holman Jones, 2000), performance studies reflect culture and experience. Performance studies research reflects the complexities of real life and human experience, and seek to represent multiple realities, experiences, and perspectives (Pelias, 2014). In addition, works written and presented performatively create space for alternative voices (Davis, 2014).

Performance studies are also a critical method because they shed light on cultural hegemony by identifying dominant characters who regulate norms in situational and environmental membership. Alexander (2005) notes that as a moral discourse, performance studies fill the gaps between the known and the unknown, as well as the self and others.

Performance based scholarship is also an empathetic form of scholarship because it, says Pelias (2014), "encourage[s] us to see and to define situations by their unique human and spiritual poetic, the interpenetrations of self, Other, and context, by our complexity and interdependence rather than by some simpler linear or causal logic" (p. 12). Performative writing lets each of us take each other's perspective and discover each other's experiences.

Performance studies contributes to the understanding of social life as a whole, by examining the intent of social behavior, and considering the moral and theoretical assertions inherent in the action. Performative writing is a form of critical research, as it challenges politics and power and uncovers issues of social justice (Pelias, 2014). Holman Jones (2000) highlights the value of performance in social activism (i.e., women's movement, civil rights, AIDS activism, etc.). Such performance asks the audience to examine critically the issue at hand. Performance matters because it is action in the world, and voice is intrinsically tied to experience. Performance studies creates a space to critically examine social systems; motivates performers with rhetorical currency to make social changes; urges audience members, as a collective unit, to make changes; and teaches audience members to recognize social disparities and work to liberate the oppressed (Madison, 1998).

Documentary, Video, or Visual Ethnography

Unlike digital or online ethnography which studies digital or online texts, or types of rhetorical criticism which study visual images as text, visual ethnography uses visual images to represent experience. **Visual ethnography** uses photographic and video images rather than, or in addition to, words, in order to represent an experience through image. Visual ethnography refers to any visual medium used to represent a community or experience. Scholars use media such as still photography; film, video, or documentary representation; and hypermedia (Pink, 2007).

Image-based ethnography crosses aesthetic, intellectual, and social boundaries to explore and represent experience (Pink, 2007). Image-based research reflects a way of knowing that is different from verbal responses. Images construct a more embodied and sensory way of knowing and understanding. Images mirror our bodies and as such replicate a more corporeal sense of an experience than words. Images also, however, are independent of the body

visual ethnography
A type of ethnography which uses photographic and video images rather than, or in addition to, words, in order to represent an experience through image.

and thus are constructed representations and interpretations (MacDougall, 2005; Sherman, 2015).

Image-based ethnography uses the unique qualities of the medium to construct ideas about the experience being studied. Image-based ethnography articulates ways of "looking and being" (MacDougall, 2005, p. 5), rather than ways of judging, thinking, or explaining. Visual ethnography has the dual purposes of representation and aesthetics and requires attention to both (Cole, Quinlan, & Hayward, 2009; Quinlan, Smith, & Hayward, 2009; Mathew, 2014); however, it's important to remember that "film is the tool and ethnography is the goal" (Heider, 1976, p. 4).

Documentary ethnographies involve an interaction between the researcher and the experience being studied, the production process, and the audience (Mathew, 2014). Moving between these elements requires several decision stages. Ethnographic filmmaking is generally understood to be a non-fictional undertaking, although most scholars acknowledge that documented reality is always interpreted and constructed (Mathew, 2014). Image-based ethnographies are typically collaborative endeavors, involving at minimum the researcher or research team, the study participants, and a cinematographer (Sherman, 2015). Sometimes, visual ethnographies are collaborative endeavors between the filmmaker and the study participants. Frequently, participants are invited to suggest ideas, narrate the story, and give feedback on rough cuts (Mathew, 2014). Visual ethnographers frequently include their study participants as partners in the filmmaking effort, and this inclusion not only makes important social justice statements but also "transform[s] oppressive and stereotypical representations of people when they arise from the daily experiences of social actors who assert agency over—and participate in—representations of themselves and their own lives" (Cole, Quinlan, & Hayward, 2009; p. 80).

Other Types of Arts-Based Research Methods

Ethnodance
An arts-based form of representation which uses dance to convey the meaning of an experience.

In arts-based research methods, you might present your research as works of art, recreating the essence of the experience into an art form—painting, sculpture, music. Arts-based scholars use drawings to explore the complexity of human experience (Guillemin & Westall, 2008); others use dance (**ethnodance**) to uncover and explore knowledge and meaning (Cancienne & Bagley, 2008); and others use music to understand the construction of meaning (Aldridge, 2008) and provide insights into social understandings (Daykin, 2008).

Visual Research

We live in a society that is dominated by images and objects. Whether we remember or forget the things we see around us, we need to accept that even for a moment they stimulate our imagination by way of either memory or expectation (Berger, 1972: 129). The ability to critically examine the effects images and objects have on people's lives is particularly important for all designers regardless of their disciplinary focus. Therefore, the type of visual research that I will introduce here is concerned with the study and interpretation of images and objects. This means that this research is 'hermeneutic' in nature. Hermeneutics is a philosophical inquiry that focuses on the interpretation of linguistic and non-linguistic expressions that can be found in symbolic communication, symbolic interaction, and culture in general (Ramberg and Gjesdal, 2013).

What is Visual Research?

There are many ways of looking at visual research, but for the purpose of this book visual research will be defined as a study of images, forms, and objects in both visual and material culture. For the same purpose, culture can be described as 'the arts and other manifestations of human intellectual achievement regarded collectively' (Oxford Dictionaries, 2013c). A form can be described as 'The visible shape or configuration of something' (Oxford Dictionaries, 2014a); an object can be described as 'A material thing that can be seen and touched' (Oxford Dictionaries, 2014b); while an image can be described as: 'A representation of the external form of a person or thing in art', or 'A visible impression obtained by a camera [. . .] or other device, or displayed on a computer or video screen' (Oxford Dictionaries, 2013d).

As such, this kind of research can cover everything from typography, illustration, and advertising, to product design and architecture. The reason why visual and material cultures are grouped together under the banner of visual research is because we perceive both of these cultures in visual terms, regardless of whether we deal with two-dimensional images or three-dimensional forms.

The focus of this section will be on the study of existing images, forms, and objects that have been found or identified by the researcher. One traditional way of visual analysis (or a critique) has been termed as 'the good eye' principle. This type of analysis is neither methodological nor theoretically explicit practice. Therefore, this practice can best be described as 'visual connoisseurship' (Rose, 2012: 52). Visual connoisseurship focuses on various aspects of the social modality of the production of images, forms, and objects in the following terms:

- Who commissioned the work?
- Why was the work commissioned?
- Who was the creator behind the work?
- How is this work being used?
- Who is using this work?

Visual connoisseurship also examines compositional and technological modalities of the making of an image, a form, or an object, but with the purpose of identifying the influences of other creators in a particular work. Experts who use this method have acquired extensive knowledge works of art and design, and can confidently attribute these works to artists or designers, or particular schools and styles. These people can establish the sources of the works they are studying, and likely the influences behind them—and as a result they can judge and critique the quality of these works.

Developing a 'good eye' requires a lot of experience, as well as broad and specialist historical and contextual knowledge in the area of study (Rose, 2012: 52–7). This approach has been long established in the field of art history and theory, and from there it has been adopted to design history and theory. Nevertheless, this way of looking at things will not be introduced further here, because it requires a substantial knowledge of the field as a prerequisite; and as such it is more appropriate for providing a critique rather than conducting research. Here, I will introduce you to other ways of looking at images, forms, and objects that are more practice-based and that do not require extensive previous knowledge in the field. This includes three research methods: **compositional interpretation**, **content analysis;** and **semiotics**. You can use these methods to conduct systematic and empirical visual research under the framework of visual and material culture studies.

Compositional Interpretation

From the first year of their studies, design students are trained to develop an ability to describe and discuss their work and the works of others. Therefore, designers should be able to critically examine and describe images, forms, and objects by using correct terminology and vocabulary, and compositional interpretation is a method that can be used for this purpose (Rose, 2012: 51). However, unlike its name suggests, compositional interpretation is a descriptive research method with limited interpretative abilities.

The main benefit from using this method is its inherent vocabulary that allows you to describe in correct terminology what it is that you are seeing. While this method focuses strongly on the visual appearance and pays most attention to compositionality, it also pays attention to the production aspects —but only when the knowledge of the technique of production helps in describing some characteristics of the image or the objects. Compositional interpretation does, however, have its limitations. This method focuses on the visual aspects of the work in question, but it ignores socially specific ways of seeing and experiencing things, as well as the visual and material representations of the social. In visual research, images and objects cannot be seen as isolated occurrences and they also need to be looked at and interpreted in terms of how they are produced, for whom, and why (Rose, 2012: 55). That is why other methods such as content analysis and semiotics are necessary for further exploration. Nevertheless, despite its limitations, compositional interpretation offers a particular way of looking at content and form (2012: 55–6).

Compositional interpretation is a method that examines images, forms, and objects by breaking them down into a number of components related to things such as content, colour, type of form, spatial organization, light, movement, expressive content, and so on. Nevertheless in practice most of these components are related to each other and the notion of composition refers to all of these components seen together (Rose, 2012: 58–79).

There are a number of questions that you can ask in the process of compositional interpretation. First, you should begin with some really basic questions and then progress to those that require specific details. These questions are for the purpose of providing pure description of the image, and answers should not contain value judgments, analysis, or interpretation. You can use the following set of questions to describe some of the key elements of the image or the object, but please note that not all questions will be applicable in all cases:

- What do you see? Does this work represent a form of art, architecture, design, advertisement, a motion picture, or something else? Are there any iconographic elements that you can identify (e.g. is this image a form, or an object based on, or inspired by, a historical event or a period, particular style, or something else)?
- Can you provide the location and date of when the work was made, and by whom?
- What is the medium in which the work is presented? Is it painted, photographed, filmed, made out of stone, metal, and so on?
- What kind of techniques and tools were used in the production of the work? Are there any particular or characteristic tools and techniques used in the production of the work?
- What is the size, scale, or length of the work? Depending on what it is that you are analyzing, you can assess the relationship of the work to a person—in terms of scale; you can provide the actual dimensions if you are studying a product or a building; or if the image is a film, you can provide information on its length. In some cases, you can assess these issues in terms of context as well.
- What kinds of objects or forms are represented in the image, or vice versa? Can you identify any elements, structural systems, or general shapes within the composition?
- What kind of direction does the composition follow? Is the axis of the direction vertical, horizontal, centred, or diagonal? If it is diagonal, does the axis go from left to right, or from right to left?
- What kinds of lines dominate? Is the line soft, hard, thick, thin, variable, irregular, planar, jagged, intermittent, indistinct, curved, and so on?
- What is the relationship between the shapes in the work? Are they grouped in terms of large and small, are they overlapping, are they positioned gradually next to each other, and so on?

- Can you describe the texture of the surface, or provide any other comments about the execution of the work if the issue of texture is not applicable?
- Can you describe the dominant color, or the color palette of the work? There are three terms that you can use to describe the color palette: hue—this is a reference to the basic, dominating colors in the image (e.g. red, blue, and green); saturation—this is a reference to the purity of a color in relation to the color spectrum (e.g. the saturation is high if the color is vivid, and low if it is nearly neutral); and value—this is a reference to the lightness or darkness of a color (e.g. if a color is in its near-white form, than its value is high; if it is its near-black form, than its value is low).
- Can you describe the composition of the design? Is it stable, repetitious, rhythmic, unified, symmetrical, harmonious, geometric, varied, chaotic, horizontal or vertically oriented, and so on?
- Can you describe the spatial organization? How is the work positioned within the space or the environment where it is found? If the work is an image, then you can answer this question in terms of perspective: How are elements of the image presented in relation to each other—in terms of height, width, depth, and position when viewed from a particular point? How is the effect of distance is achieved? While answering these questions, you can also describe from what kind of point of view the image is being presented—is it 'bird's-eye' (a top-down perspective, also referred to as an 'aerial view'); is it a an eye-level angle (when the image is presented as seen through the eyes of the image maker); is it a 'worm's-eye' perspective (the opposite to a bird's eye view); and so on? The second question refers to two-dimensional images that try to give an impression of depth (Barrett, 1994; Rose, 2012: 51–80).

These are only some of the questions that you can consider when providing a compositional interpretation. As your knowledge and experience progress, you will be able to describe images, forms, and objects in even greater detail by using some additional descriptive elements to do so. In time, by developing a proficiency in this method you will be also able to develop visual connoisseurship skills.

Content Analysis

Content analysis is a quite different method from compositional interpretation. This is a quantitative method that involves counting and summing phenomena in images or texts. As with other quantitative research methods, this method can also be used to support your qualitative research. One of the main advantages of content analysis is that it can enable you to conduct primary research and come up with new and original data that you can use as evidence in your argument (Stokes, 2011: 56). This method is based on a set of rules and procedures that must be rigorously followed for the analysis of images, including images of objects and forms—but not of the objects and the forms themselves (Rose, 2012: 81).

Content analysis is best used for visual culture studies related to mass media, such as TV, newspapers, magazines, and the like. As a designer, you may need to study the frequency with which certain types of images appear in the media. For example, let us say that you are conducting a study on advertisements in fashion magazines and you would like to know how multicultural high fashion is, or what kind of products have placements on a particular TV show. You can get a definitive answer to this by comparing the number of product placements in that TV show, or by counting models with different ethnicities that have appeared in selected magazines within a given period.

In the case of the TV show, you can choose to watch all seasons of the show and categorize all product placements. Or, in the case of fashion magazines, you can select a representative number of issues from, for example, *Vogue*, *Elle*, and *Cosmopolitan* from the selected period, and you can count the number of models in each of these categories—'Black', 'White', 'Asian', and 'other'. In addition to this, you can have other categories representing selected product brands in the first example, or fashion labels in the second. Using the same principle, you can also identify how much each brand is presented, or how multicultural each of the fashion labels is. Once this study is completed you will have factual evidence on which you can make an informed statement about the object of your study (see Rose, 2013: 82; Stokes, 2011: 56–7).

In any case, please bear in mind that the above examples are only a generalization. If you are conducting such a study you will probably need to develop a more detailed system of analysis. For example, you could conduct content analysis based on counting the frequency of certain images, or visual elements in a clearly defined sample of images. This approach also includes an analysis of these frequencies. In order for this research process to be reliable and replicable, each aspect of the process needs to follow certain requirements (Rose, 2012: 87). The breakdown of the process has been outlined by Jane Stokes in her book *How to Do Media & Cultural Studies* (2011: 61–4), and this process can be easily adapted to content analysis in visual research. Here is a 12-step process that you can follow to achieve this:

Step 1: Establish your research question or hypothesis
Step 2: Read widely on the topic
Step 3: Define your object of analysis
Step 4: Define your categories
Step 5: Create a coding sheet to record your findings
Step 6: Test your coding categories
Step 7: Collect your data
Step 8: Summarize your findings
Step 9: Interpret the findings

Step 10: Relate this back to your research question
Step 11: Present your findings
Step 12: Discuss the findings

As with any other research process, first you will need to establish your research question or hypothesis. This is important, because you will need to have a clear idea of what you would like to find out before you start looking. Then look at previous work focused on the medium in which you are interested. Has there been any previous research done on the topic of your interest? Has any of this research been done by using content analysis? If not, examine some other similar work based on content analysis so you can see how and why this method has been applied. Then you can refine your research question and hypothesis to incorporate your secondary findings (Stokes, 2011: 61).

Now you will need to isolate the material that you have chosen to study and think about how your selection will help you answer your research question or test your hypothesis. State what kind of images you will study and why. You also need to think about how many images you are going to examine. As with any quantitative research, your sample should be large enough to be representative, but also manageable (Stokes, 2011: 61). For research students, it is best if you first consult your supervisor on the amount of images you are planning to study before you proceed.

Icon

An iconic sign is a sign in which the signifier provides an instant recognizability to the signified. This type of sign is especially important for all types of design forms and visual images. For example, a photograph of a baby is an iconic sign of that baby (Rose, 2012: 119). In some cases, certain design objects can also acquire an iconic status. For example, the Eames lounge chair and ottoman developed by Charles and Ray Eames in 1956 can also be described as an icon of modern design. This is because the object is an instantly recognizable design artifact that is highly characteristic for its era. The chair's design has endured time and style and over half a century later it still remains a desirable object. The chair is even exhibited in places such as the Museum of Modern Art in New York, the Art Institute of Chicago, and the Vitra Design Museum in Germany, and it continues to be featured in various design publications.

Symbol

The word 'symbol' comes from the Greek *symbolon*, which means contract, token, insignia, and a means of identification. The symbol, regardless of whether it is in the form of a picture, a sign, a word, an object, or a gesture (or all of them, or parts of them together), requires an association with a certain and consciously held idea in order to fully express its meaning. As a rule, a symbol depends upon a group of people agreeing upon its meaning—thus this is a somewhat unfamiliar meaning of 'contract' (Goldammer, 1995: 591).

If we take this into consideration, a baby can also be interpreted as a symbol that stands for a new beginning or can represent notions of 'the future' (Rose, 2012: 119). Some other examples of widely accepted symbols include the following signs (see Figure 7.3, 7.4 and Figure 7.5)—all of them standing for peace, and Che Guevara's stencilled image, which is often seen as a symbol of revolution and rebellion (see Figure 7.6).

© Shutterstock.com

Figure 7.1. Signage for a restroom

© Shutterstock.com

Figure 7.2. Signage for a changing room for infants

© Shutterstock.com

Figure 7.3. The peace symbol

This sign was created by the British artist Gerald Holtom in 1958. The sign was originally designed as a symbol for the Direct Action Committee Against Nuclear War (DAC) and was an emblem for the Campaign for Nuclear Disarmament (CND) in Britain, but in 1960 in the USA the sign was used as a symbol of the peace movement.

© Shutterstock.com

Figure 7.4. Dove of peace

This illustration, drawn by Pablo Picasso as an emblem for the First International Peace Conference in Paris in 1949, became one of the world's most recognizable symbols of peace.

This sign has a number of meanings that range from victory (most famously used by Winston Churchill during the Second World War), to insult, or happiness. Nevertheless, one of the most popular meanings of this sign is that of representing a symbol of peace by anti-war protestors and counterculture activists.

Figure 7.5. The 'V' hand sign

A word or an image, and even a gesture, becomes a symbol when it implies something more than its obvious and immediate meaning. The symbol has a wider and 'unconscious' appeal, which is never precisely defined or fully explained. Symbols work precisely because in the everyday context we do not perceive anything fully, or comprehend completely. We can see, hear, touch, smell, and taste; but how far we can see, how well we can hear, what our touch tells us, and what we taste, depends upon both the quality of our senses and our willingness and capacity to process all of this.

It is our senses that limit our perception of the world. In this regard, it can be argued that we often rely on unconscious appeals when it comes to perceiving reality. Even when our senses react to real phenomena, such as sights and sounds, they are translated from the realm of reality into the realm of the mind. Within our mind they become psychic events whose ultimate nature is inexplicable (Jung, 1964: 4).

Since we cannot know the ultimate nature of matter itself, it can be argued that every experience contains an indefinite number of unknown factors, while every concrete object remains unknown in certain respects. In reality, events constantly occur, but they often remain hidden below the threshold of our consciousness. Since people select with reason and knowledge, logical analysis is the prerogative of consciousness. The unconscious thought, on the other hand, seems to be guided mainly by instinctive trends and is represented by a different set of corresponding thought forms—archetypes (Jung, 1964: 67). When 'unconscious' events occur, they are subliminally absorbed. People become aware of them only in a moment of intuition; by a process of profound thought that leads to an unconscious conclusion; or as a sort of after-thought that such events must have happened—even though they have been originally ignored (1964: 5).

Without us realizing it, our unconscious perception of subliminal messages influences the way in which we react to both events and people (1964: 20). Consequently, when a mind explores a symbol, it is led to ideas that lie beyond the grasp of reason. Since there are innumerable things beyond the range of human understanding, we frequently resort to the use of symbols in order to communicate concepts we cannot exactly define or fully comprehend. As Carl, Jung (1964: 4) argues, this is the reason why the employment of symbolic language and images is common to virtually all religions.

During the historical development and use of symbolization, a variety of categories and relationships have been developed. While some symbols, such as those of religion, have been and still are used to convey concepts concerned with people's relationship to the sacred, or holy, such as the Christian cross in Christianity (Figure 7.6) and also to the social and material world, such as the *Dharmacakra*—the Wheel of Buddhist Law (Figure 7.7), other non-religious types of symbols have achieved increasing significance as well.

In the nineteenth and twentieth centuries, for example, symbols dealing with people's relationship to the material world and its conceptualization such as scientific-technical symbols) have assumed ever-increasing importance in modern science and technology. These types of 'secularized' symbols are also rooted, to a degree, in the realm of religious symbolism. They function in a similar manner to religious symbols and their purpose is to associate particular meanings to particular signs. There are numbers of tropes and modes of signification that can operate within the concept of the religious symbol. This includes allegory, personifications, figures, analogies, metaphors, parables, pictures (as in pictorial representations of ideas), emblems and individually conceived artificial symbols with added verbal meaning, as well as attributes used as a mark to distinguish certain individuals. They are all formal, historical, literary, and artificial categories of the symbolic. Whether it is religious or not, the symbol is intended primarily for the circle of the initiated and

© Shutterstock.com

The cross is a Christian symbol that represents the crucifixion of Jesus Christ. This symbol is fully integrated within the whole process of worship. It appears on churches, in paintings, in books, on vestments, in jewellery, and at different stages in the church service as part of the ritual. With an intimate and all-embracing hand movement, the cross is even made by individuals—both priests and worshippers.

Figure 7.6. The Christian cross

© Shutterstock.com

The wheel represents the teachings of Buddha. The wheel has a number of meanings, including that it also stands for an endless cycle of birth and rebirth.

Figure 7.7. The Wheel of Buddhist Law

involves the acknowledgement of the experience that it expresses. Therefore the meaning of the symbol is not to be kept hidden—on the contrary, it should have a revelatory character. The symbol indicates the need for communication, but at the same time it conceals the details and the innermost aspects of its contents (Goldammer, 1995: 591–2).

Essentially, semiotics is a method that is concerned with the analysis of meaning-making processes that are socially significant. As such, semiotics can provide you with an excellent foundation for understanding the fundamentals of both visual and material culture. If you want to develop a better understanding of people's aspirations and motivations within our consumption-driven society, a particularly interesting area for conducting semiotic analysis is the field of advertising. That is why mainstream semiotics often looks at advertisements and the messages they convey. Often, these messages are core to the ideologies that structure contemporary society (Rose, 2012: 109). Given that advertising is a form of brand communication, similar semiotic analysis can also be extended to the field of branding. Below, I will provide you with some examples on how you can examine both fields from a semiotic perspective.

Conclusion

Visual research is concerned with the study and interpretation of both visual images and material objects. This way of research can also be defined as a study of visual and material culture. This type of research is hermeneutic in nature and can enable you to look for patterns and meanings in sketches, drawings, illustrations, paintings, photographs, videos, objects, products, or architecture. The ability to critically examine meanings of images and objects, and the messages they convey, is particularly important for designers because it can enable them to better understand the effects of their work.

Summary

In this section I have introduced visual research as a hermeneutical process of inquiry and I have presented you with a list of principles that you can follow when interpreting visual research. In addition to this, I have introduced you to visual and material culture studies—areas of study that examine images, forms, and objects that provide information, meaning, function, or pleasure. These are not independent fields, but cross-disciplinary subjects that exist within a broader social, historical, and cultural context. In addition to this, I have introduced three key research methods that you can use when conducting visual research: compositional interpretation, content analysis, and semiotics.

Compositional interpretation can offer you different ways of describing images, forms, and objects. This is a method that you can use at the first stage of your research to describe the visual impact that images, forms, and objects have. Compositional interpretation cannot be used for conducting an analysis because it does not encourage critical reflection (besides a discussion on the technological or the compositional production aspects), nor can this method engage with broader cultural meanings and contexts. That is why visual researchers need to combine compositional interpretation with other methods, such as those described below, in order to address the shortcomings that come with the use of only this method (Rose, 2012: 77–9).

Content analysis is a persuasive method that can generate reliable and replicable facts. This is a flexible and creative method for which a researcher requires only basic mathematical skills. The results can be presented in tables and charts that can be easily read, making this method broadly acceptable and comprehensible. The disadvantage is that content analysis can sometimes be an insensitive and blunt instrument (Stokes, 2011: 58). This method is only as sophisticated as the categories that the researcher defines in the course of the research.

That is why the categories should be theoretically grounded and justifiable. If improperly developed and applied, this method will generate meaningless data (2011: 58–9). Nevertheless, content analysis offers a clear method for engaging systematically with large numbers of images (Rose, 2012: 101). However, you need to bear in mind that even though content analysis can provide you with factual evidence, the process itself is not entirely quantitative. At each stage of the process, ranging from formulating the research topic to developing coding categories and interpreting the results, you will need to make a range of subjective decisions. There are broader issues related to cultural meaning and significance of images that content analysis alone cannot address, and that is why you also need to support your visual research with a semiotic analysis.

Semiotics is one of the most influential methods for interpreting the materials of visual and material culture (see Rose, 2012: 105–6), and advertising especially (Stokes, 2011: 72). As a major part of the creative process of advertising, semiotics can provide us with a good vocabulary for talking about how advertisements add value to products by making them meaningful and socially relevant to the prospective buyers. Because of this, ads make excellent subjects for semiotic analysis (Stokes, 2011: 73). Furthermore, semiotics can be easily combined with other research methods, such as with content analysis.

For example, you could use content analysis to determine how many images of a certain kind can be found in a particular medium, and then you can use semiotics to analyse a smaller selection of them in more detail. In addition to this, you can also include a participant observation or interviews with content creators or content providers, such as magazine editors, fashion photographers, creative directors, or publicists, in order to include their perspective as well. Or, once you conclude your analysis, you could conduct a small focus group to which you could present your findings in order to confirm or disprove your theory. In this way, you can add more breadth and depth to your research (2011: 75–6).

As a critic of both visual and material culture, you will be concerned with the examination of the effects of images and objects that are already out there in the world, and not by works that you are producing. This is the data that you are collecting. Your sampling process may range from highly rigorous to very subjective, and it is best if you frame your selection around some kind of ideological platform. There are no set formats on how you could prepare a report on visual research, and as with most research reports, formats can vary depending on your audiences or style of work.

The Creative Process

The Design Process in the Academic Environment

This chapter has explored how the design process is used within the industry, but it can also play a key role for design students completing an undergraduate degree. Firstly, learning about the processes used in the professional sphere will introduce you to the depth and breadth of research, critical thinking, analysis, creative problem-solving and graphic skill demanded by agencies. Secondly, these very processes will also provide a clear working framework for any curricular work, by breaking up the requirements of an initial brief into sequential steps that will both guide your project and support time management. Used in conjunction with an accurate personal time-plan, this will not only help you keep to deadlines, but will also allow you to allocate an appropriate amount of time to each stage of the process.

Documenting all your work, too—either through a 'process book' or a blog—will enable you to record and, later, justify any design decisions, making the final submission a much simpler process. Justifying your decisions by demonstrating the process you used to reach them proves you are both creative and a design professional.

As you gain a greater understanding of your own personal creative processes, you may find it helpful to map out a flow chart for future reference.

The Use of Social Media in Research

In recent years there has been a marked increase in the use of social media, and a resulting growth in consumer conversations relating to brands taking place on the Internet.

With so much being discussed about brands online by their customers, and so much information readily available, new research approaches are needed to make sense of it all. There is an evolving demand for systems to analyze social media data so as to be able to develop new communication strategies, and companies are increasingly investing in advanced social media monitoring tools such as Brandwatch to help them navigate this new landscape.

Of course, brands themselves must operate effectively within social media, too, raising many new concerns. Brands have learned to utilize social media to help drive awareness, and highly influential bloggers are invited to introduce brands and drive online conversation through social media channels such as Facebook and Twitter. But if brands themselves have a blog, what are they blogging about? What are the products and services they offer? What are their special offers? Do they have any thought leadership?

Posts launching a product can generate thousands of 'likes' and comments on Facebook, indirectly influencing millions via the connections of those who have engaged with the brand. This kind of engagement has opened up new research opportunities, such as using instant polling tools to fuel online discussions, or connecting online discussion boards directly to an online survey.

This type of research reveals a level of transparency that surveys and focus groups would find difficult to capture—a result of the security users feel in the relative anonymity of the online world, which can encourage a degree of honesty that many people would not feel comfortable with in person.

Social media research does not require the physical cooperation of respondents, so there are reduced financial and practical barriers to finding participants, too. A further advantage is the opportunity to work with a much larger and more diverse number of people. This method also requires little planning, is time efficient and therefore inexpensive. However, it does have its disadvantages: the freedom of speech offered by anonymity of the Internet can also result in responses that are either unexpected or negative. Due to the openness of communication on the Internet, these responses can 'go viral' or be widely circulated, causing damage to the reputation of a brand.

Visual Research Boards

The design industry uses a variety of visual enquiry boards to explore ideas and capture emotions and styles. Traditionally these were created from a range of photographs, illustrations, colours and sometimes textures, often with accompanying descriptive words, to help capture a particular theme. The images were printed and applied to a 'board'—usually an A3 (or 11 × 17 in) sheet of card—hence the term. Some agencies still use this approach, although many now create them digitally, maintaining them as a presentation tool for clients and as part of their team research process.

There are three key types of board: mood boards, inspiration boards and consumer-profile boards, each having a unique purpose within the design process.

Mood Boards

A mood board (sometimes known as a tone of voice board) is a visual collage that projects a particular emotion or theme with a selection of pictures, colours and other visual elements. This visual analysis technique helps to define an aesthetic 'feel' or style, and is frequently used in the conceptual phase of the design process.

Consumer-Profile Boards

The consumer-profile board captures, through a variety of images, a visual outline of the type of person the brand is targeting. As designers are predominantly visual people, this type of research is usually better represented through tangible characteristics, rather than a set of data or a list of abstract descriptors. Consumer-profile boards are made up from a range of images about the consumer, and will include details such as:

- What they look like—age, gender, ethnic group
- Their job—profession, skill, income
- Their family and friends—children, wider family group, types of friends

Design the layout carefully, including negative space to give each image breathing space. Use a white background—colour can introduce an unwanted subliminal effect Make sure that any typefaces are consistent. With the look of the board and reflect the personality of the consumer

- Develop a range of boards rather than trying to explore all lifestyle choices on one board

▼ ....

Other Forms of Research

Questionnaires

People's time is very valuable, so if you wish to encourage them to take part in any questionnaire, ensure that the number of questions is limited. Anything over 25 becomes a chore, and the questionnaire should ideally only take between 5 and 7 minutes to complete.

- Make sure the questions are clearly written, short and unambiguous
- The design of the questionnaire is also important for clear communication of both questions and response boxes, speeding up the process
- Avoid open-ended questions that mean a respondent has to provide a long written reply
- Try to write questions that will prompt a simple 'yes', 'no', 'maybe', 'often' or 'never' response, or use an appropriate numerical scale

- Capture the interest of your respondents by explaining the project and what the findings will support, as this can incentivize them to take part
- Be persistent: many people may be interested in helping but may have forgotten. Politely remind them and try to give them incentives or encouragement
- Finally, proofread and polish the questions with a friend or colleague to ensure you have framed them to obtain the most accurate responses

SWOT analysis

SWOT analysis is a technique that can be used to evaluate any product or service. Firstly the objective or aim has to be defined, and then the factors that are favourable or unfavourable to achieving that aim are identified. This type of analysis is useful because it enables researchers to not only identify a brand's unique selling point but also any existing threats to the brand.

- Strengths: characteristics of the brand that give it an advantage over others
- Weaknesses: characteristics that place the brand at a disadvantage relative to others

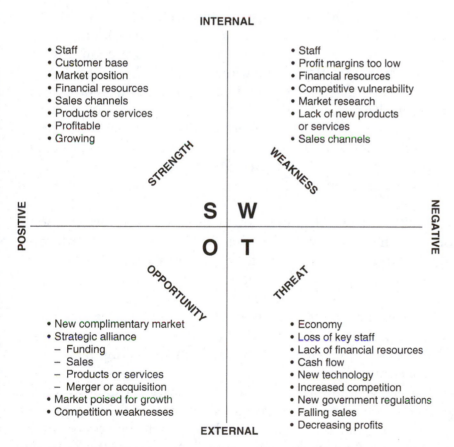

An example of a SWOT analysis diagram, used to highlight strategic unique selling points in an existing brand or brand concept, as well as to identify any strengths and weaknesses, and any possible threats.

- Opportunities: elements that the brand could exploit to its advantage
- Threats: elements in the retail environment that could cause trouble for the brand

Personal Research

In addition to the formal research explored in this chapter, many designers also undertake personal inspirational research, often collected in journals and sketchbooks or by using digital tools such as Pinterest.

*Generally the goal of research is to describe, interpret, or explain phenomena, but if the desire to see enquiry as having the capacity to change human understanding, then our sight needs to be set on a bigger picture. . . . This quest for understanding sees individual and social transformation as a worthy human enterprise for 'to know' means to be able to think, and act and therefore to change things. . . . The process of making art and interpreting art adds to our understanding as new ideas are presented that help us to see in new ways (Sullivan, 2005, p. 74).

▼ ·

Analogue Thinking

One of the values of art is that it is not static and there is never a definitive answer. A simple question can inspire an artwork and the artwork in turn can generate questions, which, upon reflection can be transformed into understanding that in turn elicits further questions. This cyclical approach not only describes an aesthetic process of self-realisation but also describes a research process in the form of reflective practice (Sullivan, 2005). Artist-researchers who engage with such a reflective practice inhabit a space of possibility in which there is no distinction between the activities of making and those of thinking. By creating the conditions that make manifest the idea, an artwork becomes an invitation to construct meaning or a way of interpreting the world.

In the context of a research project the artist-researcher draws upon a vast range of experiences and reconsiders them in the context of their history, theories and other related information along with the physical activities and processes that inform the practice. Through reverie and by making imaginative associations between such disparate elements the creative researcher is able to formulate the questions to be answered through the research project. The ways that the project is subsequently carried out are dependent upon other processes—those of making and physically manipulating materials—and through reflection.

The idea that art is a physical and material activity through which the artist can generate new knowledge by engaging with materials and processes, is gaining ground in creative arts research. Art, it could be argued always produces new knowledge especially in the ways that it advances its own particular field. However, the distinction I will make here between art practice as research and professional art practice as a creative activity is in the ways that research through art involves a self-conscious reflection that is not necessarily a part of art practice for its own sake. If art practice is to be considered as research it needs to reveal its processes and illuminate the thinking that underpins the material manifestations and it needs to be experienced. Art as research requires a viewer. For the purposes of this discussion I am referring to visual art, although of course this can just as easily apply to all other arts such as sonic art or poetry: art needs an audience.

These differences in approach to making art, between art as research and art professional practice, could be considered to be the differences between a conscious and an unconscious artist or practitioner. The conscious artist, in the terms of research project, is able to reflect on the making and what has been made and what has been made and is able to contextualise it in terms of the question or questions to be answered and its epistemology. All art as research needs to be supported in some way usually through exegetical material and this can take the form of other images or artworks that reveal processes or as a text or a combination of the two. In this way new knowledge, be it experiential, perceptual, procedural, tacit or personal can be explicated through both textual and visual means and be communicated.

By marrying a careful theoretical reading with an analysis of case studies, the researcher comes to understand the inter-related demands of industry, technique and storytelling. The researcher reflects upon this process in the exegesis, forming useful insights into the writing process that may be passed on in scholarly fashion to other screenwriters and practitioners.

In this way, the researcher may contribute the research findings to other researchers involved with exploration and innovation within the field. This may contribute to ongoing debates around structure and process or may add to an understanding of industry and the larger media culture. The researcher may publish or present new findings to the academic and/or industry communities that support the production of the project. Thus the researcher makes a meaningful contribution to the screen culture sustaining scholars, industry producers and fellow creative practitioners.

Glossary

Arts
In this type of research paradigm, scholars tend to see research as a performance.

Ethnodance
An arts-based form of representation which uses dance to convey the meaning of an experience.

Performance ethnography
Representation of a culture through performance.

Performance studies
A method in which researchers represent cultural experiences by observing and reenacting culturally situated communicative acts to reflect an interpretation of cultural practice through human expression.

Visual ethnography
A type of ethnography which uses photographic and video images rather than, or in addition to, words, in order to represent an experience through image.

References

Adams, T., & Holman Jones, S. (2017). Queer studies. In J. Matthes, R. Potter, & C. Davis (Eds.). *International encyclopedia of communication: Methods of communication research*. Wiley-Blackwell.

Adams, T., Ellis, C., & Holman Jones, S. (2017). Autoethnography. In J. Matthes, R. Potter, & C. Davis (Eds.). *International encyclopedia of communication: Methods of communication research*. Wiley-Blackwell.

Adams, T., Holman Jones, S., & Ellis, C. (2013). Conclusion: Storying our future. In S. Holman Jones, T. E. Adams, & C. Ellis (Eds.). *Handbook of autoethnography*. (pp. 669–677). Walnut Creek, CA: Left Coast Press.

Aldridge, D. (2008). Therapeutic narrative analysis: A methodological proposal for the interpretation of musical traces. In P. Liamputtong & J. Rumbold (Eds.), *Knowing differently: Arts-based and collaborative research methods* (pp. 205–228). New York: Nova Science.

Alexander, B. K. (2005). Performance ethnography: The reenacting and inciting of culture. In N. K. Denzin & Y. S. Lincoln (Eds.), *The Sage handbook of qualitative research* (pp. 411–441). Thousand Oaks, CA: Sage.

Boylorn, R. M., & Orbe, M. P. (Eds.). (2014). *Critical autoethnography: Intersecting cultural identities in everyday life*. Walnut Creek, CA: Left Coast Press.

Breede, D. (2017a). Communication activism. In J. Matthes, R. Potter, & C. Davis (Eds.). *International encyclopedia of communication: Methods of communication research*. Wiley-Blackwell.

Breede, D. (2017b). Feminist research/feminist methods. In J. Matthes, R. Potter, & C. Davis (Eds.). *International encyclopedia of communication: Methods of communication research*. Wiley-Blackwell.

Breede, D. (2017c). Holistic ethnography. In J. Matthes, R. Potter, & C. Davis (Eds.). *International encyclopedia of communication: Methods of communication research*. Wiley-Blackwell.

Cahnmann-Taylor, M. (2008). Poetry in qualitative research. In L. M. Given (Ed.). *The SAGE Encyclopedia of Qualitative Research Methods*, Volume 2, pp. 637–640. Thousand Oaks, CA: Sage.

Cancienne, M. B., & Bagley, C. (2008). Dance as method: The process and product of movement in educational research. In P. Liamputtong & J. Rumbold (Eds.), *Knowing differently: Arts-based and collaborative research methods* (pp. 169–186). New York: Nova Science.

Caulley, D. N. (2008). Making qualitative research reports less boring: The techniques of writing creative nonfiction. *Qualitative Inquiry*, 14(3), 424–449.

Cole, C. E., Quinlan, M. M., & Hayward, C. C. (2009). Aesthetic projects engaging inequities: Documentary film for social change. In L. M. Harter, M. J. Dutta, & C. E. Cole (Eds.). *Communicating for social impact: Engaging communication theory, research and pedagogy*. pp. 79–90. Cresskill, NJ: Hampton Press.

Creswell, J. W., Hanson, W. E., Clark, V. L. P., & Morales, A. (2007). Qualitative research designs: Selection and implementation. *The Counseling Psychologist*, 35(2), 236–264.

Davis, C. S. (2008). A funeral liturgy: Death rituals as symbolic communication, *Journal of Loss and Trauma*, 13(15), 406–421.

Davis, C. S. (2009). A family jigsaw puzzle: Secrets and gaps. *The International Review of Qualitative Research*, 1(4), 433–452.

Davis, C. S. (2010). *Death: The beginning of a relationship*. Cresskill, NJ: Hampton Press.

Davis, C. S. (2014). *Conversations about qualitative communication research: Behind the scenes with leading scholars*. New York, NY: Routledge.

Davis, C. S., & Breede, D. C. (2015). Holistic ethnography: Embodiment, emotion, contemplation, and dialogue in ethnographic fieldwork. *The Journal of Contemplative Inquiry*, 2(1), 77–99.

Davis, C. S., & Ellis, C. (2008). Autoethnographic introspection in ethnographic fiction: A method of inquiry. In P. Liamputtong & J. Rumbold, *Knowing differently: Arts-based and collaborative research*, pp. 99–117, Hauppage, NY: Nova Science.

Davis, C. S., & Warren-Findlow, J. (2011). Coping with trauma through fictional narrative ethnography: A primer. *Journal of Loss and Trauma, 16,* 563–572.

Davis, C. S., & Warren-Findlow, J. (2012). The mystery of the troubled breast: Examining cancer and social support through fictional narrative ethnography. *Qualitative Communication Research, 1*(3), 291–314.

Daykin, N. (2008). Knowing through music: Implications for research. In P. Liamputtong & J. Rumbold (Eds.), *Knowing differently: Arts-based and collaborative research methods* (pp. 229–244). New York: Nova Science.

Denzin, N. K. (2003). The practices and politics of interpretation. In N. K. Denzin & Y. S. Lincoln (Eds.), *Collecting and interpreting qualitative materials* (pp. 458–498). Thousand Oaks, CA: Sage.

Dethridge, L. (2003). *Writing your screenplay.* Sydney, New S Wales: Allen and Unwin.

Deveaux, M. (1994). Feminism and empowerment: A critical reading of Foucault. *Feminist Studies, 20,* 223–248.

Ellis, C. (1999). Heartfelt ethnography. *Qualitative Health Research, 9,* 669–683.

Ellis, C (2007). Telling secrets, revealing lives: Relational ethics in research with intimate others. *Qualitative Inquiry, 13,* 3–29.

Ellis, C. (2009a). Renegotiating *Final Negotiations*: From introspection to emotional sociology. In C. Ellis, *Revision: Autoethnographic reflections of life and work* (pp. 95–120). Walnut Creek, CA: Left Coast Press.

Ellis, C. (2009b). Writing revision and researching ethically. In C. Ellis, *Revision: Autoethnographic reflections of life and work* (pp. 303–318). Walnut Creek, CA: Left Coast Press.

Ellis, C., & Bochner, A. (2000). Autoethnography, personal narrative, reflexivity: Researcher as subject. In N. Denzin & Y. Lincoln (Eds.), *The handbook of qualitative research* (2nd ed., pp. 733–768). Thousand Oaks, CA: Sage.

Ellis, C., & Bochner, A. P. (2003). Autoethnography, personal narrative, reflexivity: Researcher as subject. In N. K. Denzin & Y. S. Lincoln (Eds.). *Collecting and interpreting qualitative materials* (pp. 199–258). Thousand Oaks, CA: Sage.

Ellis, C., Bochner, A., Denzin, N., Lincoln, Y., Morse, J., Pelias, R., & Richardson, L. (2008). Talking and thinking about qualitative research. *Qualitative Inquiry, 14*(2), 254–284.

Farmer, M., & Chevrette, R. (2017). Critical theory and research. In J. Matthes, R. Potter, & C. Davis (Eds.). *International encyclopedia of communication: Methods of communication research.* Wiley-Blackwell.

Foley, D., & Valenzuela, A. (2000). Critical ethnography: The politics of collaboration. In N. K. Denzin & Y. S. Lincoln (Eds.), *The Sage handbook of qualitative research* (pp. 217–234). Thousand Oaks, CA: Sage.

Gatson, S. N. (2003). The methods, politics, and ethics of representation in online ethnography. In N. K. Denzin & Y. S. Lincoln (Eds.). *Collecting and interpreting qualitative materials* (pp. 513–527). Thousand Oaks, CA: Sage.

Geertz, C. (1973). *The interpretation of cultures.* New York, NY: Basic Books.

Grbich, C. (2007). *Qualitative data analysis: An introduction.* Thousand Oaks, CA: Sage.

Grierson, E. M. (2004). Methodology and interpretive procedures in education: Risk imagination and reflexivity. In *Educational research, risks and dilemmas.* Proceedings of the NZARE AARE (New Zealand and Australia) Association of Research in Education Conference, Auckland, New Zealand Nov. 29 – Dec. 3, 2003. Retrieved Oct. 28, 2008, from http://www.aare.edu.au/03pap/gri03172.pdf.

Grierson, E. M. (2005). Art academy and the creative community in a globalized place. In S. Jones (Ed.), *Artists, designers and communities.* Proceeding of the Australian Council of University and Design Schools (ACUADS) Conference, Canberra, Australia, September 23–25, 2004. Canberra, ACT: ACUADS.

Grierson, E. M. (2006). Creativity: Cultural identities in a state of becoming. Questions of art and art education in a global knowledge economy. *Australian Art Education, 29*(2), 5–19.

Guillemin, M., & Westall, C. (2008). Gaining insight into women's knowing of postnatal depression using drawings. In P. Liamputtong & J. Rumbold (Eds.), *Knowing differently: Arts-based and collaborative research methods* (pp. 121–140). New York: Nova Science.

Harter, L. M., Dutta, M. J., & Cole, C. E. (Eds.). (2009). *Communicating for social impact: Engaging communication theory, research and pedagogy.* Cresskill, NJ: Hampton Press.

Harter, L. M., Ellingson, L. L., Dutta, M., & Norander, S. (2009). The poetic is political . . . and other notes of engaged scholarship. In L. M. Harter, M. J. Dutta, & C. E. Cole (Eds.). *Communicating for social impact: Engaging communication theory, research and pedagogy.* pp. 33–46. Cresskill, NJ: Hampton Press.

Harter, L. M., Shaw, E., & Quinlan, M. M. (2016). *Creative abundance.* Athens, OH: WOUB Center for Public Media.

Harter, L. M., Quinlan, M. M., & Shaw, E. (n.d). *Acoustics of care.* Athens, OH: WOUB Center for Public Media.

Harter, L. M., Shaw, E., Quinlan, M. M., Ruhl, S. M., & Hodson, T. (2015). Beautiful remedy. Athens, OH: WOUB Center for Public Media.

Heider, K. G. (1976). *Ethnographic film.* Austin, TX: University of Texas Press.

Holman Jones, S. (2000). Autoethnography: Making the personal political. In N. K. Denzin & Y. S. Lincoln (Eds.), *The Sage handbook of qualitative research* (pp. 763–791). Thousand Oaks, CA: Sage.

Huffman, T. (2017). Participatory/action research/CBPR. In J. Matthes, R. Potter, & C. Davis (Eds.). *International encyclopedia of communication: Methods of communication research.* Wiley-Blackwell.

Kaur, S., & Dutta, M. J. (2017). Digital ethnography. In J. Matthes, R. Potter, & C. Davis (Eds.). *International encyclopedia of communication: Methods of communication research.* Wiley-Blackwell.

Kozinets, R. V. (2002). The field behind the screen: Using netnography for marketing research in online communities. *Journal of Marketing Research, 39,* 61–72. doi:10.1509/jmkr.39.1.61.18935

Liamputtong, P., & Rumbold, J. (2008). *Knowing differently: Arts-based and collaborative research methods.* New York: Nova Science.

MacDougall, D. (2005). *The corporeal image: Film, ethnography, and the senses.* Princeton, NJ: Princeton University Press.

Madison, D. S. (2005). *Critical ethnography: Methods, ethics, and performance.* Thousand Oaks, CA: Sage.

Marsh, J. S., & Davis, C. S. (2017). Ethnodrama and ethnotheatre. In J. Matthes, R. Potter, & C. Davis (Eds.). *International encyclopedia of communication: Methods of communication research.* Wiley-Blackwell.

Mathew, W. (2014). Reality in ethnographic film: Documentary vs. docudrama. *Visual Anthropology, 27*(1–2), 17–24.

Maynard, K., & Cahnmann-Taylor, M. (2010). Anthropology at the edge of words: Where poetry and ethnography meet. *Anthropology and Humanism, 35*(1), 2–19.

McDonald, J. (2017) Critical methods. In J. Matthes, R. Potter, & C. Davis (Eds.). *International encyclopedia of communication: Methods of communication research.* Wiley-Blackwell.

Meade, M. R. (2017). Critical ethnography. In J. Matthes, R. Potter, & C. Davis (Eds.). *International encyclopedia of communication: Methods of communication research.* Wiley-Blackwell.

Metta, M. (2013). Putting the body on the line: Embodied writing and recovery through domestic violence. In S. Holman Jones, T. E. Adams, & C. Ellis (Eds.). *Handbook of autoethnography.* (pp. 486–509). Walnut Creek, CA: Left Coast Press.

Miller, L. (2008). Foucauldian constructionism. In J. A. Holstein & J. F. Gubrium (Eds.), *Handbook of constructionist research* (pp. 251–274). New York: Guilford.

Motion, J., & Leitch, S. (2007). A tool box for public relations: The oeuvre of Michel Foucault. *Public Relations Review, 33*(3), 263–268.

Moulding, N. (2006). Disciplining the feminine: The reproduction of gender contradictions in the mental health care of women with eating disorders. *Social Science & Medicine, 62*(4), 793–804.

Patti, C., & Ellis, C. (2017). Co-constructed interview. In J. Matthes, R. Potter, & C. Davis (Eds.). *International encyclopedia of communication: Methods of communication research.* Wiley-Blackwell.

Pelias, R. J. (2014). *Performance: An alphabet of performative writing.* Walnut Creek, CA: Left Coast Press.

Phillips, J. (2017). Interactive interviewing. Co-constructed interview. In J. Matthes, R. Potter, & C. Davis (Eds.). *International encyclopedia of communication: Methods of communication research.* Wiley-Blackwell.

Pink, S. (2007). *Doing visual ethnography*. Thousand Oaks, CA: Sage.

Ponterotto, J. G., & Grieger, I. (2007). Effectively communicating qualitative research. *Counseling Psychologist, 35*(3), 404–430.

Prince, S. (1998). *Sam peckinpah and the rise of ultraviolent movies*. Texas, TX: University of Texas Press.

Quinlan, M. M., Smith, J. W., & Hayward, C. (2009). This car seems to be alive—Perspectives on the documentary Plan F. *Journal of Research in Special Educational Needs, 9*, 59–61.

Richardson, L. (1993). Poetics, dramatics, and transgressive validity: The case of the skipped line. *The Sociological Quarterly, 34*(4), 695–710.

Richardson, L. (2000). Writing: A method of inquiry. In N. K. Denzin & Y. S. Lincoln, (Eds.), *Handbook of qualitative research* (pp. 923–948). Thousand Oaks, CA: Sage.

Richardson, L. (2003). Writing: A method of inquiry. In N. K. Denzin & Y. S. Lincoln (Eds.), *Collecting and interpreting qualitative materials* (pp. 499–541). Thousand Oaks, CA: Sage.

Romney, J. (2006). The digital cusp: How new technologies are reshaping the distribution of content. In *Centre for screen business* research papers, Australian Film, Television and Radio School (AFTRS) Retrieved July 15, 2006, from http://csb.aftrs.edu.au/go.cfm?path=/go/research&

Saldaña, J. (2011). *Ethnotheatre: Research from page to stage*. Walnut Creek, CA: Left Coast Press.

Sherman, S. R. (2015). *Documenting ourselves: Film, video, and culture*. Lexington, KY: University Press of Kentucky.

Tapp, H., de Hernandez, U., & Smith, H. (2017). Community based participatory focus groups. In J. Matthes, R. Potter, & C. Davis (Eds.). *International encyclopedia of communication: Methods of communication research*. Wiley-Blackwell.

Trethewey, A. (1999). Disciplined bodies: Women's embodied identities at work. *Organization Studies, 20*(3), 423–450.

Tullis, J. A. (2013). Self and others: Ethics in autoethnographic research. In S. Holman Jones, T. E. Adams, & C. Ellis (Eds.). *Handbook of autoethnography*. (pp. 244–261). Walnut Creek, CA: Left Coast Press.

Whitehead, K., & Kurz, T. (2008). Saints, sinners and standards of femininity: Discursive constructions of anorexia nervosa and obesity in women's magazines. *Journal of Gender Studies, 17*(4), 345–358.

Winkle-Wagner, R. (2008). Not feminist but strong: Black women's reflections of race and gender in college. *The Negro Educational Review, 59*(3–4), 181–195.

CHAPTER 8

Designing a Research Proposal: Writing the Script

This chapter works as a praxis week—providing students an opportunity to apply knowledge and skills gained throughout the course. This week students will identify a topic of interest and propose a discipline-specific approach for investigating the topic.

Upon successful completion of this chapter, you will be able to:

- Determine the relevance of information in evaluating an argument or conclusion.
- Identify a research topic/work that will contribute to knowledge in your discipline.
- Write a problem statement, purpose/interest statement, and corresponding research questions.
- Generate conclusions based on credible research, analysis, and interpretation.

▼

Introduction

Perhaps you've never worked on construction, but use your imagination and common sense. . . ever seen a blueprint? Worked with a list or a plan of any kind? Ah, I knew that would get you. List-lovers unite! Those who color-code your planners, jump in. This chapter is all about designing a plan.

As with any good list, we start at the very beginning . . . just kidding, it's not that simple. You have to figure out what paradigm you're working from, you have to know what previously existing work is out there, and be familiar enough with it so that you can see what might be missing or needed; after all, the gap is where your question or hypothesis or will come from.

KEY to remember: everyone's plan or list will look different! For example, one part of the formulation of a research problem in quantitative research is the construction of a hypothesis, or a hunch, of what you hope to (or think you'll) find as you begin your research. Hypotheses bring clarity, specificity, and focus to a research problem, but are not essential for a study.

Think about the varying data that each discipline uses . . . the Creative Arts relies heavily on design process and how things have been done in the past. Qualitative research mostly uses descriptive or narrative statements as the "units of measurement," whereas quantitative research places greater emphasis of measuring responses on one of the four measurement scales.

And what about variables?! Value, value, value. Whether we accept it or not, we all make value judgments constantly in our daily lives: "This food is excellent"; "I could not sleep well last night"; "I do not like this"; and "I think this is wonderful." These are all judgments based upon our own preferences, indicators, or assessment. Because these statements explain feelings or preferences, the basis on which they are made varies from person to person. There is no uniform standard of measurement. A particular food (sushi) may be judged "excellent" by one person but "awful" by another, and something else could be wonderful to one person but ugly to another. When you express these feelings or preferences, you do so, on the basis of certain criteria in your mind, or in relation to others' expectations. If you question your friends or colleagues, you will discover that their judgment is based upon indicators and/or expectations that lead them to conclude and express a particular opinion.

Researching and Writing in Different Disciplines

▼
What are The Objects of Study? and How Might The Research Be Carried Out?

Creative Arts and humanities researchers focus on a range of products and issues, their production, the ways in which they construct and represent the world, and their reception. Historical, art history and some literary researchers might use documentary or archival research.

Documentary Analysis

This is analysis of documents, both as primary and secondary sources, looking at their origins, contexts, how they are constructed and expressed, who produced them, when and why, and the effect they have had.

Archival Research and The Sources Themselves

Researchers might need to explore archival material, which is original material stored, and catalogued. They could be asking questions about and looking at work produced at the time of study, tracking down and classifying these primary sources, to develop an argument about their original meaning, intention, how they grew from the artist/writer's time or background.

They might look at an author's or artist's papers to identify how and in what ways they were influenced, used the materials in their own work, contributed to ongoing dialogues, kept up correspondence.

They might be looking at the production and publication of or the reception of primary sources or products, focusing on the cultural reception of films or texts, looking at audiences and audience response in order to identify who responded to what, and in what ways and why.

Literature Research—Other Variants

For literature researchers, the actual process of research, the critical practice and the framing of questions, methods, decisions made about approaches, is quite likely to be assumed, taken for granted. In literature, other humanities, performance and creative arts, students sometimes claim they have no need to be as 'jargon ridden' as their social science colleagues and often they might even argue that explaining the process of the research kills the creativity. But actually, they are overlooking the research processes they are using. All students ask research questions, develop theoretical perspectives, research design and methods, conceptual frameworks, and produce results, although they are in different forms and use different expressions from those produced by students using social science designs and methods. You need to be able to communicate your intentions, design, processes, and what is achieved to aid both your own understanding and that of others.

Some creative and humanities research uses social science strategies, particularly in subjects close to the social sciences, such as history, and cultural studies. However, much of the research in the arts and humanities uses quite different strategies. You will need to interpret any product or data and turn this into findings and some conclusions which are themselves underpinned by the theories and the research question.

The whole research piece is then written up and presented in an appropriate form. This can be conventional in shape, such as a dissertation in literature which focuses on asking a research question about the work of an author or group of authors. Or if appropriate it can be creative in shape. Answering questions about response to texts in context, engaging with personal response to cultural difference, exploring self-development, family history, the creative responses of others to events, have produced creative work accompanied by critical, discursive, analytical work. These include quilts, videos, song cycles, multilayered texts, poetry sequences, and photo sequences.

A student might be looking at how an artist or author goes about their own artistic and creative work. They might need to interview the artist, match what they say critically about their own work to what the work presents, and how other view it, in context.

They might want to know about the explicit creative processes the artist uses to creatively change and develop their sketches, thoughts, influences, into their own work.

They might be looking at the work itself and exploring themes and issues, cultural engagement, innovation, and so they would need to critically engage with the work, use the thoughts of theorists and the work of the other critics and commentators, and look at it in context—cultural, social—in terms of critical trends (modernism, writing the body . . .), cultural trends (socially relevant art, the adult education movement and its work with adults as artists in the community) and so on.

Or they might be researching to carry out their own piece of creative work.

There can be a focus on the discovery, collection, analysis and critical commentary upon data, which would be gathered from different sources including documents, collections, images, literary and other texts. They might have interview data from authors or artists who are interviewed, and they might combine critical responses to the artist's work with the comments they make in interview, and some personal, critical and/or creative responses themselves.

All of this needs to be in a framework which is explained, defended, and which helps to address the research question. If the aim of the piece of research is towards a creative product rather than the critical analysis of others' work it could be accompanied by a reflective and analytical piece looking at decisions made about research processes and the development of the work, the creative piece.

Sometimes the research process itself enables the creative process, or indeed the creative process *is* the research process. You might decide to explore your own responses to a cultural or historical issue (for example) by producing a series of poems and pictures. You would need to use theory about creative writing and art as expression and comment, keep a journal or log about the decisions made in the creative process in response to stimuli and critical reading, problems, discoveries, thoughts. You would need to analyze and explain the ways in which the creative work addresses your question.

Creativity and Research

Sometimes you could be researching your own creative processes and sometimes you are carrying out research FOR your own creative processes. You need to acknowledge your involvement in the work.

Creative Arts and humanities research can be seen as lying on a continuum related to:

- information gathering, questioning and documenting
- critique, analysis, explanation
- conceptual work, theorizing the work in relation to theories, to help interpret and understand it
- creative work, whether this is what is being studied, or being produced (and then studied)
- personal involvement—subjectivity and rigor

A literature or fine art researcher might be dealing with their own critical responses and those of other critics to a group of writers, a writer, a group of texts, or a phenomenon, theme or issue in texts, to the work of an artist or group of artists. They might be making something new out of this mixture of the personal and the established critical responses.

The researcher might be writing a creative piece, a novel or poem sequence, and accompanying that with analytical, critical and reflective versions, and with commentary. A creative artist might be carrying out visual research using sketchbooks, to build up a creative response, keep notes, work at ways of creating something out of a situation or feeling, and/or they could produce an installation, a set of paintings, sculptures, or chairs or other functional objects designed by them.

Their research:

- informs their creative thinking and production—collection, identification, selection, analysis, then the spin-off creative thinking and ideas, plans, practice, refining, product of the piece whether written or artistic (fashion, design, glass, a poem, both mixed together, a film piece . . .);
- informs their reflective and analytical processes—helps them work out what influenced this, what happened to create a response, what it might mean to them and others, how it can be interpreted in a critical and conceptual frame-work so that the ideas within it are bought out, and so that the thoughts, theories, work and ideas of others are brought to bear on exploring, even explaining it.

Researching Your Own Creative Work/Using The Creative in Your Research Work

Many students engage in literary, artistic, musical or performance work directly, rather than through the lens of a critic. So, your research is not merely in the arts and humanities but in relating your own performance and production, your own creative practices.

The final stage of your research involves writing a research report. The report is a straightforward document that introduces your research problem, outlines what you have done to resolve it, and presents your findings. A research report is not a work of literature—it is a factual, logical, and comprehensible document. When this document is written in the form of a postgraduate-level thesis, the report also becomes a reflection of your scholarship and it is used to measure your educational achievement (Leedy and Ormrod, 2010: 291).

Learning how to write professional research reports is a skill that you will find valuable in your professional life too, and not only within a university setting. The formal and impersonal style of writing that is characteristic to most research reports represents a model of writing and reporting that is often used in the corporate world as well. If, for example, your career takes you to the path of working for corporate or government clients, you will most certainly be expected to present your research and/or elaborate your design solutions in this way.

▼ ....

Research Report

When researching in the sciences, a research report should act as a documented record of your contribution to the knowledge in your field. Research reports can take many forms: theses, journal articles, conference presentations, business reports, and so on. This means that there are various ways of preparing and writing research reports. Therefore, here I will simply highlight the key principles that you should take into consideration when planning a research report, regardless of what your research is about:

1. Introduction
2. Research Rationale
3. Research Methods and Methodology
4. Summary of Findings
5. Discussion
6. Conclusion

First you should begin by introducing your readers to the research problem. Then you will need to explain why this problem needs an in-depth investigation. Following this, you should describe how you attempted to resolve this problem (in other words, here you will need to explain your research procedure and discuss how you gathered the research data). Then you should present the research data. Finally, you should provide an interpretation of the data and conclude by demonstrating how your findings have resolved the research problem.

Writing a Research Report

Once you have made a plan of how you will prepare your research report, you can start with your writing. The structure of your report should follow your plan, but in greater detail. This structure can also form the subheadings of your report:

1. Introduction
2. Research Problem
3. Research Objectives
4. Research Question
5. Knowledge Gap
6. Hypothesis
7. Research Rationale
8. Research Aims
9. Methodology and Methods
10. Review of the Literature
11. Theoretical Discussion
12. Summary of Key Findings
13. Conclusion

A typical stumbling block for most people is figuring out how to start writing—especially a formal report of such nature. In the first issue of the *Design Research Quarterly*, Eric J. Arnould (2006) provides a set of useful techniques on getting a typical research report to publication standards.

According to him, a good way of starting is by preparing a two- to three-page synopsis of the report that focuses on the highlights of your theoretical and/or practical contribution in design. The synopsis should begin with an opening sentence that introduces your field of study, states the purpose of your research, and makes links to existing key research in this area that is either canonical (accepted as being accurate and authoritative) or cutting edge—or covers both. Then, based on this, you should frame your research problem by including few sentences explaining what is known about the phenomenon in question, what yet needs to be established (what is the gap in the knowledge), and why this is important. This can be written in one or two paragraphs (Arnould, 2006: 21).

Next, you should state your objectives. Arnould (2006: 21) recommends that this should be done in three steps. The first step should state your long-term vision. What is your broad goal? Frame this within a broad problem area. Then, state your immediate research objective (this is your key research question), and explain how this relates to the knowledge gap that you have identified in your literature review. Following this, provide a hypothesis that states what needs to be done in order for this problem to be addressed.

Now, you will need to include a brief rationale, in one paragraph, that states what the outcome of your research will be, or explains how your research will enable any practical or theoretical steps that can follow in the future, if they cannot occur now. Also, here you should state why is this a feasible solution (Arnould, 2006: 21). Please note that it is perfectly fine if the information appears to be somewhat repetitive in a research report. As mentioned above, this is not a work of literature and different rules of writing apply.

Following this, you should state your conceptual aims. These are different from your descriptive aims, as their purpose is to explain *what* you aim to accomplish, rather than *how* or *why*. Anywhere between two and five aims is good. These aims should be logical, brief, concise, and hopefully exciting. Collectively, they should either test your hypothesis or fulfil the needs that you have identified. Then, you will need to describe your empirical studies, summarize your findings, and make an impact statement. You should begin by briefly explaining what your methodology is and what research methods have you used. Then you need to set the theoretical context of your study. As Arnould (2006: 21–2) points out, the theorizing part consists of activities such as abstracting, generalizing, relating, explaining, synthesizing, and idealizing from contexts found in the relevant literature. The contexts will make your argument appear well rounded, reliable, and engaging. Then, you will need to outline your key results and findings, and elaborate on them without adding any irrelevant or unnecessary information. Be brief and to the point. If appropriate, include figures and tables that can visually aid the presentation of your results. Finally, write a concluding statement that sums up the impact of your study. Mainly, your conclusion should explain how your study advances theory or practice in your field (2006: 22).

Once you have completed your synopsis, Arnould suggests that you should share the synopsis with your peers and get feedback on it. Use this feedback to rewrite any parts that need improving. Finally, write your report as an extended version of your synopsis. The report can include more details, additional background information, detailed descriptions of your methodology and methods, and so on (Arnould, 2006: 22). In addition to this, you will often be asked to provide a list of keywords that best describe the topic of your research and to write an abstract outlining your report. Here, I will give you a brief introduction on what these are and why you need them. Also, I will provide you with a structure that you can use as a guide or a template when preparing your research report and the accompanying elements.

This type of research report is suitable for academic audiences, but if you need to prepare a research report for corporate clients, you may have to reformulate some components and perhaps include some additional information that may be of relevance to your clients. If the research is done primarily for the purpose of producing some kind of design outcome, then you will need to follow up on your research with some additional documentation that will support your design solution. The main purpose of this kind of research is for you to make informed design decisions.

Keywords

By looking at the keywords, the reader should be able to understand the key topics that you are addressing. Keywords are also useful for search engine purposes. Think about them in the following way: if you were trying to find something about your topic on the Internet, what terms would you search for in Google? The same principle applies here as well. In most cases anything between three and six keywords separated by commas is sufficient (e.g. aging, rural Australia, user-interface design).

Abstract

An abstract is a condensed summary of your research report. The abstract is a stand-alone document that should provide clear and concise information about your research. This means that it should make sense on its own, even when it is not paired with the research study. For example, most academics will make a decision on whether to read a research paper or not on the basis of the abstract.

Abstracts are often used when submitting research papers for journals and conferences, or when preparing research proposals. Sometimes they can serve as a proposal as to what you intend to do research on, but most often their purpose is to describe your research after it is completed. Therefore, if you have begun your research with an abstract, you can continue to refine and update your abstract as you progress with your research and finalize your abstract once your research is completed.

Abstract Structure

Writing an abstract is not easy for a novice, so I have developed a formula that you can follow. An abstract should be brief and to the point, so try to write your abstract in five sentences. Use the following instructions as a guide:

- **First sentence (the topic):** What is this project about?

    You should begin by establishing your topic. Good abstracts often start with: 'This study examines . . .' Then, fill in the gaps. For example: '(. . .) the influence of social media on the Generation Y decision-making habits', or: '(. . .) the current trends in Australian wine label design and packaging for export purposes'.

- **Second sentence (conventional wisdom):** Based on your literature review, what would you say the current situation on this topic is?

    Give very brief background information on the issue that you are addressing in one, or if necessary two sentences. Here is an example: 'The latest findings suggest that social media can influence the decision-making habits of Generation Y when it comes to travel choices, entertainment and clothing, but there is a limited information on how social media can influences their political preferences.' This sentence also moves into the next area—the research gap.

Another example could be: 'The wine industry is one of the largest industries in Australia. The role that design and branding play in this industry is significant when it comes to maintaining the competitive advantage that Australian wines have on the domestic market; yet, the situation is different when it comes to foreign exports.'

- **Third sentence (gap in the knowledge):** What unanswered questions remain in your literature review?

  Is there a particular issue that yet needs to be addressed? Often, in the conclusions of their research reports, researchers will highlight opportunities for further research. This is a good indication of the possible gaps in the knowledge that you can address. It is important that you find an area that has not been thoroughly examined and where more information is needed. This is an area where you can contribute with new research. This is the most important part of any research project. For example, you can write something along the following lines: 'A comparative case study analysis shows that the Australian wine industry can be more competitive on the European markets if it readjusted its branding strategy for export.'

- **Fourth sentence (the findings):** What have you discovered in your research?

  Your findings need to be original and interesting. Explain how your findings contribute to the issue that you were examining. For example, you can say something like this: 'The research findings show that social media influences 68 per cent of the respondents when it comes to voting preferences', or: 'The key reason for this is the difference in the public expectations in Europe of how quality wine should be labelled and packaged, which is distinctively different from the that in Australia.'

- **Fifth sentence (social or practical implications):** What are the implications for practice? Or, if applicable: What is the impact on society?

  What you need to address in this section is the 'So what?' factor. For example, you could say something along these lines: 'This means that social media can play a significant role in election campaigns, and this study provides a list of recommendations on developing social media communication strategies for political purposes, in addition to the overall printed and online campaigns', or: 'This study highlights the key design elements that need to be taken into consideration when developing wine branding strategies for European markets, both in terms of label design and packaging.'

Unless you are specifically asked to provide an extended abstract with references, try to limit your abstract to a maximum of 300 words and do not include any references in the abstract. Remember, the abstract is meant to work as a stand-alone document and may not be accompanied by the reference list that will follow your report. Based on the

above comments, I have compiled the following tv ...
convenience. However, please note that these exa ...
are for illustration purposes only.

....

Example

Abstract 1

Title and Subtitle Generation Y and F... Media in the Election Process

Abstract

This study examines the influence of social media on the ... Y decision-making habits. The latest findings suggest that socia... can influence the decision-making habits of Generation Y when it co... to travel choices, entertainment, and clothing, but there is limited information on how social media can influence their political preferences. The research findings show that social media influences 68 per cent of the respondents when it comes to voting preferences. This means that social media can play a significant role in election campaigns, and this study provides a list of recommendations on developing social media communication strategies for political purposes, in addition to the overall printed and online campaigns.

....▼

Example

Abstract 2

Title and Subtitle Australian Wine in Europe: Design and Branding of Australian Wine for Exports

Abstract

This study examines the current trends in Australian wine label design and packaging for export purposes. The wine industry is one of the largest industries in Australia. The role that design and branding play in this industry is significant when it comes to maintaining the competitive advantage that Australian wines have on the domestic market; yet, the situation is different when it comes to foreign exports. A comparative case study analysis shows that the Australian wine industry can be more competitive on the European markets if it readjusted its branding strategy for export. The key reason for this is the differences in the public expectations in Europe of how quality wine should be labelled and packaged, which is distinctively different from that in Australia. This study highlights the key design elements that need to be taken into consideration when developing wine branding strategies for European markets, both in terms of label design and packaging.

Contents of The Research Report

The following is a contents list for a practice-based research report. This research report framework is accompanied by a framework on preparing a design brief, design report, and an executive summary—and I will present all of them below:

1. Title and Subtitle
2. Abstract
3. Keywords
4. Research Problem
5. Research Purpose
6. Stakeholders
   a. The Client
   b. Primary Audience
   c. Secondary Audience
7. Review of the Literature
8. Primary Research
9. Argument
10. Conclusion
11. Recommendations
12. Opportunities for Further Research
13. Reference List and a Bibliography

As with the research proposal, the research report should begin with a title and subtitle. Here you can use the same title and subtitle as for the proposal. However, it is common for your line of thinking to have changed after conducting your research and so you may need to change or refine the title and the subtitle of your project. This is perfectly normal. It means that you have broadened your understanding of the research problem and now you need to adjust your research report accordingly. Again, make sure that you use a clear title that sets the theme of your study and a subtitle that is descriptive in nature.

The introduction is next. The purpose of the introduction is to set the stage for the reader. Consider the following questions when writing the introduction:

■ What is this study about?
■ Why are you studying this?
■ How will you go about this study?
■ What should the reader expect to read?
■ How is this study relevant, and to whom?

These are the things that you will need to reflect on in your introduction. Nevertheless, keep your introduction reasonably brief. You will explain all of this in more detail as you progress with the report. Then, you will need to reflect on the research problem by providing a clear statement:

■ What is the problem that you trying to solve?

You should have already stated this in the first sentence of your abstract—repeat it here as well. If a client has commissioned the research, then you should consult the client prior to defining the research statement. If this is an independent research project, then you are expected to deliver the research statement. You can also formulate the problem as a research question or as a hypothesis. Following this, you also need to explain further why this issue is worthwhile exploring:

- What do you expect to achieve by resolving this problem?
- What is novel and interesting about this?
- What are your primary predications for the design outcome?
- Who will be affected by your work?

Everyone that has an interest in, or is directly or indirectly affected by, your research or the outcomes of your research should be treated as a stakeholder. Basically, you have to consider three key stakeholders: the client, and the primary and secondary audiences. First, you will need to provide details of your client, or a prospective client if you do not have a client yet. In other words, you will need to explain who has an interest in commissioning this type of research and associated design project, or may find it relevant, and why. This can be a company, a government agency, a non-government or not-for-profit organization, or an individual. Then, you will need to reflect on your primary target audience:

- Who will directly benefit from the findings of your research and who will be the end-user of the design outcome?

Often, the outcomes of any project or policy can affect third parties that are directly or indirectly associated with the client or with the key target audience. Here you should briefly outline any additional stakeholders that may be indirectly affected by the design outcome, both in a positive and a negative way. Once you have covered the practical aspects, you need to present what kind of research has already been conducted on this topic, or in this area so far:

- Are there some existing cases or historical examples that are related to your research question?
- Have there been any similar studies already conducted from which you have learned how this particular problem has been resolved?

Here you should focus on the most influential works in this field of research. Provide sufficient detail and reflection for each example:

- What makes these examples good or bad?
- How are they related to your research question?

Do not underestimate the importance of your review of the existing work. The information that you are providing here should demonstrate that you have an in-depth understanding of the question that you have addressed. Do not use Wikipedia as a source of reliable information. Also, make sure that you have cross-referenced the information you have found in order to verify it.

Once you have completed the section for the literature review, you will need to discuss your primary research—the original data that you have gathered or created through applying different methods of empirical data collection. By 'empirical' I mean data collection 'based on, concerned with, or verifiable by observation or experience rather than theory or pure logic' (Oxford Dictionaries, 2013f).

As recommended earlier, for this part of your research you will have conducted a triangulation of mixed methods. Here, you should briefly describe the methods that you have chosen, and why. Then, briefly describe the questions asked, the participant response, the strengths and weaknesses of each method, and the key findings. Explain why these findings are relevant to the development of your project. You can include the full documentation of your primary research as an appendix at the end of the research report. If ethics approval has been sought, in the appendix you can also include your ethics authorization letter, consent letters, and so forth.

Use the information you have gathered so far to advance or build your position. Agree with and/or challenge other researchers by questioning their position if you do not agree with it. Avoid faulty reasoning. Develop a strong argument by providing sufficient detail, comparisons, illustrations, and causal analysis. Be specific in your examples and restate your position in different ways to bring your message home to the reader. Maintain a coherent line of reasoning. Key questions to consider while structuring your argument are:

- What am I focusing on here?
- What am I talking about?
- Why am I focusing on this?
- What are my reasons?
- How do I want to develop this discussion?
- What do I want to discuss and in what order do I want to discuss these topics?

In the conclusion you should bring together the findings of your paper. Then, process your findings for the reader. Here you should ask yourself:

- What do I find most interesting or important about my findings?
- What is new about the idea and the position that I have developed?
- Who can benefit from this?

Then, proceed with recommendations and state clearly what the implications of your findings are. On the basis of what you have learned from this process, discuss what you think needs to numbered bullet points (e.g. Recommendation 1, Recommendation 2, and so on). These recommendations can set the framework for the design brief.

Design Brief

Once you have completed your research, you can begin making informed design decisions about the problem that you have been tasked with resolving. The next stage would be for you to prepare a design brief. A design brief is a written document that outlines the expectations for a design project.

Many designers are often tempted to begin their projects straight from this stage, without conducting a proper research on the problem that they have address beforehand. It is quite common in the design industry for designers to ask their clients to provide a design brief for them. I will encourage you to do the opposite. Design briefs are much more effective when designers work with the clients on developing a final design brief after the research has taken place. In other words, the client's initial design brief should not be the final design brief. Instead, this should serve as a first point of discussion about the problem that the client wants to be resolved.

This is somewhat different approach to the 'traditional' model, where the client identifies a problem and then thinks of a solution in the form of a 'brief' that is then suggested to the designer, who in return decides how this idea is best realized. The problem with this approach is that the client may not always have the research skills or the design background to identify the core of the problem or the most appropriate design solution. In other words, the client is not necessarily qualified to drive the design thinking process.

To better exemplify this, I will draw a parallel with medical practitioners or attorneys. While a patient or a person in a need of a health advice or legal assistance may be well aware that they have a problem, they are not qualified to suggest types of medications or legal actions to their doctors or lawyers—nor does anyone expect them to do so. The same principle of work should be applied in the design profession. That is why it is better if the design brief is based on a research report. Professional designers should be able to identify the problem, suggest solutions, provide expert advice, and deliver design outcomes.

Contents of The Design Brief

There is not one standardized way in which you can prepare a design brief. In order to help you get started, here is a content structure that you may use when preparing one:

1. Project Title
2. Problem Statement
   a. Client Profile
   b. Client's Needs
   c. Target Audience
   d. Key Competitors

3. Proposed Outcome
   a. Design Consideration
   b. Design Constraints
4. Budget
5. Timetable

The title can be the same as the one that you are using in your research report, or you can provide a new title that describes the project rather than the research. Then, begin by providing brief information of what the project is that you are working on. Follow this by providing some background information about your client. This can include information related to the client's business history, areas of operation, brand values, key objectives, and future vision. Next, explain what the problem is that you are addressing:

- What are your client's needs?

If necessary, include a list of sub-problems. Here you should also provide a brief analysis of the primary target audience (end-users and/or consumers). Also, you should provide some information on the client's key competitors by listing any competing organizations and/or products.

The problem statement can simply be based on the problem stated in your research report. However, based on the findings of your research, here you can realign the focus of the problem if necessary. The purpose of this information is for you to show that you understand the context in which you are working and by doing that to reassure your client that you understand their business and their expectations. Once you have established this, you should discuss what kind of design outcome you propose to deliver:

- What is the design solution that you believe will work best, and why?

Answer this by explaining how this solution will address the above-mentioned problem. Here you can discuss similar examples from industry— but only if necessary. In addition to this, you need to be aware that there may be a number of things that you need to take into consideration while working on this project. Therefore, you should also provide brief information on the issues that you will take into consideration when designing. Depending on what the client's primary needs are, some of these issues may be related to the following:

- Function
- Purpose
- Aesthetics
- Key Design Elements

- Environment
- Sustainability
- Performance
- Materials
- Production
- Manufacture
- Human Factors and Ergonomics
- Semantics and Semiotics
- Marketing and Communications
- Packaging
- Distribution
- Design and/or Trademark Registration

Please note that this is not a definitive list and that all considerations may not be applicable to your project or some possibilities might not have been included in this list. Also, design considerations may vary from project to project. Therefore, it is best to frame the design considerations in consultation with your client.

Once you have listed the design considerations, you should also list whether there are any constraints in terms of production, colors, or materials that you also need to take into consideration. Likewise, design constraints may vary from project to project and there are many factors that you will need to be made aware of before you address this issue. Therefore, you should consult your client on this as well.

Another thing that you need to discuss with your client is the budget. As with any design project, there will be either a set budget allocated up front, or you will need to calculate a budget based on the expected expenses. If you are preparing a design brief as a part of your studies, budgeting might be an unrealistic expectation and it is rarely a necessary component of any student project. However, a timetable is often required in both cases. Therefore, here you should present a timeline of your activities. What you need to include is information on when you expect to complete the project, and what are your milestones (the different stages of your project).

▼

Design Report

Once the design work is completed, you will need to prepare a report that outlines what you have done and for whom. Your design solution or an artifact should be accompanied by a design report. The purpose of the report is to provide an explanation of the work that you have done and to justify your design decisions. Ideally, your design report should be stylistically well designed, and well written. The design of the report should reflect the proposed design solution and the writing style of the design report should be similar to the writing style of the research report.

Contents of The Design Report

There are no standardized ways of preparing design reports. Nevertheless, here is a content structure that you may use when preparing a design report:

1. Project Title
2. Project Summary
   a. Client Profile
   b. Client's Needs
   c. Target Audience
   d. Key Competitors
3. Project Presentation
   a. Design Specifications
   b. Design Rationale
   c. Design Evaluation: SWOT Analysis
4. Costing
5. Appendix 1: Research Proposal
6. Appendix 2: Research Report
7. Appendix 3: Design Brief
8. Appendix 4: Design Documentation
9. Appendix 5: Invoice

The way you present your project is very important. The production values of your presentation and of your design report should match the production values of your design outcome. The title of the design report should be the same as the title of your design brief. At the beginning of your design report, provide a brief project summary. Here you can refer back to the design brief and you can sum up key details from your client's profile, their needs, their key target audiences, and key competitors.

You can present most of this information as bullet points. Then, once you have set the context of the project, you should present your design solution. Here you can include visuals such as drawing, renderings, and photographs of the design artifact, or of prototypes and models. In addition to this, you should provide a list of the design specifications, such as technical information related to size, dimensions, production technologies, materials, mediums, and so on. Then, you will need to provide a justification of the design solution by writing a design rationale.

Following this, provide an evaluation of the design solution. There are several ways by which you can do this, such as conducting user testings or focus groups. You can report on this by proving a SWOT analysis—a brief outline of the strengths, weaknesses, opportunities, and the threats associated with this project. Following this, include a list of expenses and associated costs. Here you can provide a breakdown of your activities, list of the materials and the resources that were necessary for the completion of this project, and any other expenses that you have incurred by working on this project. This, of course, will need to be linked to the original budget that was approved by your client.

In addition to your design report, you can gather together all of the materials that you have produced so far—the research proposal, the research report, and the design brief—and include them as an appendix. In addition to this, you can also include any supporting design documentation, such as copies of your sketches, drawings, photographs, and notes from meetings with the client. This is very important for record-keeping purposes, both for you and your client At the end, you can include your invoice.

Conclusion

The research report is a report on what you have done over the course of your research effort. The purpose of the report is for you to help the reader understand:

- What was the problem you were trying to resolve?
- What was the data that have led to the resolution of that problem?
- What were the means by which these data were gathered?
- How were these data analysed?
- What conclusions were reached?

The interpretation and presentation of the findings should be written in the *present tense*. The writing style of the report must be formal and impersonal—with the exception of reports written as a part of ethnographic or historical studies, which may be written in personal and literary (storytelling) fashion (Leedy and Ormrod, 2010: 304). In addition to the research report, you can also prepare an executive summary. This is a simplified synopsis that can be presented alongside your reports or as an independent document that sums up your activities. The main purpose of conducting research in a design context is either to help you improve your design practice, or to help you make informed design decisions that will result in high-quality design outcomes. Therefore, the research report can help you draft a better design brief, which can lead to a more appropriate design solution. Also, you should be able to use your research report when writing your design report.

Summary

In this chapter I have highlighted the key points that you will need to take into consideration when preparing research and design reports, including supporting documentation such as abstract, keywords, and executive summaries, as well as a design brief. In this book I have covered some of the key essentials that you need to know when embarking on a research path, and why these things are relevant to many different disciplines and areas of study. Beginning your research is an exciting thing and this text has given you the tools to begin. Build well.

▼

Glossary

Australian wine
Branding
Decision-Making
Design
Elections
Europe

Generation Y
Packaging
Politics
Social Media

INDEX